ESG Investing

ESG Investing

Current Theory and Practice

Edited by
John Hill

DE GRUYTER

ISBN 978-3-11-117813-4
e-ISBN (PDF) 978-3-11-117860-8
e-ISBN (EPUB) 978-3-11-117872-1

Library of Congress Control Number: 2025932081

Bibliographic information published by the Deutsche Nationalbibliothek
The Deutsche Nationalbibliothek lists this publication in the Deutsche Nationalbibliografie;
detailed bibliographic data are available on the internet at http://dnb.dnb.de.

© 2025 Walter de Gruyter GmbH, Berlin/Boston, Genthiner Straße 13, 10785 Berlin
Cover image: John Hill
Typesetting: Integra Software Services Pvt. Ltd.

www.degruyter.com
Questions about General Product Safety Regulation:
productsafety@degruyterbrill.com

To my beloved wife Nicole,
whose unwavering love and support, intellect, and determination have been my
constant source of strength,

To my children and grandchildren,
whose joy and curiosity inspire me daily,

And to my students, past and present,
whose hunger for knowledge fuels my passion for learning, writing and teaching,

This work is a testament to all of you—
my motivations to dream, create, and persevere.

Acknowledgments

This book would not have been possible without the support, guidance, and encouragement of many remarkable individuals.

To my family, your love, enthusiasm, and work ethic remind me why I do what I do. You bring immeasurable joy and inspiration to my life.

To my students, past and present, your intellectual curiosity and diligence continue to impress. Your questions, insights, and aspirations have enriched my understanding of the world, challenged me to grow, and given me confidence that the future is in great hands.

I am deeply grateful to friends and colleagues at Fairfield University, especially Zhan Li, Kristen Fitzgerald, and Dina Franceschi, the staff at De Gruyter, especially Jaya Dalal, and most importantly, the authors of this book who despite the demands of their "day jobs" found the time to conscientiously provide exceptional contributions, elevating this work beyond what I imagined.

Finally, thank you to all the readers who bring these words to life. This book is a labor of love, created with you in mind.

https://doi.org/10.1515/9783111178608-202

Contents

Acknowledgments —— VII

List of Contributors —— XI

Preface —— XV

Jon Lukomnik and James P. Hawley
1   Modern Portfolio Theory, Capital Market Structural Changes, and ESG —— 5

Dan Daugaard and Moses Kangogo
2   Universal Ownership Perspective: Incorporating ESG Metrics to Monitor
     and Manage Externalities —— 25

Disen Huang Albrecht, Divya Anantharaman, Keyi Zhao
3   A Review of ESG Measurements and Ratings —— 49

Preeti Bhattacharji and Patrick Wong
4   A Practical Guide to Sustainable Investing by Asset Class —— 85

Carol A. Casazza and Sarah J. Herman
5   Environmental, Social, and Governance in Private Equity —— 109

Eric Darrisaw and Bruce Bolger
6   ESG—The Convergence of Social Justice and Value Creation —— 129

Richard Morrison
7   The Case Against Mandatory ESG Standards —— 143

About the Editor —— 167

List of Tables —— 169

Index —— 171

List of Contributors

Disen Huang Albrecht is Assistant Professor of Accounting & Information Systems at Rutgers, the State University of New Jersey. She completed her PhD in Accounting from the New York University Leonard N. Stern School of Business in 2019. Before joining academia, she worked as an International Tax Consultant at Deloitte and passed the CPA exams in Massachusetts. She was an undergraduate recipient of the Trustee Scholarship at Boston University, where she majored in Business Administration and minored in Anthropology. Her research interests include accounting regulation and enforcement, ESG disclosures, and corporate political activity.

Divya Anantharaman is Professor of Accounting and Information Systems and Dean's Research Professor at Rutgers Business School, Newark and New Jersey. Divya conducts research on defined-benefit pensions in both corporate and governmental settings, and on environmental, social, and governance (ESG) aspects of corporate performance. As an accountant, Divya is particularly interested in how the measurement and reporting of economic activities can have real impacts on those activities, and her work on pensions has demonstrated that pension accounting standards can play a significant role in driving pension risk-taking. She brings the same interest in measurement and reporting to her work on ESG. Her work has appeared in top-tier journals in accounting and finance, been discussed in the popular press, and cited in regulatory rulemaking.

Preeti Bhattacharji is the Head of Sustainable Investing for J.P. Morgan's US Private Bank. In this role, she works with advisors and their clients to incorporate sustainability into their investment portfolios, develops thought leadership, and works with portfolio managers and due diligence colleagues to expand the Private Bank's sustainable investing platform. Preeti has a decade of experience stewarding sustainable investments across asset classes and return profiles. Prior to J.P. Morgan, Preeti worked on post-investment engagement at Calvert Research & Management. Before that, she served as Vice President of Integrated Capitals at the F.B. Heron Foundation, working to better align the foundation's endowment with its mission, informing Heron's long-term strategic direction, and helping to steward its investments across asset classes. Preeti has also served as the Assistant Director for the Heilbrunn Center for Graham & Dodd Investing and a research associate at the Council on Foreign Relations, where she reported on global issues that included the global financial crisis and climate change. Preeti earned a B.A. from Columbia University and an MBA from Columbia Business School.

Bruce Bolger is CEO of the Enterprise Engagement Alliance at TheEEA.org, and is one of the founders of the field of Enterprise Engagement, an implementation process for what is now known as stakeholder capitalism. Since 1988, he has combined a career in business publishing and marketing with stakeholder management, human capital reporting, and investor relationships in all people aspects of ESG (environmental, social, governance). Based on nine years of research conducted by the Forum for People Performance Management at the Medill School at Northwestern University, he founded the EEA in 2009 to create a framework for the implementation of stakeholder engagement.

Carol A. Casazza is Senior Advisor to private equity firms advising on ESG risks and opportunities associated with deploying capital in private markets. A seasoned ESG professional, she was Vice President, Assistant General Counsel, Global Environment, Health and Safety (EHS) at Pfizer Inc where she managed the company's worldwide EHS program. She has guided global companies on enhancing their sustainability programs as part of the Ernst & Young Climate Change and Sustainability Services Practice. She started her career at the United States Environmental Protection Agency where she held positions first, as Environmental Scientist and then, as Assistant Regional Counsel. She earned a B.A. in systems ecology from Rutgers College, Rutgers University and a J.D. from Maurice A. Deane School of Law, Hofstra University.

https://doi.org/10.1515/9783111178608-204

Eric Darrisaw is Principal of Lazarus Advisors LLC, a ESG consulting firm, and a member of the governing board of the Interfaith Center on Corporate Responsibility. ICCR is a coalition of over 300 global institutional investors representing more than 4 trillion in managed assets. Eric has 30 years' experience in the securities industry providing corporate governance and quantitative research services to asset managers and pension funds. He is Impact Shares Corporate Engagement Advisor, a SEC-registered Investment manager of NACP ETF (NYSE: ARCA) which replicates the NAACP corporate scorecard and tracks the performance of the Morningstar Minority Empowerment Index.

Dan Daugaard is Associate Professor and Head of Discipline for Finance, Tasmanian School of Business and Economics, University of Tasmania. Dan is also honorary Associate Professor and Deputy Director for the Centre for Corporate Sustainability & Environmental Finance, Macquarie Business School. His current research investigates the key drivers for ESG performance, the pathways to operationalize universal ownership to mitigate risk, the financial and economic implications of renewable energy transformation, and the behavioral enablers for corporate leaders to improve sustainability practice. Prior to academia, Dan managed institutional investment portfolios and developed innovative investment products including one of Australia's first environmental superannuation funds.

James Hawley is Professor Emeritus School of Economics and Business, Saint Mary College of California. He is the author/co-authors of four books, most recently *Moving Beyond Modern Portfolio Theory: Investing that Matters* (with Jon Lukomnik), and editor/co-editor of three handbooks on corporate governance and responsible investment, in addition to numerous scholarly articles and papers on topics including corporate governance, responsible and sustainable investment, the international monetary and financial system, and environmental issues. He has been an invited guest professor at the University of Cambridge, Université de Paris, Université de Montpellier, Maastricht University, St. Gallen University, and the Kennedy School, Harvard University. He has spoken before numerous professional investor conferences and is frequently quoted in business and other media.

Sarah J. Herman is an accomplished secondary school educator and administrator. Her experience includes teaching courses in American and World History, World Literature. She developed an experiential Law elective as former Humanities Department Chair at a high school in Brooklyn, NY. Prior to her transition to education, she was a Law Clerk in the Corporate Transactions and Securities practice group at a midsize firm in New York City. She earned a B.A. in English with a Minor in History from Boston College (Honors Program), a J.D. from Fordham University School of Law, and an M.A. in Secondary English Education from Brooklyn College, City University of New York.

Moses Kangogo is a lecturer in Finance and Economics at the Tasmanian School of Business and Economics, University of Tasmania. Moses is also an early career researcher. He is an expert in systemic and systematic risk, banking, asset pricing, corporate finance, credit risks and housing finance, with econometric and statistical analysis skills for large databases. His current research investigates the drivers of regional spillovers in the housing market, effects of COVID-19 on banking sector and the effects of global supply chain disruptions on energy commodities.

Jon Lukomnik is a long-time institutional investor and has been named by Forbes as one of the pioneers of modern corporate governance. Jon is Adjunct Professor of International and Public Affairs at Columbia University, and a Senior Fellow at the High Meadows Institute. He served for more than a decade as the executive director of the IRRC Institute and is a former Pembroke Visiting Professor at the Judge Business School at Cambridge. The managing partner of Sinclair Capital, Jon has been the investment advisor or a trustee for more than $100 billion and has consulted to institutional investors with aggregate assets of more than $1 trillion dollars.

Richard Morrison is a senior fellow at the Competitive Enterprise Institute (CEI), a non-profit economic policy organization in Washington, D.C. His research focuses on the relationship between economic and political freedom, including regulation of corporate governance and cultural attitudes toward capitalism. He is a frequent contributor to news and commentary publications such as *National Review*, *Fortune*, *Discourse*, *Law & Liberty*, and *Real Clear Politics*. He is also the host of the weekly Free the Economy podcast, and a former host of the Tax Foundation's Tax Policy Podcast and the CEI podcast Liberty Week. He is a graduate of Claremont McKenna College.

Patrick Wong is the Content Lead for OpenInvest, a J.P. Morgan company. A former journalist, Patrick has spent the majority of his career leading content strategy and execution at various startups spanning foodtech, fintech, and public safety. He has written extensively about sustainable food, finance, and banking-as-a-service. Patrick earned a bachelor's degree in journalism from the New York University Arthur L. Carter Journalism Institute.

Keyi Zhao is Associate Professor at the School of Accounting at the Southwestern University of Finance and Economics in Chengdu, China. She earned her Ph.D. at Rutgers, the State University of New Jersey. Her research interests include ESG disclosure and measurement and textual analysis.

Preface

This collection of writings spans a range of important topics at a time when ESG has hit something of an inflexion point. ESG investing has attracted substantial assets yet has been subject to increasing attacks from critics. One might take this as a sign of maturity. Twenty years ago, the amount of money going into ESG investments was relatively small and had the attention of only those committed to their success. Now, however, ESG investing has become pervasive and the amounts at stake have become material. The simple, noncontroversial investing style of an earlier age has given birth to more complex strategies subject to oversight that is often skeptical. Also, while returns to well-designed ESG funds have been shown to be comparable to equivalent, conventional portfolios, returns to naïve divestment funds have more often than not underperformed conventional funds. In an increasingly divided and contentious world, ESG investing has been challenged aggressively by those who question its effectiveness, its fidelity to fiduciary responsibility, and its perceived affiliation with a far left "woke" agenda. This backlash has resulted in outflows from some of the most successful ESG ETFs with resultant damage to the reputation and bottom line of several financial firms, most visibly BlackRock. It has been noted that in response, BlackRock pivoted from using the label "ESG" to the less triggering term "transition investing."[1]

Some of the critics of ESG investing have undoubtedly been politically motivated. Others have focused on poor portfolio returns. Some analyses of financial performance have relied on evaluating historical performance of naïve divestment strategies which have underperformed[2] and generalized those results to conclude that more sophisticated index portfolio vehicles would also underperform. The many meta studies which show positive sustainable portfolio performance refute those conclusions. There are also several diversified investment products (such as the S&P 500 ESG ETF) which have a positive ESG tilt yet closely follow a conventional diversified index in terms of both risk and return.

But a more disturbing criticism is that many investment products have been incorrectly marketed as ESG or Sustainable. Some have been found to bless companies that have either engaged in greenwashing or have been rated inaccurately by one or more of the ESG rating services. And some financial institutions have not lived up to

---

1 J. Pitcher & A. Ramkumar (2024, March 3), Step aside, ESG. BlackRock is doing transition investing now, *WSJ*, https://www.wsj.com/finance/investing/step-aside-esg-blackrock-is-doing-transition-investing-now-59df3908?st=gl1tgoqnkrgx2sb&reflink=article_email_share

2 On November 14, 2022, investment firm Wilshire provided the Investment Committee with its annual analysis of CalPERS divestment activities that stated, "Since inception, the active divestment programs have reduced the potential market value of the CalPERS Total Fund by an estimated $3.378 billion in present value terms, CALPERS." Board of Administration. Agenda Item 8C (2023, March 13), https://www.calpers.ca.gov/docs/board-agendas/202303/full/item8c_00_a.pdf

https://doi.org/10.1515/9783111178608-205

their claims of properly vetting companies for their ESG practices. Now that ESG investing has reached a certain level of maturity, investors and analysts are able to not only assess risk and financial return but also do a thorough investigation of company ESG practices. Seeking to understand the details of their investments, many sustainable investors have taken a deeper dive into the specifics of their portfolios. They are asking questions such as: are evaluations of investee companies accurate? And are these companies truly performing in ways that are consistent with the aims of investors? An investor might start with the goal of having her money invested in a manner which will support activities which she believes will further ESG issues she considers most important to her. The investor is not taking direct action herself in, for example, improving corporate diversity, equity and inclusion. These activities are carried out by the companies in whose assets she has invested. For most investors, even some of the larger, more sophisticated institutional investors, it is difficult or prohibitively expensive to determine which companies are furthering their desired ESG goals. The fact that many companies make claims of superior ESG qualities only clouds the issue. "Greenwashing" has become a popular marketing tactic for many companies. To take one example, a company may claim that it has instituted policies to manufacture and sell clothing that contains "sustainable" or "eco-friendly" fibers. These claims are easy to make but the reality is all too often something different. The U.S. Federal Trade Commission (FTC) has fined several companies for making misleading or fraudulent claims. Kohl's and Walmart are two examples of retailers who were fined for their transgressions.

> The complaint against Kohl's charges that the company falsely represented that sheets, pillows, bath rugs, and towels advertised as made wholly or in part from bamboo were, in fact, made of rayon. What's more, the company described them with terms like "sustainable," "highly renewable," and "environmentally friendly." Kohl's also advertised some of the products online with a "Cleaner Solutions" seal that linked people to a "Sustainability at Kohl's" webpage describing initiatives suggesting that the company "care[s] about the planet."[3]
>
> According to the complaint against Walmart, the company also made false bamboo claims in promoting sheets, towels, blankets, and nursing bras. In addition, Walmart marketed the items with phrases like "eco-friendly & sustainable" and "renewable and environmentally sustainable."

As stated by the FTC, Kohl's and Walmart knew these claims were misleading at best, and the FTC had sent warning letters to these companies as early as January of 2010.

The [2022] complaints against Kohl's and Walmart charge them with making false or unsubstantiated claims, in violation of Section 5 of the FTC Act. According to the FTC, they "misrepresented that the products were made of bamboo and that they pro-

---

3 FTC (2022, April 8), $5.5 million total FTC settlements with Kohl's and Walmart challenge "bamboo" and eco claims, shed light on Penalty Offense enforcement, https://www.ftc.gov/business-guidance/blog/2022/04/55-million-total-ftc-settlements-kohls-and-walmart-challenge-bamboo-and-eco-claims-shed-light

vided environmental benefits when, in fact, the rayon manufacturing process uses toxic chemicals and emits hazardous pollutants."

In the E.U. several regulators have also investigated inaccurate claims. For example, the Netherlands Authority for Consumers and Markets (ACM)

> has carried out investigations into sustainability claims in the clothing sector, among other sectors. This has resulted in commitments made by the sporting goods retail chain Decathlon and clothing retail chain H&M. They have promised to adjust or no longer use sustainability claims on their clothes and/or websites. They have additionally committed to informing consumers more clearly in order to minimize the risk of misleading practices involving sustainability claims. ACM will continue to keep a close watch on the clothing sector.[4]

These are just a few examples of greenwashing or "virtuous" claims that turn out to be confusing at best, and misleading or fraudulent at worst, and demonstrate the difficulty in relying on company advertising campaigns. If the investor understandably mistrusts the claims of individual companies, they might then look to industry ratings. But in the past, some industry ratings have also been questioned. Sticking with the apparel industry, the Netherlands Authority for Consumers and Markets (ACM) and the Norwegian Consumer Authority (NCA) in 2022 issued guidelines for clothing claims to address allegedly misleading statements that relied on industry ratings:

> The ACM and the NCA have drawn up guidelines for the way in which the clothing industry can use the Higg Material Sustainability Index (Higg MSI) in their communications involving sustainability claims targeting consumers. Major clothing brands use the Higg MSI to bolster their sustainability claims of materials. However, without any explanation, the data from the Higg MSI about the materials used could be unclear to consumers and can easily become misleading. In the guidelines, ACM and the NCA have put forward recommendations for improving the use of the Higg MSI in communication about sustainability claims of materials to consumers.
>
> [In 2022], the NCA conducted an investigation into a Norwegian clothing company. That company used the Higg MSI in its customer communications about the sustainability aspects of the materials used in its products. The NCA concluded that these sustainability claims on the basis of the Higg MSI were misleading and demanded that the company stop using these claims. Following the NCA's investigation, the Sustainable Apparel Coalition (SAC), which is the organization behind the Higg Index suite of five tools, one of which is Higg MSI, decided to suspend temporarily the use of Higg MSI in communicating sustainability claims to consumers. The SAC subsequently contacted various European regulators, including ACM and the NCA, for further guidance.

As the above examples point out, many companies have made misleading claims to be producing sustainable products, or otherwise operating in a manner consistent with the desires of ESG-oriented investors. And at least some organizations which represent that they are providing oversight or validation of those claims have been

---

4 ACM (2022, October 11), ACM and its Norwegian counterpart issue guidelines for the clothing sector regarding the use of a material index in marketing communications, https://www.acm.nl/en/publica tions/acm-and-its-norwegian-counterpart-issue-guidelines-clothing-sector-regarding-use-material-index-marketing-communications

found not to be doing so. Critics of ESG investing can point to these and other examples to reinforce their skepticism. If companies might make misleading claims, and if industry trade groups are often unreliable sources, where can an investor turn to get reliable information on company practices? Many investors rely on financial service providers such as brokers and mutual fund and Exchange Traded Fund (ETF) originators. These organizations are expected to have the resources needed to research candidate investments. In fact, one could argue that one of the fundamental economic justifications for the existence of financial institutions is that they are able to provide just this sort of expertise in assessing investment choices. Two well-known firms, Deutsche Bank and Goldman Sachs, have built substantial businesses on just this sort of financial product: a diversified portfolio, thoughtfully constructed to have risk/return expectations consistent with conventional portfolio benchmarks and invested in companies with superior ESG scores. Yet, each of these firms has been fined by the United States Securities and Exchange Commission (SEC) for misrepresenting their ESG portfolio construction processes. In the case of Deutsche Bank, the SEC's order finds that DIMA [DWS Investment Management Americas, Inc., a subsidiary of Deutsche Bank A.G,] made materially misleading statements about its controls for incorporating ESG factors into research and investment recommendations for ESG integrated products, including certain actively managed mutual funds and separately managed accounts. The order finds that DIMA marketed itself as a leader in ESG that adhered to specific policies for integrating ESG considerations into its investments, however, from August 2018 until late 2021 DIMA failed to adequately implement certain provisions of its global ESG integration policy as it had led clients and investors to believe it would. The order finds that DIMA also failed to adopt and implement policies and procedures reasonably designed to ensure that its public statements about the ESG integrated products were accurate.

"Whether advertising how they incorporate ESG factors into investment recommendations or making any other representation that is material to investors, investment advisers must ensure that their actions conform to their words," said Sanjay Wadhwa, Deputy Director of the SEC's Division of Enforcement and head of its Climate and ESG Task Force. "Here, DWS advertised that ESG was in its 'DNA', but, as the SEC's order finds, its investment professionals failed to follow the ESG investment processes that it marketed."[5]

As for Goldman Sachs,

[t]he SEC's order finds that, from April 2017 until February 2020, GSAM [Goldman Sachs Asset Management, L.P.] had several policies and procedures failures involving the ESG research its investment teams used to select and monitor securities. From April 2017 until June 2018, the com-

---

5 SEC (2023, September 25), Deutsche Bank Subsidiary DWS to pay $25 million for anti-money laundering violations and misstatements regarding ESG investments, https://www.sec.gov/news/press-release/2023-194

pany failed to have any written policies and procedures for ESG research in one product, and once policies and procedures were established, it failed to follow them consistently prior to February 2020. For example, the order finds that GSAM's policies and procedures required its personnel to complete a questionnaire for every company it planned to include in each product's investment portfolio prior to the selection; however, personnel completed many of the ESG questionnaires after securities were already selected for inclusion and relied on previous ESG research, which was often conducted in a different manner than what was required in its policies and procedures. GSAM shared information about its policies and procedures, which it failed to follow consistently, with third parties, including intermediaries and the funds' board of trustees.[6]

Subsequent to these enforcement actions, these firms have hopefully brought their policies and procedures into compliance, but the SEC findings point to the difficulty for an investor to know if their investments are going into the kinds of assets that sell side firms are representing to them.

Investor enthusiasm for ESG ETFs hit a speed bump in the 2023–2024 period as many of the funds either underperformed conventional funds or were expected to have future underperformance. Also, some of the funds were targeted by the 19 states' Attorneys General as being too focused on ESG issues[7] or, conversely, were seen to not be living up to representations made of their consistency with ESG issues. In 2023 alone, investors pulled $13 billion out of some publicly traded ESG funds. But other ESG investments continued to raise funds. Some index-tracking funds had inflows and private equity funds focusing on renewable energy attracted $75 billion in 2023 and about $500 billion for the five-year period ending in 2023.[8]

Exchange Traded Funds (ETFs) originated in the early 1990s and soon attracted explosive growth due to their ease of construction and several other advantages over mutual funds. They provide diversification, easy execution, low fees, and can be constructed to mirror investors' specific interests. ESG investing on the surface may seem like a simple matter of finding an ETF with superior ESG ratings and an historical risk/return profile that mirrors a conventional portfolio. But what is really in that ETF? Are the companies that are included actually delivering on ESG issues which the investor favors? To have some hope of having a reasonable belief that an investor's goals are being addressed, it is important to dive into the details and investigate the process used to rate the portfolio companies. There are a plethora of firms providing ESG ratings although there is perhaps only a dozen or so that are used most commonly by the majority of investors and asset managers. The proliferation of raters and ratings points to the fact that there is no one methodology which is superior to the others. The complexity of the process results in a wide range of solutions with

---

6 SEC (2022, November 22), SEC charges Goldman Sachs asset management for failing to follow its policies and procedures involving ESG investments, https://www.sec.gov/news/press-release/2022-209
7 Texas Attorney General et al. (2022, August 4), Letter to BlackRock, https://www.texasattorneygen eral.gov/sites/default/files/images/executive-management/BlackRock%20Letter.pdf
8 Pitcher & Ramkumar, "Step Aside, ESG . . .".

varying degrees of arbitrary and ambiguous steps. First, the rater has to decide which factors to include as indicative of matters of concern for each broad category of Environmental, or Social, or Governance. Secondly, how are these factors measured and compared across industries? Some factors lend themselves to objective or third-party quantitative measures but many are self-reported. Some are measured by inputs versus outputs. For example, how do we think about measuring diversity, equity, and inclusion by reported budget for this corporate function (inputs) as opposed to employee data (outputs)? And thirdly, there are the matters of scaling and weighting: do all factors get an equal weight and, if not, how to justify subjective weights? How do we weigh carbon emissions versus board governance issues? And how do we get all of these factors resolved into a single metric? When we look at the full range of complexity and judgement required it should come as no surprise that these questions are answered in many different ways, allowing for a broad array of competitors to offer their solutions.

As of 2025, ESG investing could be said to have achieved a new level of maturity and sophistication. Critics have caused investors and financial service providers to exercise increased care in evaluating ESG investments. Simplistic divestment strategies have been superseded by sophisticated portfolio analysis. Company provided ESG claims are being challenged and vendor provided ESG ratings are being scrutinized. This book seeks to provide insights into this new phase of ESG investing. The chapters that follow shed light on the theoretical underpinnings of ESG finance; methods and differences of ESG ratings; practical issues in investing in various asset classes; and conclude with an argument for the economic and financial justification for ESG investing beyond government mandate originating in environmental and social activist circles.

The chapters in this book start with a review of financial theory. In "Modern Portfolio Theory, Capital Market Structural Changes, and ESG," authors Lukomnik and Hawley make the case that ESG investing is an evolutionary extension of Modern Portfolio Theory (MPT). They argue that structural changes to the capital markets would have caused ESG to flourish with or without the non-capital market environmental developments of the last few decades. This chapter presents a summary of MPT and its importance to modern finance theory and practice. But three related concepts –rationality of economic actors, random walk of asset prices and the hypothesis of efficient markets – assume away many real-world issues that ESG investing concepts seek to address. In contrast to the restrictive theories underlying MPT, and its myopic benchmarks, ESG considers the broader real-world issues of environmental, social and governance impacts.

Combining ESG concepts with MPT has led to "systems-level" investing. Systems level investors actively consider how the real world financial, social, and environmental systems affect their portfolios on both the individual company level and for the portfolio as a whole and how their investing activities affect those systems. Viewed in this context ESG investing can be seen as an organic extension of the valuable but overly restrictive implementation of MPT alone.

Chapter Two, "Introduction to Universal Ownership Perspective: Incorporating ESG Metrics to Monitor and Manage Externalities," considers further extensions of the restrictions of financial theory. "Universal Ownership" refers to the concept that institutional owners of large diverse portfolios have more at stake than simply the financial profits of their investee companies. Large institutional investors have highly diversified and long-term portfolios that are inevitably exposed to growing and widespread costs from the environmental damage which might be caused by certain companies. They can positively influence the way business is conducted in order to reduce these externalities and minimize their overall exposure to these costs. Long-term economic wellbeing and the interest of beneficiaries are at stake. This chapter focuses on the incorporation of externalities, impact investment, and shareholder engagement, all of which are instrumental in fostering an ESG performance focus within companies.

The authors delve into sustainable finance practices, including ESG integration, impact investment, and green bonds, highlighting their benefits and challenges. The chapter also profiles investors, companies, and other organizations that have embraced these approaches, showcasing their best practices and outlining the opportunities and obstacles they have encountered.

Chapter Three addresses the fundamental issue of how an investor can know if their investments are actually achieving positive ESG results. In their paper "A Review of ESG Measurements and Ratings," authors Albrecht, Anantharaman, and Zhao provide a thorough review of how ESG factors are measured and how the plethora of ESG Ratings are determined. They review the publicly available data sources, the stated methodologies, and shortcomings of ESG ratings. Seeking to understand the details of ESG ratings, many sustainable investors have undertaken a thorough investigation into the specifics of their investments. They are asking if evaluations of investee companies are accurate. For most investors, even some of the larger, more sophisticated institutional investors, it is difficult or prohibitively expensive to determine which companies are furthering their desired ESG goals. The fact that many companies make claims of superior ESG qualities only clouds the issue. "Greenwashing" has become a popular marketing tactic for many companies. Claims of virtuousness are easy to make but the reality is all too often something different. So, if an investor cannot verify ESG claims on their own, it should not be surprising that a plethora of firms have rushed to fill this information gap by providing ESG ratings, although there is perhaps only a dozen or so that are used most commonly by the majority of investors and asset managers. The proliferation of raters and ratings points to the fact that there is no one methodology which is superior to the others. The complexity of the process results in a wide range of solutions with varying degrees of arbitrary and ambiguous steps. First, the rater has to decide which factors to include as indicative of matters of concern for each broad category of Environmental, or Social, or Governance. Secondly, how are these factors measured and compared across industries? Some factors lend themselves to objective or third-party quantitative measures but many are self-reported. Some are measured by inputs versus outputs. And thirdly, there are the matters of scaling and weighting: do all factors get an equal weight and, if not, how to justify subjective weights? When we look at the full range of complexity and judgement required it should come as no surprise that these questions are answered in many different ways, allowing for a broad array of competitors to offer their solutions.

In this chapter, the authors provide a thorough review of the publicly available data sources and the methodologies used by various sources to evaluate and weigh that data into ESG metrics. They highlight the critical importance of understanding the various measurement methodologies and how different methodologies lead to different conclusions. The authors go on to analyze the difficulties in measuring ESG performance, identifying the many unsettled questions about ESG disclosure and measurement.

Now that we have laid the theoretical groundwork for ESG investing and identified the difficulties in measuring ESG performance, in Chapters Four and Five we review the classes of financial instruments available to investors. In Chapter Four, "A Practical Guide to Sustainable Investing by Asset Class," the authors Bhattacharji and Wong present the many different assets available, with a focus on ESG characteristics. The authors first identify several different approaches to sustainable investing: exclusionary screening; ESG integration, whereby the investor incorporates ESG factors into the investment process; thematic investing, which focuses on specific threads or topics; and impact investment. Each of these investing approaches have differences but each can generate measurable, positive social or environmental impact. One particularly useful distinction the authors make is that the investor or researcher should consider a company's impact from two different sources: the company's product and, separately, the company's conduct. It is then possible to assess a company on a "cradle to grave" basis, beginning with how the company sources its raw materials, the complete supply chain, its operations including fuel sources at each stage, its human resources practices, sales practices, impact on local communities, recycling and end of life disposals, and any other relevant factors.

An important section of this chapter is the cautionary discussion of challenges to the investor pursuing a sustainable investing approach. These challenges include portfolio performance, politicization, greenwashing, and resource challenges involving not just financial commitment but also the time, effort, and other resources required to conduct holistic due diligence, monitoring, and corporate engagement. The authors go on to provide a useful overview of sustainable investing by asset class for public equity, private equity, public debt, and private debt.

The Private Equity (PE) market represents a large and growing segment of the financial markets yet it is little understood by many investors. PE investing entails ownership of assets of companies which are not publicly traded. PE funds are managed by General Partners (GPs), with investing capital provided by Limited Partners (LPs) who may be institutional investors such as pension funds, insurance companies, university endowments, and corporate entities as well as high net worth individuals. Historical outperformance by PE funds has raised their profile in recent years and forecasts of global assets under management in PE range upwards of $10 trillion by the late 2020s.

In Chapter Five, "ESG in Private Equity," Casazza and Herman investigate the large and growing role of ESG considerations in the private equity market. Historically, ESG issues were less central to PE participants due to two factors. First, the typical investment horizon of only five to ten years may be too short for many of the changes needed to affect ESG concerns such as GHG emissions. Secondly, PE investments are more opaque than investments which are traded on public markets. Decision makers and investors may be less responsive to ESG concerns where it's more difficult for activists to identify the investors or ESG issues. While some aspects of these two factors persist, in recent years there has been a substantial increase in focus and sensitivity of GPs, LPs, and activists generally in assessing and addressing ESG concerns in PE. This is especially true where European investors are involved and in cases where regulators have oversight. For many GPs, ESG has become a top strategic priority. The authors provide a detailed list of some of the important stakeholders who are instrumental in driving the ESG focus for many fund managers. In addition to investor involvement in advancing ESG interests, regulators in both the EU and the US have increasingly pushed forward pro-ESG agendas which are seen as key drivers in investment decisions in private markets, as they are in public markets. Casazza and Herman go on to discuss the impact ESG is having throughout the various stages of the PE Investment cycle: defining the fund's investment approach, fundraising, asset acquisition, managing portfolio investments, and, finally, investment exits. Considering the backlash against some aspects of ESG investing, the authors conclude that "Holistic and sustained integration of ESG will depend ultimately upon whether GPs and their investors believe ESG actually results in better long-term returns in their portfolios."

Chapters Six and Seven step back from the details of the ESG investing process and provide historical context. The focus of supporters of ESG investing has most often been on environmental risks and social justice issues which make the case for more environmentally friendly and equitable business practices. However, in Chapter Six, "ESG—The Convergence of Social Justice and Value Creation," authors Darrisaw and Bolger point out that progress has been slow in convincing companies to focus more strategically on engaging the broadest possible cohort of customers, employees, distribution partners, and communities in their management practices. They argue that, ironically, shareholder activists are increasingly succeeding not based on ethical or moral grounds but rather on compelling evidence that a corporation's focus on creating value for customers, employees, supply chain and distribution partners, and local communities will produce more sustainable returns for investors. This is the economic argument for a greater emphasis on stakeholder engagement in business and it comes precisely at a time when many critics believe ESG issues are arbitrary nonpecuniary factors and a violation of management fiduciary responsibility to generate profits for investors. By making the case that there is a direct link between having highly engaged, diverse stakeholders and more sustainable profitability, the argument shifts from a debate about just how much responsibility corporations have to society to one that focuses on the fiduciary responsibilities of leadership to find the best path to sustainable returns.

Divestment as an ESG strategy has been frequently criticized in two dimensions: that it often results in subpar investment performance and, somewhat more controversially, it often does little to impact desired behavior by the target firm or industry. The authors spend some time discussing a dramatically successful case of divestment, the targeting of firms operating in apartheid South Africa in the 1970s. The Reverend Louis Sullivan became deeply concerned about the role of multinational corporations operating in South Africa during the era of apartheid. He believed that these companies had a responsibility to promote positive social change and improve the conditions of black South Africans. To address this issue, he developed a set of principles that corporations should follow to ensure ethical practices and respect for human rights. In time, the Global Sullivan Principles, the NAACP Fair Share Model, and the European Union (EU) Sustainability Reporting Directive have converged to represent a shared commitment towards promoting corporate responsibility, social equity, and sustainable practices to benefit both shareholders and all stakeholders. Although these initiatives have distinct origins and contexts, they all contribute to the broader goal of fostering ethical business conduct and advancing societal well-being in a way that enhances long-term returns for both shareholders and society.

The authors discuss the convergence of the social responsibility movement with ESG, the rise of analytics demonstrating the return on investment of having highly engaged stakeholders, and the European Union Corporate Sustainability Reporting Directive (CSRD), which may mark a watershed moment in the world of management in which racial equity is viewed as a source of value creation, rather than a redress for past inequities.

In the concluding Chapter Seven, "The Case Against Mandatory ESG Standards," Morrison addresses the complications that have arisen due to the development of ESG investing in environmental and social activist circles, without a parallel evolution in legal and policy making arenas. This relative lack of attention paid to law and policy impacts is surprising and problematic. As U.S. government agencies have increasingly solidified voluntary ESG goals as mandatory standards, mostly on a partisan basis, the risks of potentially adverse economic and political impacts have increased. While there are obvious political motivations for much of the backlash to ESG investment, it would be reductionist to dismiss all objections as unfounded, and Morrison considers it important to the future of ESG investing that existing shortcomings be addressed.

Morrison is concerned that regulatory proposals for ESG policymaking have had an overbroad scope, with the potential to impact virtually all aspects of the economy. And that impact is not immaterial. He quotes estimates of the 2022 burden of ESG-themed federal regulations in the U.S. as $2 trillion. He is also concerned about the risks of "regulatory capture" whereby regulation can be influenced by profit-seekers in opposition to the presumed regulatory goals of correcting anti-social behavior. In analyzing corporate behavior, one can find many instances of greenwashing where companies claim environmentally friendly practices but are found to be at best exaggerating any environmental benefits of their operations, and in some cases making fraudulent claims. The case of ethanol is presented as just one example of a disappointing federally mandated environmental policy that has both negative economic and environmental effects.

He goes on to make the case that many ESG values are too subjective to be legally enforceable. Fundamental to Morrison's concern is the lack of Congressional authority for U.S. executive actions promoting ESG goals. In 2024 the U.S. Supreme Court in several opinions gave substantial weight to those concerned with overreach by the agencies and the White House.

The author's solution is to trust in market signals favorable to ESG investments, emphasize voluntary corporate initiatives, and remove government mandates that too often have the perverse effect of masking price signals which would point the way to the most efficient ESG solutions. Modern companies have a great deal of flexibility to undertake ESG initiatives without the market-distorting impact of government mandates. Many states allow a board of directors to consider the interests of other stakeholders in addition to those of shareholders, and dozens of states have enacted benefit corporation statutes based on either the Model Benefit Corporation or the Public Benefit Corporation model.

Morrison's approach could be seen as putting the "private" into "private-public" partnerships, relying on the efficiency of pricing signals and believing in the ability of citizens to make informed choices. It can be argued that the long-term viability of ESG investing rests on successfully addressing these concerns voiced by Morrison.

Chapter One: **Modern Portfolio Theory, Capital Market Structural Changes, and ESG**

Introduction

In this chapter, authors Lukomnik and Hawley make the case that ESG investing is an evolutionary extension of Modern Portfolio Theory (MPT). As ESG gained traction in recent years it was the general media and politicians, viewing ESG through their political science perspective, which gave it the appearance of a social movement in contrast to understanding the convergence of financial theories and structures which are far more fundamental to the development of ESG development and growth. The authors recognize the importance of factors such as the "financialization" of the economy, the breakdown in the neo-liberal economic consensus, and concurrent polarization that made people perceive government as unable or unwilling to address social concerns but argue that structural changes to the capital markets would have caused ESG to flourish with or without the non-capital market environmental developments.

This chapter presents a summary of MPT and its importance to modern finance theory and practice. But three related theories – rationality of economic actors, random walk of asset prices, and the hypothesis of efficient markets – assume away many real-world issues that ESG investing concepts seek to address. They point out the following: "by assuming rationality, randomness and efficiency, MPT creates an investing dynamic where definitions of risk and return, success and failure, are self-referential. The real world is messy? OK, let's just measure investing success relative to the capital markets, not relative to liabilities. So, we measure whether a portfolio has beaten the S&P 500." In contrast to the restrictive theories underlying MPT, and its myopic benchmarks, ESG considers the real-world issues of environmental, social, and governance impacts.

Combining ESG concepts with MPT has led to "systems-level" investing. Systems level investors actively consider how the real world financial, social, and environmental systems affect their portfolios on both the individual company level and for the portfolio as a whole, as well as how their investing activities affect those systems. Viewed in this context ESG investing can be seen as an organic extension of the valuable but overly restrictive implementation of MPT alone.

https://doi.org/10.1515/9783111178608-001

Jon Lukomnik and James P. Hawley

1 Modern Portfolio Theory, Capital Market Structural Changes, and ESG

Why did ESG[1] explode onto the investing landscape in the first quarter of the twenty-first century? Is ESG, as some critics claim, a fad, foisted onto capitalism by so-called elites? Or is it a natural evolution in investing with an economic basis?

Examining ESG through the lens of finance suggests there was nothing sudden or exogenous about its emergence. Rather the apparent rapidity of ESG's ascension was just the inflection point when a combination of long-term structural changes in capital markets and advances in technology made ESG manifest. What appears to be a rapid change is really just the tip of the iceberg breaking above the waves. The iceberg itself has been forming for three quarters of a century, the result of two massive evolutionary changes: 1) the institutionalization of the capital markets; and 2) a recognition by investors of the limitations of – and unintended effects of – modern portfolio theory (MPT). Once the iceberg started floating above the water-line, it was noticed by the general media and the politicians, most notably in the U.S. It was viewing ESG through their political science lens which gave it the appearance of a social movement untethered from the financial theories and structures which nourished it below the waterline for more than a half-century.

Certainly contextual issues – such as scientific advances which detected and proved the threat of climate change, the "financialization" of the economy which gave for-profit corporations more influence over citizens' daily lives, the breakdown in the post-World War II neo-liberal economic consensus and concurrent polarization that made people perceive government as underpowered – have provided tail winds, but structural changes to the capital markets would have caused ESG to flourish with or without the non-capital market environment.

Ironically, to understand those structural changes that enabled ESG to flourish, one needs to appreciate the role that modern portfolio theory has played for investors over the past 70 years. This is ironic because MPT both facilitated the institutionalization of the asset management industry, thereby providing the condition necessary for

---

1 ESG, which stands for Environmental, Social and Governance factors, have become a somewhat controversial semantic, with even advocates such as London Business School Professor Alex Edmans and BlackRock CEO Larry Fink suggesting the three letters have served their purpose. We continue to use them in this chapter for consistency with the rest of the textbook, and because there is no consensus around how to replace them. For the sake of clarity, we define ESG as real-world factors that impact investments and/or the environmental, social and financial systems on which capital markets rely.

Note: The authors are the co-authors of *Moving beyond modern portfolio theory: Investing That Matters* (Routledge, 2021).

https://doi.org/10.1515/9783111178608-002

ESG to flourish, and created the need for ESG because it has no mechanisms to directly consider ESG risks and opportunities.[2]

1.1 Institutionalization of the Capital Markets

In 1952, the post-World War II world was trying to figure out how to invest in a rapidly changing world. Harry Markowitz, a young Ph.D. student, answered the question with his Nobel-prize winning paper on modern portfolio theory (MPT) (Markowitz, 1952). At the risk of oversimplifying, MPT's great step forward was to provide the mathematical basis for diversifying investment portfolios.

Certainly, diversification was not a new concept. Miguel de Cervantes had warned to not put all your eggs in one basket in *Don Quixote*, back in 1615. But, until Markowitz, no one had given investors a methodology to diversify efficiently, or even suggested how the theory of diversification could work. Markowitz gave us the math that unlocked our ability to mix and match securities in the purpose of creating the best risk-per-unit-of-return portfolio.

Make no mistake about it. As routine as MPT seems today, it was a revolution. And revolutions have consequences. Before MPT there was only security analysis, focusing on an individual stock or bond or other investible instrument. MPT plowed the intellectual groundwork for pre-packaged, diversified investing products. So, thank Markowitz for the rise of mutual funds, ETFs, index funds, and the rise of the institutionalized asset management industry generally. When Markowitz wrote "Portfolio Selection" in 1952, the US equity market was 92% retail (Aguilar, 2013). In other words, mom and pop investors as well as very wealthy ones, reading stock tables in newspapers (there was no internet) or via banks managing trust funds, dominated the markets. Only 8% of the market was professionally managed. Indeed, none of the world's three biggest investment managers were even founded until at least two decades later. Blackrock, the world's largest investor, didn't exist until 1988, more than a third of a century after Markowitz's break-through theorem.[3] Today, institutional investors account for more than 80% of the market.[4] And that trend towards institutionalization has held (with variations in details) across different jurisdictions globally, and across differing asset classes, both public and private.

---

2 MPT advocates would say that MPT incorporates the market's reaction to ESG factors through the metrics of price and volatility. As discussed later in this chapter, price and volatility are summary measures, and MPT does not provide investors with a way to mitigate or enhance ESG risks/opportunities as MPT is not interested in the origins of risk.

3 https://corporate.vanguard.com/content/corporatesite/us/en/corp/who-we-are/sets-us-apart/our-history.html. https://www.ssga.com/us/en/institutional/ic/about-us/who-we-are/our-history. https://www.blackrock.com/corporate/about-us/blackrock-history

4 https://www.investopedia.com/ask/answers/06/institutionalinvestor.asp

1.2 Isolating Investing from The Real World

To quote British statistician George Box, "All models are wrong. Some are useful (Box, 1976)." MPT is a mathematical model. As evidenced above, it has proven not only incredibly useful but also performative in that by convincing the investing universe to follow its precepts it has changed that universe from retail-driven, security-by-security-analysis-oriented to an institutional, portfolio-oriented. But how is MPT, if not wrong then silent with regard to ESG issues, also relevant in explaining why ESG has seen widespread adoption.

ESG, at its heart, is the consideration of how real world issues – climate change, diversity, how a board of directors functions – affect individual companies and the capital markets generally. By contrast, MPT's math isolates investing from the real world.

MPT is enabled by three related theories. First is economic rationality (Markowitz, 1990), which means that humans are risk adverse, valuing potential opportunity and potential loss equally. But we know that's not true from a later Nobel prize winner, behavioral finance pioneer Daniel Kahneman who, with Amos Twersky, proved that humans are loss adverse, not risk adverse.[5] In other words, there's truth to the old saying that we think that a bird in the hand is worth two in the bush.

The second enabling theory is random walk, the idea that the next movement of any security is not predictable (Malkiel). Since there is no path dependency, there is no predictability. But if we are loss adverse as Kahneman and Twersky proved, then there is path dependency; you have to know how much you paid for a security to know if you had a loss, and so movements around that price are not random. Expand that to "the market" writ large and you have the basis for the charting of security prices. Other non-random, predictable events include contagion events[6] – for instance when high quality liquid securities are sold during crises because there is an impaired market for riskier securities, thereby spreading risk to a number of markets beside the one where the risk originated. Momentum strategies are built on path dependence.

Finally, there is the efficient market hypothesis. There are weaker and stronger versions of this but all versions say that the market absorbs and acts upon knowable information. EMH has been rightly criticized for decades. For the purpose of this chapter, we note that if EMH were correct there would be no arbitrage desks at investment banks and no need for insider trading laws.[7]

---

5 See Kahneman & Tversky (1979 March). Implicit in this is that emotion and non-rational behavior play an important role in financial markets, e.g. herding, panic, greed.

6 https://www.investopedia.com/terms/c/contagion.asp

7 For an introduction to the academic and practitioner debate around of the various forms of EMH, see (Lukomnik and Hawley, 2021).

Together, these three enabling theories combine to create the perfect myth: easily understood, intuitive, remarkably explanative. And wrong.

1.3 The Divorce of Investment Theory from Real World Complexities

The three theories also serve a purpose which is both elegant and troubling: where ESG is all about considering real-world risk and opportunity, these three theories assume away any problems caused by the messy complexity of the real world. Insulating MPT's math from the world makes the math of MPT elegant.

But by assuming rationality, randomness, and efficiency, MPT creates an investing dynamic where definitions of risk and return, success and failure, are self-referential. The real world is messy? OK, let's just measure investing success relative to the capital markets, not relative to liabilities. So, we measure whether a portfolio has beaten the S&P 500, not whether you are more or less able to retire, buy a home or pay for college. The two – relative returns and absolute returns – measure very different things and rarely align. For example, if your portfolio return is down only 8% in a market that, overall, is down 10%, you have succeeded, at least in an MPT sense. Relative return, in other words, measures the success of an investor in navigating an extant market to create an appropriate risk/return profile for a portfolio from the available opportunity set.

However, in the real world, you would only have 92 cents on the dollar to retire on or buy that home. Conversely, your investments would underperform relatively if your portfolio trailed the S&P by 200 basis points in an up 10% market environment. But in the real world you would be better off, with $1.08 on the dollar to buy that home. Absolute return is what investors rely upon to offset real-world liabilities, including just having money with which to live. But the distinction between relative and absolute return is often ignored in measuring investing success. We are so used to the MPT assuming away the real world that the fact that you can "win" and have less money or "lose" and have more money doesn't even register with most investors.

The distinction between relative and absolute return is easy to understand. But it is how MPT considers risk that both brings it into conflict with considering ESG and, paradoxically, increases the need for investors to consider ESG. In an MPT framework, risk is only volatility, the variation in the price of a security. Again, this suits the hermetically-sealed math of MPT, in that having an expected return is a needed input into creating an efficient portfolio, and the variability around that return is therefore viewed as a risk. MPT doesn't care if the source of risk is how an individual company executes its business plan, a global financial crisis, a pandemic or the climate crisis.

This is circular reasoning at its worst: since the math of MPT assumes away the real world, the causes of volatility are unexamined. And as there is no discussion about how to mitigate those causes of volatility, volatility is assumed to be exogenous.

1.4 ESG/MPT Collision #1: ESG Integration

This is the first instance where ESG and MPT collide head-on. ESG is an investing process that considers how real world factors – environmental, social and governance – pose risks and opportunities to companies. ESG investors believe that ESG factors can affect the enterprise value of an individual company. Therefore, investors use an ESG lens to consider both ex-poste impacts that have happened and are quantifiable to the second decimal point and ex-ante impacts that are thought about more as a probabilistic distribution around a central tendency that may, or may not, be changing. For instance, it would be the height of folly to invest in a property and casualty insurer or an agricultural producer without considering not only the experienced weather in the geography in which the company operates as well as the projections for how climate change will affect those weather patterns in the future. Or to invest in a beverage company without considering its ability to source the quality and quantity of water it needs now, and into the future. Mindy Lubber, CEO of the NGO Ceres, which works on sustainability issues with both companies and investors, told several hundred academics who specialized in researching ESG that she had been speaking with the board of a fashion company whose cotton crop had been devastated by extreme weather, which was likely enabled by climate change. When the news was released, the enterprise value of the company decreased by 3% (Lubber, 2023). This type of outside in materiality – wherein the ESG factor is directly related to the enterprise value of the company and, therefore, material to its securities –is often called ESG integration.[8]

ESG integration is not new. Rather, it is a return to the way investing was done before MPT. Farmers value their land based on the quality of the soil, the climate, the availability of water, and the ability to bring their produce to markets. None of those factors show up on a set of financial statements but their related costs and revenues do. Richer soil and rain and sun when needed means more units of production to sell. Ease of access to market means less transportation cost. No one would think those ESG factors are not "pecuniary"; they affect the financial prospects of the farm. Considering whether or not the weather is changing, or water is drying up or flooding, is simply having situational awareness of the inputs to the business. MPT does suggest that investors can incorporate their analyses of such factors into their investment portfolios by making thoughtful estimates of how such factors will affect expected re-

---

8 Principles for responsible Investing (2010, April 25), What is ESG integration

turn, expected risk, and even the expected correlations between the various securities. However, the more correlated the volatility – such as volatility due to climate change affecting much of the market, or country risk affecting every security in a particular jurisdiction, or a failing or overheating economy – the less effective diversification is as a risk mitigation tool. ESG investors can go further – by engaging with companies, policy-makers and using other tools (Burckart & Lydenberg, 2021), – thereby actually trying to mitigate those risks and enhance those opportunities through affecting real world situations.

Indeed, it is MPT's view of investing as somehow separate from the real world – whereby all that is necessary to invest is known by understanding capital market assumptions (specifically return, volatility and correlation) – that is contrary to most economic analyses. Integrating the non-financial world and investing has been the default for centuries; economists with views as conflicting as Adam Smith, Karl Marx, Ronald Coase, Milton Freidman, and Oliver Williamson have all, in their own way, considered the linkages between the real society and economy and the capital markets (Lukomnik & Hawley, 2021). Part of the reason is that those esteemed economists considered societal and economic impacts over time. That encouraged them to account for feedback loops as people, society, economy, and even their economic theories affected capital markets and then, in another feedback loop, as capital markets affected the next iteration of people, society, the economy, and academic theory.

By contrast, since MPT provides no tool for investors to improve or degrade risk/opportunity, MPT limits the role of the investor to extracting the best risk/return portfolio from the extant marketplace at a moment in time by diversifying (as well as weighting and hedging, all based on volatility and price) rather than considering how investors can impact the market over time by reducing ESG risks or increasing ESG opportunities.

The problem with that framing – that volatility is exogenous and that the only role for an investor is to diversify as much risk (volatility) as possible – is that diversification only works on idiosyncratic risks such as those that affect company a versus company b or, more accurately, security a versus security b. But it doesn't affect the overall risk/return profile of the markets.

1.5 The MPT Paradox

This is the MPT paradox. Even if you are only concerned with financial risk and return and not with people and planet, the fact is that idiosyncratic risk – the type that you can diversify – only accounts for 6–25% of your return. The rest, 75–94% of your return, depending on which academic study you select, is the result of non-diversifiable, or systematic, risk (Brinson, Hood, & Beerbower, 1996, Ibbotson, 2010).

1.5.1 Investors' Impacts on the Capital Markets

MPT asserts that systematic risk – the beta of the market – will affect your portfolio but you can't affect it; diversification, the only risk management tool MPT has, doesn't work on systematic, non-diversifiable risk. But the fact is that all investments do impact the overall capital markets. Just think of some of the common phrases you hear: "We're in a risk on (or risk off) market." That's the result of people's investment decisions. Or "index effects," where a security performs differently if it's in a popular index such as the S&P 500. Again, that's because of how people invest. Examining how investors' actions impact market levels and non-diversifiable systematic risk exposes the simplifying assumptions which make MPT's math so elegant, so powerful, and so wrong.

Why doesn't MPT consider the impact of investing? Remember, Markowitz wrote his article in 1952. Observable market conditions were different; his market was dominated by small, retail investors. While each investment a retail investor makes has impact, it is tiny. Think of it this way: if you walk across the room you will have affected the gravitational relationship between the earth and the moon. But no one, other than perhaps a theoretical astrophysicist, would care. The impact is too small to measure and, in all likelihood, someone else is probably walking in the other direction at the same time. That was the market back then – many small investors doing their own thing. Markowitz – and MPT – were blinded by the market that existed then.

Ironically, the reason it's not the market now is at least in part because of the dominance of MPT, leading to the institutionalization of the market through the demand for pre-packaged diversified products. Other factors, such as less friction in trading, widespread computerization, and improved communications technology also play a role. The slow-moving, random-moving retail investor dominated markets of 1952 have been replaced by technologically advanced, interconnected, and institutionalized markets of today. Investors are more interconnected. Because of their size, some investors are price makers,[9] and social media and instant communications enable other market participants to see trades in milliseconds.

In other words, the price level, directional movement, and magnitude of movement are not exogenous to today's investors. They cause it. Investors affect the market, creating risk on/risk off markets, index effect, super-portfolios, and so forth. But those impacts are unintentional.

The key question then is: can investors deliberately affect the risk/return characteristic of the market overall? To put it in investor speak, can we affect the Sharpe

---

9 Jonathan Harris notes that supply/demand economics suggests all investors are both price takers and price makers because the elasticity function of supply and demand is not binary (not 0 or 1). However, that may not be apparent for smaller investors as the size of the investor matters in terms of where on the spectrum that investor is between absolute price maker and absolute price taker. J. Harris (2022, July 1), *Pricing Investor Impact*, https://ssrn.com/abstract=4263206, http://dx.doi.org/10.2139/ssrn.4263206

ratio[10] of the overall market, so that the diversification tool of MPT can be applied to a better opportunity set?

Yes.

That is exactly what today's investors do. To do that they have broadened, or perhaps restored, the definition of investing to include more than MPT-oriented activities such as security analysis, trading, portfolio construction, and risk management. They understand that modern portfolio theory should be only a subset of modern investment theory.

1.5.2 ESG/MPT Collision #2: Universal Ownership Leads to System-Level Investing

As noted, the market was retail in 1952; pre-packaged diversified products were not the norm. As a non-diversified owner, you owned the stock or a bond of a particular company and that company's financial performance was what you focused on. To the extent investors cared about ESG factors, it was what resembles ESG integration today: how did those factors affect the company or outside in materiality.

But today, investors are diversified. Diversification often makes investors acutely aware that they are "universal owners," invested in the economy, not just in portfolio companies. In the words of Martin Skancke, at the time a Norwegian Ministry of Finance official charged with overseeing that country's sovereign wealth fund, "The nature of the Fund's diversified portfolio has been referred to as universal ownership. When most economic activity affects your portfolio (negatively or positively) on the margin, there is no rationale to support exploitative behavior in any one portfolio company (Skancke, 2010)." As Skancke noted, being a diversified owner means what a company is doing to the environmental, social, and financial systems on which the capital markets rely matters. What is traditionally called an externality because its impact is on others (firms, communities, individuals) and therefore not priced into the entity's valuation is "internalized" into a universal owner's portfolio through its impact on the real world, which marginally affects the price levels of the capital markets. This "inside out" materiality creates the second dimension where ESG and MPT collide.

The European Union tries to account for the impact of a company on the financial, social, and environmental systems through the idea of dual materiality. The EU calls ESG integration or outside in materiality "Financial Materiality" and inside out

---

10 The Sharpe ratio measures an investment's (or a universe or portfolio of investments) risk-adjusted return by comparing it to the return of a risk-free asset.

materiality, or what the company does to the world, "Environmental and Social Materiality."[11] As much as that's an improvement over only considering outside materiality, it "ghettoizes" inside out materiality as not being as financially material. The EU is thinking about materiality from the point of view of a company and only considers enterprise value for that company. But for universal owners (which includes just about every institutional investor and many retail investors today[12]), the EU's semantics are problematic as they ignore the feedback loops between the real world and the capital markets. For example, a manufacturing facility which pollutes clearly causes an environmental impact on the community. But that pollution, over time, causes increased health costs, clean-up cost funded by higher taxes, and can affect property values and housing patterns. Over time, any universal investor will see some of those impacts reflected financially. Much like MPT, the distinction between "Financial Materiality" and "Environmental and Social Materiality" is based on enterprise value at a point in time. That is why the double materiality rubric seems like an attempt to graft outside in materiality onto an outdated vision of how investors think.

Think about the math of universal ownership this way. If you had an equal-weighted portfolio of the stock of 100 global companies, and one of those an individual companies could double its enterprise value by externalizing costs onto the general economy, that likely would hurt a universal owner (as Skancke noted in 2010). The gain in the portfolio attributable to that individual a company would be 1%, making the portfolio value 101. But if those externalities decreased the general price level by even 0.00102% (one and two hundredths of a basis point) the investor would lose, with a portfolio value less than 100, even including the single "winning" company's stock.

1.5.3 System-level Investing

Today's cutting edge is "system-level" investing. System-level investors take the universal ownership approach and extend it to be both proactive and encompass all aspects of investing. In so doing, they actively consider how the real world financial, social, and environmental systems affect their portfolios (both individual companies and overall) and how their investing activities (defined broadly) affect those systems. For example, here is one of the investment beliefs which govern how the University Pension Plan Ontario invests: "As a long-term investor, UPP has a responsibility to promote the health of the capital markets and the financial, social, and environmental systems on which capital markets rely."[13]

---

11 https://ec.europa.eu/newsroom/fisma/items/754701/en
12 E. Quigley, Principal Research Associate and Special Advisor to the CFO of Cambridge University notes that because of diversified portfolios, "We are all universal owners now" (Quigley, 2020).
13 University Pension Plan, Statement of Investment Beliefs, Belief #2.

How does that work in the real world? Some agricultural and industrial food companies regularly feed antibiotics to their livestock. It somewhat reduces illnesses and therefore increases yield. Those companies benefit. However, the side effect is that it also causes the growth of antimicrobial resistant bacteria (AMR) which cause disease in humans and do not respond to traditional medical treatments. The UK government estimates the worldwide cost of AMR at $100 trillion (as well as an unnecessary 10 million deaths) by 2050 if no new actions are undertaken (HM Government, 2019). Even today, in the United States, which is perhaps the most advanced medical jurisdiction in the world, the Center for Disease Control estimates that AMR costs the US economy some $55 billion each year (Dadgostar, 2019). You can see how even a small reinternalization of the cost to the economy into the general price level of the market, and therefore into the other companies in an investor's portfolio, is likely to offset the price gain to the portfolio from the few companies that benefit from abusing antibiotics.

System-level investing was turbocharged by two seminal books published within weeks of each other in 2021. "21st Century Investing: Redirecting Financial Strategies to Drive Systems Change" by William Burckhart and Steve Lydenberg provided the "how" of system-level investing as well as the name "system-level investing"[14] and "Moving Beyond Modern Portfolio Theory: Investing that matters," as cited above, provided the why.

1.5.4 The Arc of Dynamic Materiality

If the lens investors use to determine materiality has broadened from simple enterprise value to systems, so, too, have the issues. There are two paths to an issue becoming material. First, morals, mores, and practices of society change over time. As existing practice increasingly divides from what is considered acceptable by society that issue has a chance to become material. The arc of dynamic materiality often follows a path that, when complete, includes: concern, reputational risk, regulatory risk, and illegality. With historic hindsight, that path has been traveled by these issues, all of which were, at one point in time, common practice: slavery, child labor, a lack of health and safety standards, and ethnic, racial, gender, and sexual orientation discrimination. To be sure those practices still continue in some shadowy corners of the global capital markets, but most jurisdictions have laws prohibiting them. And investors consider them material.

---

14 "System-level investing" is becoming the most used semantic for this theory/practice of investing. Other terms which apply to fundamentally similar investing practice include "beta activism" which was used by Lukomnik and Hawley and "3D," standing for the three dimensions of risk, return and impact, which is used by PGGM, the Dutch pension manager.

The second pathway is more evolved scientific knowledge. Climate change, for example, wasn't an issue for investors when Markowitz wrote in 1952 because the scientific community hadn't yet discovered it as an existential issue.

In other words, what is material changes over time and in different jurisdictions. Materiality – whether outside in or inside out (whether ESG Integration or Impact) – is characterized by a bright immutable line. It is not a state of being. It is of a state of becoming.

1.5.5 "Isn't that Politics?"

If ESG investing is a natural outgrowth of the institutionalization of capital markets combined with investors trying to mitigate both corporate-specific and systematic market-wide risk, why is it subject to charges of being political?

First, for the risk to affect the capital markets it has to be big. So, it's newsworthy and gets attention, often from a point of view other than the economic issues. Questions of diversity, for example, get caught up in gender politics, visions of gender roles, structural racism discussions, cultural norms, etc.

Second, if investors are trying to mitigate that risk, then the chances are some set of people have been benefitting from the ability to externalize costs onto society. And since the risks have to be big enough to matter, those who have been reaping private benefits by externalizing costs are not about to yield without fighting. For example, the risk of climate change is well-documented. Estimates vary but to use just one, Deloitte estimates that a failure to adequately address climate change would cost the United States 900,000 jobs a year and $14.5 trillion in total by 2070. Of course, there's opportunity as well: rapid transition would add $3 trillion in economic activity and a million jobs in total over the same time period.[15] However, to significantly reduce greenhouse gas emissions to a level necessary to keep climate change within tolerable bounds would mean business models have to change for such powerful industries as fossil fuel companies, real estate, agriculture, construction, logistics, manufacturing, and even banks, insurance companies, and asset management firms. Certainly some will see opportunities (sometimes accelerated or made obvious by government policies (Deese, 2023)) and shift their business models, but others will fight to save their ability to increase profits by externalizing costs.

Third, investing is a discipline that rewards thinking probabilistically about the future. That often involves being "ahead" – at least in terms of time – where society is about any of those issues. The arc of dynamic materiality describes the process an issue traces from non-material to codified in legislation. The probabilistic, future ori-

---

15 https://www2.deloitte.com/us/en/pages/about-deloitte/articles/press-releases/deloitte-report-inac
tion-on-climate-change-could-cost-the-us-economy-trillions by 2070.html

entation of investing means that investors' judgements raise issues at the "concern" or reputational risk segment of the arc, before the specific issue has yet metastasized into an issue that all of society agrees should be illegal or regulated.

So, to use a climate change example, in 2015 a broad coalition of investors effectively lobbied for the Paris climate accord to create governmentally sanctioned greenhouse gas targets. The investor coalition was partially organized by CERES, an NGO which has been working with investors since it was founded in 1989. Indeed, the original CERES principles were written in the office of New York City Comptroller Harrison J. Goldin, who was the investment advisor for New York City's pension funds. One of the authors of this chapter, Jon Lukomnik, who worked for Goldin and later served as the Deputy Comptroller responsible for the pension funds, remembers a discussion in the mid-1990s with the then investment committee chair for the California Public Employees' Retirement System. Unlike 2015, there was little consensus around environmental issues as "material" at the time; the NYC Comptroller's office was working with an issue at the "concern" stage of the materiality arc. The discussion involved trying to get CalPERS to vote for a set of proxy resolutions put forth by one of the New York City funds, asking companies to sign the CERES principles, with the CalPERS investment chair adamant that environmental issues were not material to how CalPERS invested at the time and wanting to only focus on the "G" of ESG. Today, of course, CalPERS is a leader in viewing climate change as an investing risk, with its current position that "As an investor in the global economy, the scale and multifaceted nature of climate change presents a systemic risk to our portfolio."[16] Clearly, climate change has moved up the materiality arc.

Fourth, going beyond MPT means that the tools used by today's investors include some which might indeed be considered political. Investors are interacting with the real world, not just trading electronic dots on computer screens. Where MPT diversifies idiosyncratic risk in the capital markets, today's diversified investors also try to mitigate systemic risks by intervening in the real economy. That means interacting with the political system to try to change policy, engaging with companies, forming coalitions with both other investors and NGOs around issues like extractive industry practices or gender diversity on boards, participating in intellectual debate by publishing white papers, etc. The motivation of most of such investors likely is risk reduction/ opportunity maximization but, in the end, motivation is not absolutely knowable and, so, using political tools subjects investors to charges of playing politics.

---

16 https://www.calpers.ca.gov/page/investments/sustainable-investments-program/climate-change

1.5.6 Legitimacy

Given that ESG involves the reintegration of investing with the real world, what are "legitimate" issues for investors, and what would, in fact, be considered solely political? What would be the investor equivalent of ESG impact activism comparable to a company reaping profits by externalizing costs onto society? In other words, how do we test whether an investor is seriously considering ESG impact issues, as opposed to perverting ESG for private, political purposes?

Simply put, if the twin purposes of investing are to provide a risk-adjusted return to investors and to allocate capital where it is needed by society (Hawley & J. Lukomnik, 2018), then legitimacy must be determined by whether an investor's actions further or retard either or both goals. It would be inappropriate for an investor to take action which would benefit that investor's unique beliefs but negatively affect either purpose. But merely participating in so-called "political issues" does not, ipso facto, make an investor's actions problematic.

1.5.7 Does it Work?

So, does any of this actually help improve the risk return of the overall market? Remember, that's the system-level finance theory rationale.

Yes.

Quantification is difficult because the analysis often involves hypothetical contrafactual situations. However, there are a few data points that suggest that, directionally, investors improve the risk return of the overall market when they mitigate systemic risks.

Perhaps the best is an analysis done by three economists, including one from the Securities and Exchange Commission of the Boardroom Access Project (BAP), undertaken in 2014 by the New York City pension funds (Bhandari, Iliev, & Kalodimos, 2019). The ability of shareowners to directly nominate directors to companies incorporated in various United States jurisdictions[17] has long been a controversial issue. "Proxy access" (which allows shareowners to nominate someone to be a director with or without corporate approval, as long as certain conditions are met) had gone through a long and twisted legal history where it was allowed, then disqualified by a court, then allowed if, and only if, each individual company approved it. As a result, only six American companies featured proxy access when the BAP began.

The New York City funds attempted to establish proxy access at 75 companies with a history of ESG problems, both to pressure those companies into dealing with

---

17 The vast majority of companies incorporated in the United States are actually incorporated by one of the individual states, often Delaware.

those ESG issues and as a first step in trying to establish proxy access as a new market standard. The convoluted history of proxy access created a natural experiment. The researchers found that the simple announcement of the Boardroom Accountability Project caused the shares of those 75 companies to experience an excess return in the shares of those 75 companies of 53 basis points.[18] The City owned roughly $5 billion of stock in those companies, so it profited to the tune of $26.6 million in increased value. Were that re-rating applied to the entire US equity market at the time of the announcement, it would have added $132 billion to the US equity markets.

Today, proxy access is the norm for large public American companies. It is an abject lesson that changing real world risks and opportunities can create (or destroy) market value for both individual companies and the market as a whole.

However, it is noteworthy that, at the time, the Comptroller's actions were criticized as "social engagement efforts" with little focus on "improving returns" (Doyle, 2018) by an author at a NGO generally considered to be aligned with corporate executives. To that observer, the action to reduce an ESG risk by affecting a real-world problem – who sits around the board tables in America's boardrooms and how sensitive are those directors to ESG risks and opportunities – was a wrong-footed power grab and politically-motivated.

In other words, the example is a microcosm of the state of ESG in the first quarter of the twenty-first century:

- It featured a large institutional investor running a diversified portfolio who self-identifies as a universal owner who confronts a systemic ESG issue – who sits on the boards of directors of companies with ESG issues;
- Which meant the investor couldn't mitigate the risk through diversification and so required a systemic solution to a systemic issue;
- That systemic solution required action in the real world, in this case by creating a new market norm for how directors are selected; and
- Those actions elicited a negative reaction to it by an entity who did not consider the systemic solution legitimate because it didn't fit within the universe of investing as circumscribed by MPT; but
- Nonetheless, the systemic solution ultimately changed market norms and created value.

1.5.8 Conclusion

ESG is a natural outgrowth of changes in the capital markets and our understanding of them. ESG may have exploded into the general news and political consciousness in the first quarter of the 21st century, but the causes of it – the institutionalization of

---

18 Bhandari, Iliev, & Kalodimos (2019: 9).

the capital market via pre-packaged diversified products offered by asset management companies, the increased understanding that investing has impacts, and the lack of the ability to deal with non-diversifiable risk through the capital markets themselves – had been building since Markowitz wrote about modern portfolio theory in 1952.

References

Aguilar L. A. (2013, April 19), United States Securities and Exchange Commissioner, speech to Georgia State University, J. Mack Robinson College of Business.

Also R. G. Ibbotson (2010), The importance of asset allocation, *Financial Analysts Journal*, 86(2).

Bhandari T., Iliev P., & Kalodimos J. (2019, February 18), Governance changes through shareholder initiatives: The case of proxy access, fourth annual conference on financial market regulation, https://ssrn.com/abstract=2635695orhttp://dx.doi.org/10.2139/ssrn.2635695

Box G. E. P. (1976), Science and statistics, *Journal of the American Statistical Association*, 71, 791–799.

Brinson G. P., Hood R., & Beerbower G. (1996), Determinants of portfolio performance, *Financial Analysts Journal*, 42(4).

Burckart W. & Lydenberg S. (2021), *21st Century investing: Redirecting financial strategies to drive systems change* (Berrett-Koehler Publishers).

Dadgostar P. (2019), Antimicrobial resistance: Implications and costs, *Infect Drug Resist.*, 20(12), 3903–3910, doi: 10.2147/IDR.S234610, PMID: 31908502, PMCID: PMC6929930.

Deese B. (2023, May 20), The new climate law is working: Clean energy investments are soaring, *The New York Times*, https://www.nytimes.com/2023/05/30/opinion/climate-clean-energy-investment.html

Doyle T. (2018), Politics over performance, the politicization of New York City retirement systems, American Council for Capital Formation.

Hawley J. P. & Lukomnik J., *The Purpose of Asset Management* (Pension Insurance Corporation, March 2018).

HM Government (2019, January 24), Tackling antimicrobial resistance, 2019–2024, p. 9.

Kahneman, D. & Tversky, A. (1979 March), Prospect theory: An analysis of decision under risk, *Econometrica*, 263–92

Lubber M. (2023, August 24), presentation to the Global Research Alliance for Sustainable Finance and Investment, Yale University.

Lukomnik J. & Hawley J. P. (2021), *Moving beyond modern portfolio theory: Investing that matters* (Routledge), pp. 57–61.

Lukomnik J. and Hawley J. P. (2021), *Moving beyond modern portfolio theory: Investing that matters* (Routledge), pp. 15–18.

Malkiel B., A random walk down Wall Street, iPad twelfth edition.

Markowitz H. (1952), Portfolio selection, *Journal of Finance*, 7(1), 77.

Markowitz, H. M. (1990, December 7), Foundations of portfolio theory, in *The Founders of Modern Finance: Their Prize-winning Concepts and 1990 Nobel lectures*, The Research Foundation of the Institute of Chartered Finance Analysts (1991), 35.

Quigley, E. (2020), *Universal Ownership Theory in the Antropocene*, https://papers.ssrn.com/sol3/papers.cfm?abstract_id=3457205

Skancke M. (2010, June), The government pension fund global and the management of petroleum wealth, Norwegian Miniistry of Finance.

Chapter Two: **Universal Ownership Perspective**

Introduction

"Universal Ownership" refers to the concept that institutional owners of large diverse portfolios have more at stake than simply the financial profits of their investee companies. "Large institutional investors are in effect, "Universal Owners", as they often have highly diversified and long-term portfolios that are representative of global capital markets. Their portfolios are inevitably exposed to growing and widespread costs from environmental damage caused by companies. They can positively influence the way business is conducted in order to reduce the externalities and minimize their overall exposure to these costs. Long-term economic wellbeing and the interest of beneficiaries are at stake. Institutional investors can, and should, act collectively to reduce financial risk from environmental impacts."[1]

The concept of universal ownership, rooted in the understanding of interconnectedness and long-term impacts, represents a guiding theme for institutional investors' use of ESG factors. In this chapter, authors Daugaard and Kangogo focus on the incorporation of externalities, impact investment, and shareholder engagement, all of which are instrumental in fostering an ESG performance focus within companies. By reviewing the origins and logic of universal ownership, the authors reveal why institutional investors should adopt this perspective in their ESG investing. Furthermore, they examine the unique position of institutional investors and their ability to influence corporate behavior, emphasizing the importance of integrating ESG metrics into investment strategies.

Through an exploration of externalities and sustainable finance models, insights are gained into the interrelationships between the environment, society, and the global economy. The authors delve into sustainable finance practices, including ESG integration, impact investment, and green bonds, highlighting their benefits and challenges. The chapter also profiles investors, companies, and other organizations that have embraced these approaches, showcasing their best practices and outlining the opportunities and obstacles they have encountered. By bringing together these diverse perspectives, the authors conclude that the concept of universal ownership offers a framework for institutional investors to engage in ESG investing, aligning their strategies with the goals of a sustainable and equitable global economy. This chapter provides evidence that the incorporation of externalities, the adoption of sustainable finance models, and the active involvement of investors, companies, and other stakeholders can collectively advance ESG issues and promote positive social and environmental outcomes.

The first section of the chapter defines universal ownership and explores the origin and implications of the concept. After this, the authors consider how externalities

---

1 UNEP Finance Institute (2011), *Universal ownership: Why environmental externalities matter to institutional investors*, https://www.unepfi.org/filcadmin/documents/universal ownership_full.pdf

https://doi.org/10.1515/9783111178608-003

and sustainable finance models can be incorporated into ESG Investing. This is followed by an examination of the impact of externalities on the environment, society, and the global economy. In this and the following sections there are useful lists of key examples of externalities, the reasons for externalities to be included in investment management, ESG categories and methods for implementing ESG. Then the authors link sustainability with positive and negative externalities and the overall importance of incorporating externalities into investment decision-making. The final sections detail the principles and practices of sustainable finance and the benefits and challenges of sustainable finance models. Here, the authors also provide cases to illustrate universal ownership concepts in impact investing.

Dan Daugaard and Moses Kangogo

2 Universal Ownership Perspective: Incorporating ESG Metrics to Monitor and Manage Externalities

2.1 Introduction

Recognition and implementation of environmental, social, and governance (ESG) factors by institutional investors is gaining significant global traction (Eccles et al., 2017; Matos, 2020). The concept of universal ownership, rooted in the understanding of interconnectedness and long-term impacts, represents a guiding theme for institutional investors' use of ESG factors. This chapter focuses on the incorporation of externalities, impact investment, and shareholder engagement, all of which are instrumental in fostering an ESG performance focus within companies. By reviewing the origins and logic of universal ownership, we reveal why institutional investors should adopt this perspective in their ESG investing. Furthermore, we examine the unique position of institutional investors and their ability to influence corporate behaviour, emphasizing the importance of integrating ESG metrics into investment strategies.

Through an exploration of externalities and sustainable finance models, we gain insights into the interrelationships between the environment, society, and the global economy. We delve into sustainable finance practices, including ESG integration, impact investment, and green bonds, highlighting their benefits and challenges. The chapter also profiles investors, companies, and other organizations that have embraced these approaches, showcasing their best practices and outlining the opportunities and obstacles they have encountered. By bringing together these diverse perspectives, we conclude that the concept of universal ownership offers a framework for institutional investors to engage in ESG investing, aligning their strategies with the goals of a sustainable and equitable global economy. This chapter therefore provides evidence that the incorporation of externalities, the adoption of sustainable finance models, and the active involvement of investors, companies, and other stakeholders, can collectively advance ESG issues and promote positive social and environmental outcomes.

The following section defines universal ownership and explores the origin and implications of the concept. After this, we consider how externalities and sustainable finance models can be incorporated into ESG Investing. This is followed by an examination of the impact of externalities on the environment, society, and the global economy. In this and the following sections there are useful lists of key examples of externalities, the reasons for externalities to be included in investment management, ESG categories and methods for implementing ESG. The next section links sustainability with positive and negative externalities and is followed by the overall importance of

https://doi.org/10.1515/9783111178608-004

incorporating externalities into investment decision-making. The final sections detail the principles and practices of sustainable finance, the benefits and challenges of sustainable finance models, and then present cases to demonstrate universal ownership style institutional investment engaged in impact investing and consider the presence of ESG metrics and the links to systemic risk.

2.2 Overview of Universal Ownership

The concept of universal ownership has two intersecting origins. The first arises from the underlying technical nature of risk, and the second is found in the evolving dominance of different investor types. Firstly, a key motivation behind portfolio construction is to diversify risk. By combining a range of securities which differ with respect to industry sector, company size, geographical operations etc., investors can substantially reduce their portfolio risk (Bodie et al., 2023). This risk reduction process is at the foundation of "modern portfolio theory." Elements of risk associated with the issuing firm's characteristics and activities (e.g., unique aspects of management strategy and firm operations) are effectively diversified away. The remaining portfolio risk is called systemic market risk. This risk conceptually reflects the firm's vulnerability to market wide, underlying economic systems and risk factors (e.g., inflationary and employment conditions). While this feature of portfolio risk has been widely understood and implemented since the mid to late 1900s, the concept of universal ownership revolutionises this risk mitigation process. Investment management and financial advice typically treats systemic market risk as a given. It is usual practice to simply increase or decrease a portfolio's exposure to this risk in line with the associated investor's level of risk aversion. However, a universal ownership perspective goes a step further. It explicitly recognizes the close links between economic systems and the broader environmental and social systems underpinning the economy. This perspective provides an avenue for directly addressing and potentially reducing systemic market risk.

The second origin source is the changing landscape of investor types. When modern portfolio theory was first proposed by Markowitz (1952), the investor community was dominated by many wealthy individuals and few institutional investors (Lukomnik & Hawley, 2021). Fast forward to the present day and we see the opposite, with large institutional investors now the dominant type of investor. For example, institutional investors represent 72% of the market in Europe (EFAMA, 2021). Table 2.1 shows the major institutional investors participating in the developed markets and their relative holdings of equity investments. The table reveals professionally managed investment funds, pension funds, and insurance companies are the largest payers in this space followed by sovereign wealth funds and hedge funds. The equity holdings displayed in the table demonstrate "Institutional investors are thus the dominant share-

Table 2.1: Share of institutional investors in equity.

Type of institutional investor	Amount (in US $ trillion)	Share in equity markets
Investment funds	24.0	41.1%
Investment funds (excluding pension funds and insurance companies)	11.2	19.1%
Pension funds and insurance companies	22.9	39.1%
Traditional institutional investors	**34.1**	**58.2%**
Sovereign wealth funds	3.3	5.6%
Hedge funds	0.9	1.6%
Alternative institutional investors	**4.2**	**7.2%**
Total institutional investors	**38.3**	**65.4%**

Source: Schoenmaker, D.,& Schramade, W. (2018). Principles of sustainable finance. Oxford University Press.
Note: Pension funds and insurers invest directly in equity and indirectly via investment funds.This indirect investment is deducted from the equity managed by investment funds to avoid double counting. As only data for institutional investors in developed countries is available, the share is calculated as a percentage of developed equity markets.

holders of companies" (Darvas & Schoenmaker, 2018x). Institutional investors can therefore be considered a significance force of influence on investee organisations.

The term, universal ownership, is first encountered in the 1996 edition of Monks and Minow (2011). The subsequent development of this idea and its implications for institutional investors is elegantly narrated by Quigley (2019). Universal owners are understandably described as modern-day institutional investors (e.g. pension funds and financial institutions). They hold significantly diversified portfolios and represent a broad swath of end investors (e.g., employees of companies, contributors to industry funds, and even retail investors through their unit holdings in large institutional funds). The concept is illustrated by the simple fund flow links between individual fund contributors, institutional investors, and environmentally and societally impactful investments shown in Figure 2.1. The technical consequences of universal ownership draw on two sources of the universal concept. Large institutional investors have a motivation to manage the impacts of their investee organizations on systemic risk (Hawley & Williams, 1997). By holding significantly diversified portfolios, these investors are primarily exposed to market risk. This creates the problem that institutional investors are unable to divest from organizations which will have negative impacts on market risk. For, example suppose there is evidence that a mining company is poorly managing the environmental impact of its tailings dams. If institutional investors sell out of the company's shares, that would merely put downward pressure on the company's share prices (Edmans et al., 2022) and have the unintended consequence of raising its yield and making it more attract to other investors (who are just after returns without a concern for environmental impacts). These, less responsible, investors are therefore likely to continue to support the company by holding its capital. Unfortunately, when the inevitable disaster occurs, it affects everyone: the environment, society, and the economy. There will be negative market returns and a spike in market risk. The institutional investor, who sold out of the stock, has therefore not escaped the impact on its investment portfolio.

Individual fund contributors   Large institutional investors   Impact investments

Figure 2.1: Fund flows link diverse individual fund contributors, institutional investors, and environmentally and societally impactful investments.

Institutional investors obviously hold a unique position for advancing universal ownership and ESG investing. However, there are many alternative ways to implement ESG investment (Daugaard, 2020). For example, an ESG negative screen can be applied to divest from poorly scoring ESG companies. However, this raises the problem highlighted above, i.e., perhaps the divestment simply shifts the supplier of capital to the offending company. In contrast, the challenge with divestment implies an engagement or impact investment approach is better suited to achieve change in the practices of the company (Edmans et al., 2022). Impact investing is particularly appealing in the highly prudent context of institutional fund management. The evaluation of outcomes and application of impact metrics enables institutions to validate their investment choices and avoid the potential accusation of green washing. The topics of institutional ESG investing and impact investing are therefore further explored in the following section.

Although the historical roots of universal ownership were built upon the "widely held" nature of institutional pension portfolios and linked their concerns to "the interests of society at large" (Monks & Minow, 2004, p. 143), the idea has developed and been thoroughly adopted. The intellectual rigour around the concept was substantially expanded through a special issue in Corporate Governance (Quigley, 2019). Industry mirrored the academic development of the concept with major institutions such as the Norwegian Government Pension Fund Global identifying as Universal Asset Owners. The principles highlighted by Universal Owners have included intergenerational equity, the common good, advancing ESG issues, promoting sustainable development, and the importance of taking a long-term perspective in investment decision-making. Most recently, Universal Owners have particularly emphasized a systems perspective – in relation to the interconnected environmental, societal, and economic systems. Examples of institutions adopting this concept include the University Pension Plan in Canada, Aviva, Franklin Templeton, Legal & General Investment Management, Domini, Amundi, and Health Employees Superannuation Trust Australia.

The essence of the universal ownership idea is therefore that large, diversified investors have asset holdings which are exposed to the intersection of economic, environmental, and societal systems. Major disruption occurring across any of these systems have consequences for both the returns and risks encountered by universal owners. Furthermore, the universal owners are responsible, for their decisions, to a highly diversified representation of the community. From these two reasons, universal owners have an obviously important role to play in fostering responsible practices by the entities they invest in. Activities by those companies that negatively impact either the economy, the environment, or society have consequences for the performance of their investment portfolios. Negative impact is also likely to have direct ramifications for the end investors of the universal owners. Combining these responsibilities with the technical concern with market risk described above, the actions of universal owners have important consequences for all of society.

2.3 Incorporating Externalities and Sustainable Finance Models in ESG Investing

Incorporating externalities and sustainable finance models is crucial to effectively implement Environmental, Social, and Governance (ESG) investing. ESG investing involves considering ESG factors alongside financial considerations. This enables an assessment of the long-term sustainability and societal impact of an investment. In a tangential manner, externalities are the costs or benefits associated with an economic activity that are not directly reflected in market prices (Schoenmaker & Schramade, 2018). This means externalities arise when certain actions of consumers, producers, and governments have indirect effects on other consumers, producers, society, and other countries (Ziolo et al., 2019). For example, pollution from a manufacturing plant is an externality because it affects the environment and society but is not necessarily captured in the cost of production.

It is essential to combine externalities in sustainable finance models so as to accurately assess the true value and impact of investments (Schoenmaker & Schramade, 2018). This involves considering the activities that generate benefits (positive externalities) or costs (negative externalities) which are not compensated by other parties and evaluating the associated risks and opportunities (Eidelwein et al., 2018). However, according to Schoenmaker and Schramade (2018), there are different approaches and considerations for incorporating externalities and sustainable finance models into ESG investing which include:

ESG Integration: The UN PRI (2018, n.p.) defines ESG integration as "the explicit and systematic inclusion of ESG issues in investment analysis and investment decisions." In other words, ESG integration involves analyzing environmental, social, and governance factors alongside traditional financial analysis when evaluating investments (Van Duuren et al., 2016). It requires integrating relevant ESG information into investment decision-making processes to identify risks and opportunities that might impact long-term performance. Van Duuren et al. (2016) argue that ESG investing relies on the idea that both investors and society gain with the inclusion of ESG information.

–   ESG Data and Metrics: Robust ESG data and metrics are essential in incorporating externalities into ESG investing. Companies and investors use a range of different frameworks and reporting standards such as the Global Reporting Initiative, Sustainability Accounting Standards Board, and Task Force on Climate-related Financial Disclosures to disclose and evaluate ESG information (Schoenmaker & Schramade, 2018). These frameworks help quantify externalities and enable investors to assess the sustainability performance of companies. Although, it is important to recognize there can be issues regarding the transparency and reliability of the associated (Dorfleitner et al., 2015).

–   Impact Investing: The Global Impact Investing Network (GIIN) (2017, n.p.) defines impact investing as "investments made with the intention to generate positive, measurable social and environmental impact alongside a financial return." In other words, impact investing aims to generate positive social or environmental impact alongside financial returns. It involves investing in companies, projects, or funds that have measurable and intentional positive impacts. Impact investors actively seek investments that address social or environmental challenges, thereby incorporating externalities into their investment decision-making process information (Schoenmaker & Schramade, 2018).

2.4 The Impact of Externalities on the Environment, Society, and the Global Economy

Sustainability issues are closely related to externalities and thus addressing externalities is essential for achieving sustainable development. Some key sustainability issues related to externalities include:

–   Climate Change: Externalities, particularly in the form of greenhouse gas emissions, contribute significantly to climate change. Activities such as burning fossil fuels, deforestation, and industrial processes release large amounts of carbon dioxide and other greenhouse gases into the atmosphere (Ziolo et al., 2019). These externalities disrupt the world's climate system, leading to rising temperatures, sea-level rise, extreme weather events, and other adverse impacts on ecosystems and human communities.

– Biodiversity Loss: Externalities such as habitat destruction, pollution, and overexploitation of natural resources contribute to biodiversity loss (Cardinale et al., 2012; Schoenmaker & Schramade, 2018). When ecosystems are disrupted, species are driven to extinction, leading to a loss of biodiversity and ecological imbalance. Preserving biodiversity is vital for maintaining the health and resilience of ecosystems as well as for supporting essential ecosystem services that humans rely on (Cardinale et al., 2012).

– Resource Depletion: Many economic activities deplete finite resources, including minerals, fossil fuels, and freshwater. These externalities can lead to resource scarcity, increased extraction efforts, and environmental degradation. Sustainable resource management involves considering the lifecycle impacts of resource extraction, promoting circular economy principles, and finding alternative, renewable sources of energy and materials (Schoenmaker & Schramade, 2018).

– Pollution and Waste: Externalities related to pollution and waste generation pose significant sustainability challenges. Industrial activities and improper waste management practices can result in air, water, and soil pollution. Plastic pollution, chemical contaminants, and toxic substances can harm ecosystems, wildlife, and human health (Schoenmaker & Schramade, 2019). Addressing these externalities involves adopting cleaner production methods, promoting waste reduction and recycling, and implementing stringent environmental regulations.

– Social Inequities: Externalities often have social implications, exacerbating social inequities and injustices (Ziolo et al., 2019). Certain communities and regions, particularly marginalized and low-income individuals, have a disproportionate burden of negative externalities such as pollution, environmental hazards, and poor working conditions. Achieving sustainability requires addressing social inequities, promoting environmental justice, and ensuring that the benefits and costs of economic activities are distributed fairly among all members of society (Schoenmaker & Schramade, 2018).

– Global Challenges: Many externalities go beyond national boundaries, highlighting the interconnected nature of sustainability issues. Climate change, pollution, and resource depletion are global challenges that require international cooperation and collective action (Schoenmaker & Schramade, 2018). Addressing these externalities necessitates global agreements, collaborations, and frameworks to promote sustainable practices and mitigate their adverse impacts.

2.5 Linking Sustainability with Externalities

The concept of sustainability is often described using the three interconnected pillars encountered in ESG investing: environmental, social, and economic (Ziolo et al., 2019). Figure 2.2 categorizes major externalities within these pillars of sustainability. The pillars provide a framework for understanding the different dimensions of sustainability and how they relate to positive and negative externalities.

– Environmental pillar: The environmental pillar focuses on minimizing negative externalities on the natural environment and promoting positive externalities that contribute to ecological health. Positive externalities in this context include actions that conserve resources, protect ecosystems, and reduce pollution. According to Ziolo et al. (2019), these actions include not polluting the environment, obtaining production in safer ways, preventing degradation of natural environment, ensuring resources of natural environment are kept in good conditions, ensuring effective actions to reduce noise, emissions of soil, air, water pollution and actions to minimize the greenhouse emissions (Ziolo et al., 2019). Additionally, implementing renewable energy systems, practicing sustainable agriculture, and adopting waste reduction and recycling measures all have positive environmental externalities. On the other hand, negative externalities arise from activities that degrade ecosystems, contribute to pollution, or deplete natural resources. Examples include deforestation, air, water, and soil pollution from industrial processes, smog, and overexploitation of fisheries.

– Social pillar: The social pillar of sustainability emphasizes the well-being and equity of individuals and communities (Ziolo et al., 2019). Positive externalities in the social sphere are actions that enhance quality of life, promote social cohesion, and improve equity. For instance, investing in education and healthcare, promoting gender equality, and fostering inclusive communities have positive social externalities (Ziolo et al., 2019). Conversely, negative externalities occur when actions or policies result in social injustices, inequality, or adverse impacts on marginalized groups. Examples include displacement of communities due to large-scale infrastructure projects, labor exploitation, and social exclusion.

– Economic pillar: The economic pillar of sustainability relates to the long-term viability and prosperity of economic systems (Ziolo et al., 2019). Positive externalities in the economic sphere include activities that generate sustainable economic growth, promote innovation, and create employment opportunities. For example, investing in renewable energy technologies can lead to the growth of green industries and the creation of green jobs. Negative externalities in the economic domain arise when economic activities have detrimental impacts on society and the environment, such as through overexploitation of resources, income inequality, or financial instability.

Thus, to achieve sustainability, it is essential to internalize external costs, promote responsible consumption and production patterns, prioritize renewable and efficient resources, foster social equity, and ensure the protection and restoration of ecosystems (Schoenmaker & Schramade, 2019). By incorporating sustainability considerations into decision-making processes, policies, and practices, we can reduce the negative externalities and move towards a more sustainable future.

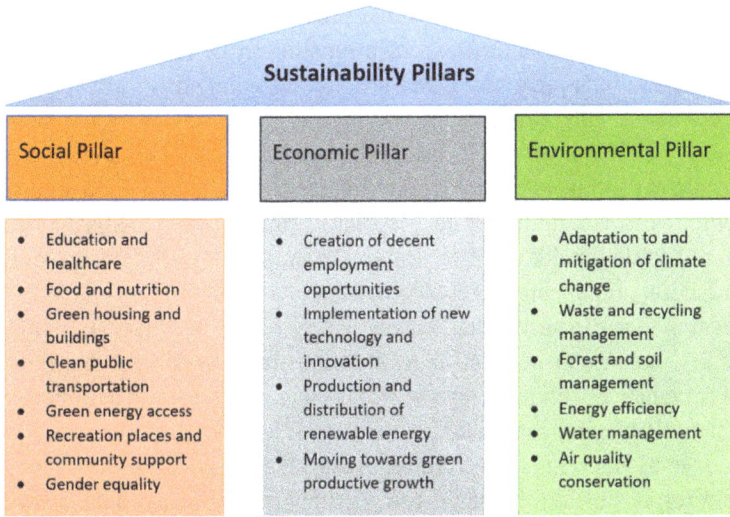

Sustainability Pillars

Social Pillar	Economic Pillar	Environmental Pillar
• Education and healthcare • Food and nutrition • Green housing and buildings • Clean public transportation • Green energy access • Recreation places and community support • Gender equality	• Creation of decent employment opportunities • Implementation of new technology and innovation • Production and distribution of renewable energy • Moving towards green productive growth	• Adaptation to and mitigation of climate change • Waste and recycling management • Forest and soil management • Energy efficiency • Water management • Air quality conservation

Figure 2.2: Externalities categorized within the sustainability pillars.

2.6 The Importance of Incorporating Externalities into Investment Decision-Making

Incorporating externalities into investment decision-making is crucial for sustainable and responsible investing. The external costs or benefits associated with externalities can have significant impacts on the long-term value and viability of investments. Investors can utilize frameworks such as ESG analysis, impact investing, or the SDGs to incorporate externalities effectively (Schoenmaker & Schramade, 2018). These frameworks provide a systematic approach to evaluating and integrating environmental, social, and governance factors into investment decision-making. There are some key reasons why incorporating externalities is important in investment decision-making which include:

– Risk assessment: Externalities can pose significant risks to investments. For example, environmental degradation, greenhouse gas emissions, global warming, climate change, exclusion, income disparities, or social unrest can directly impact the profitability and stability of sustainable businesses (Ziolo et al., 2019). By considering these external factors, investors can better assess the potential risks and vulnerabilities associated with an investment, allowing for more informed decision-making.

- Long-term value creation: Ignoring externalities can result in short-term gains at the expense of long-term value. Companies that neglect environmental and social considerations may face regulatory actions, reputational damage, or increased costs in the future. Conversely, businesses that proactively address externalities, such as by adopting sustainable practices or promoting social responsibility, are more likely to create long-term value and sustainable competitive advantages (Schoenmaker & Schramade, 2018).
- Stakeholder expectations: Investors increasingly recognize the importance of addressing externalities to meet the expectations of various stakeholders, including customers, employees, communities, and regulators. Incorporating externalities into investment decision-making demonstrates a commitment to responsible and sustainable practices, enhancing stakeholder trust and loyalty.
- Regulatory compliance: Governments and regulatory bodies are placing greater emphasis on ESG factors. Incorporating externalities into investment decisions helps ensure compliance with evolving regulations and reduces the risk of penalties or legal issues (Schoenmaker & Schramade, 2018). It also positions investors to take advantage of emerging opportunities in sustainable industries or sectors. By investing in responsible businesses, investors support companies which prioritize long-term sustainability and positive relationships with their stakeholders (Ziolo et al., 2019).
- Reputation and stakeholder trust: Financial companies that effectively address externalities can enhance their reputation by restoring their trust with stakeholders (Schoenmaker & Schramade, 2018). Consumers are increasingly conscious of the environmental and social impact of their purchasing decisions, leading to a growing demand for products and services from responsible and sustainable companies. Incorporating externalities allows investors to align their portfolios with consumer preferences and capture market opportunities.
- Positive impact: Incorporating externalities into investment decision-making provides an opportunity to drive positive change. By directing capital towards companies that actively manage and mitigate externalities, investors can contribute to the development of a more sustainable and inclusive economy (Ziolo et al., 2019). This approach promotes responsible capitalism and aligns financial goals with broader societal and environmental objectives.

2.7 The Principles and Practices of Sustainable Finance

Sustainable finance refers to financial activities and investments that integrate environmental, social, and governance (ESG) factors into decision-making processes (Schoenmaker & Schramade, 2019). Thus, its primary objective is to promote long-term sustainable development and mitigate negative externalities, which are the consequences of economic activities that impact society or the environment. To discuss the sustainable finance typology towards negative externalities, we explore various approaches and strategies that aim to address and reduce such externalities. These include:

- Positive Screening: This approach involves selecting investments based on predefined sustainability criteria (Schoenmaker, 2017). In the context of negative externalities, positive screening would involve investing in companies or projects that actively engage in reducing or eliminating negative impacts on the environment or society (Kim & Li, 2021). For example, fund managers might avoid investing in fossil fuel companies and instead focus on renewable energy projects.
- Negative Screening/Exclusion: Negative screening refers to excluding certain industries or activities from investment portfolios based on their negative impact on society or the environment (Schoenmaker & Schramade, 2018). Thus, this approach aims to avoid supporting activities that contribute to negative externalities. Examples of excluded sectors would include tobacco, weapons, or companies that are involved in unsustainable practices such as deforestation or pollution.
- Impact Investing: Impact investing involves investing in projects or companies with the intention of generating tangible positive social or environmental impacts alongside financial returns (Schoenmaker & Schramade, 2018). This approach actively seeks opportunities that address specific negative externalities and seeks to contribute to their mitigation or resolution. Examples of impact investments initiatives include funding clean energy infrastructure and supporting social enterprises that address poverty or inequality.
- ESG Integration: Another important strategy in sustainable finance is integrating ESG factors into investment analysis and decision-making processes. By considering environmental, social, and governance risks and opportunities, investors can better assess the potential negative externalities associated with an investment (Ziolo et al., 2019). This approach helps promote more informed investment choices and encourages companies to improve their ESG performance to attract capital (Schoenmaker & Schramade, 2019).
- Green and Sustainability Bonds: Green and sustainability bonds are financial instruments used to raise funds for projects with environmental or social benefits (Schoenmaker & Schramade, 2018; Thompson, 2021; Bhutta et al., 2022). According to Bhutta et al. (2022), these bonds enable investors to invest in initiatives aimed

at addressing negative externalities. The proceeds from these bonds are typically allocated to environmentally friendly projects such as renewable energy, sustainable agriculture, or affordable housing, aiming to mitigate negative impacts on the environment and society (Thompson, 2021; Bhutta et al., 2022).

– Engagement and Active Ownership: Active ownership refers to shareholders using their influence to engage with companies and encourage positive change in their ESG practices (Dimson et al., 2015). This approach involves dialog, voting on shareholder resolutions, and collaborating with other stakeholders to address negative externalities. Engaging with companies can be a powerful tool in promoting sustainable practices and mitigating negative impacts, thus addressing the environmental, social, and governance issues (Dimson et al., 2015).

2.8 Sustainable Finance Models: The Potential Benefits and Challenges of Sustainable Finance Models

Sustainable finance models, which encompass various approaches such as green finance, impact investing, and socially responsible investing, offer several benefits and present certain challenges. Some key benefits associated with sustainable finance models include:

– Environmental and Social Impact: Sustainable finance models prioritize investments that generate positive environmental and social outcomes (Schoenmaker & Schramade, 2018). These models aim to promote sustainable development, climate action, renewable energy, social equity, and other socially responsible initiatives. The main task of the financial systems and governments is allocating funding towards these areas, while sustainable finance models contribute to addressing pressing global challenges.

– Risk Management: The sustainable finance models incorporate environmental, social, and governance (ESG) factors into investment decision-making. By considering ESG risks and opportunities, institutional investors can enhance their risk management practices which may solve the sustainability issues in finance (Schoenmaker, 2017). This approach helps identify potential risks related to climate change, resource scarcity, regulatory changes, reputational issues, and other non-financial factors that could impact the long-term viability of investments.

– Long-Term Value Creation: By incorporating sustainability considerations, finance models promote long-term value creation rather than focusing solely on short-term gains (Schoenmaker & Schramade, 2019). This shift in perspective aligns financial incentives with the achievement of sustainable development

goals. Additionally, it encourages investments that generate lasting positive impacts.
- Long-Term Financial Performance: Studies suggests that sustainable finance models can deliver competitive financial returns over the long term (Schoenmaker & Schramade, 2019). Several asset managers, institutional investors, and pension funds are increasing the assessment of ESG activities and practices of companies when making investment decisions (Kim & Li, 2021). Companies with robust ESG practices tend to exhibit resilience and may be better positioned to navigate market disruptions. Additionally, sustainable finance models incorporate emerging opportunities in sectors such as renewable energy, clean technology, and sustainable infrastructure, which have the potential for significant economic growth.
- Access to funds: Sustainable finance models encourage investment in companies and projects that meet ESG criteria (Kim & Li, 2021). This expands the pool of funds available to sustainable businesses and thus promotes innovation and growth in sectors that support sustainability objectives. It also provides opportunities for emerging markets and underserved communities to access capital for sustainable development projects (Schoenmaker & Schramade, 2018).
- Enhanced Reputation and Stakeholder Engagement: Sustainable finance models enable companies to build a positive reputation by demonstrating their commitment to sustainability. This helps transforming the financial system towards an inclusive and sustainable economy (Schoenmaker & Schramade, 2019) and attracts socially conscious investors, customers, and employees who align with the organization's values. Moreover, sustainable finance models promote transparency and engagement with stakeholders, fostering trust and accountability.

2.9 The Key Challenges Associated with Sustainable Finance Models Include

- Measurement and Standardisation: Evaluating the environmental and social impact of investments requires standardized metrics and reporting frameworks (Schoenmaker & Schramade, 2018). Currently, there is a lack of consistent methodologies and data quality, making it challenging to compare and measure the impact of different investments. Developing common standards and reporting guidelines is essential for meaningful assessment and comparability.
- Information and Data Gaps: Access to reliable and relevant ESG data can be limited, especially for smaller companies and emerging markets. Investors need comprehensive information to make informed decisions. Thus, addressing data gaps and improving data availability is crucial for the effective integration of ESG factors into investment processes (Schoenmaker & Schramade, 2019).

- Greenwashing and Lack of Accountability: Greenwashing refers to the misleading practice of presenting investments as sustainable when they do not meet rigorous environmental or social standards (Nemes et al., 2022). It poses a challenge in sustainable finance as investors may struggle to differentiate between genuinely sustainable investments and those with superficial or false claims. Strengthening accountability mechanisms and ensuring transparency are essential to mitigate greenwashing risks (Schoenmaker, 2017).
- Limited Market Integration: Although sustainable finance has gained momentum, it still represents a relatively small portion of the overall financial market. Achieving broader market integration and scaling up sustainable finance requires overcoming barriers such as limited awareness, regulatory obstacles, and market incentives that favour short-term gains (Schoenmaker & Schramade, 2018). Thus, increasing the adoption of sustainable finance principles is essential to create meaningful change.
- Financial Performance Uncertainty: Although sustainable finance models have demonstrated potential for competitive financial performance, there can be variations in short-term returns. According to Schoenmaker and Schramade 2018), certain sustainable investments strategies may involve higher upfront costs or longer payback periods which may impact the financial performances. Thus, managing return expectations and navigating potential volatility is a challenge for many institutional investors (Schoenmaker & Schramade, 2018).
- Balancing Trade-offs: Sustainable finance models often require navigating complex trade-offs. For instance, investing in renewable energy may have positive environmental impacts but could also raise concerns about land use or community engagement (Ziolo et al., 2019). Finding a balance between various sustainability goals, such as social equity and environmental conservation, can be challenging and requires careful consideration.

2.10 Case Studies

The following case studies illustrate the way institutional investors are engaging with impact investments. These cases highlight good examples of how institutions have incorporated externalities into their investment decision-making. The investments particularly emphasize social and environmental priorities. The ESG connections can easily be discerned from the impact metrics used to evaluate the investments. However, the implications of these investments on underlying systematic risk exposures of the institutional investors are not clearly specified. Nevertheless, these examples hold great potential to lead to further development where direct connections to underlying systematic risks are detailed and a coordinated systems risk stewardship is developed.

2.10.1 Vanguard Laundry Services

The first case study has a societal impact focus. Vanguard Laundry Services provides institutional investors with both a financial return and measurable societal impact. The institutional investor support is through loans from a major Westpac and grants from banks, insurance companies, charitable foundations, and local investors. This business creates "employment opportunities for people previously excluded from the workforce, predominantly due to mental health reasons" (Addis et al., 2018, n.p.). The key ingredient to their success is an in-house career development center. They thereby produce solutions to social challenges (through providing access to disenfranchised people back into the workforce) and achieve a sustainable business venture.

This investment's ESG impact is reasonably straightforward. The societal benefits of better employee conditions are evident by the higher income and significant improvement in staff retention rate (relative to public employment service programs). Further to these indicators, there are additional societal benefits associated with reducing housing affordability stress and increasing employee wellbeing indices. These benefits experienced in societal systems point to potential improvements in economic and financial systems. By creating greater societal cohesion and stability, there are potential improvements on reducing market-wide systematic risk. However, the links are not entirely clear and there is little evidence of systemic risk forming part of the decision-making processes of the institutional investors.

International Finance Corporate:

This case has a broad environmentally focused sustainability agenda. The International Finance Corporate builds funds that act as catalysts for collaborative institutional sustainable investing. From initial commitments by large public investors, they are able to attract significant investing from Governments, pensions funds, and sovereign wealth funds. The focus is "on providing capital for companies that enable resource efficiency and develop low carbon products across global emerging markets" (Addis et al., 2018, n.p.). Specifics include renewable energy, green real estate, cleantech, improving air quality, and reducing greenhouse gas emissions.

The interconnection with ESG is relatively straightforward. The investment impact measures include clean energy metrics (e.g., megawatts installed, generated, and avoided and mega tonnes of CO_2 avoided). There are also implied links to reducing underling systematic risk, mainly in relation to reduced likelihood of climate change impacts but also because many of the investments are across emerging Asian markets. The contribution to reducing inter and intra country inequalities is likely to reduce geopolitical risks. However, these systematic risk connections are again not obvious and unlikely to be an explicit part of the investment selection marking process.

These cases serve as instructing examples of how institutional investors can adopt a universal ownership perspective into their investment strategies, specifically by reducing market risk through impact investing and incorporating ESG metrics to measure, monitor, and manage impact. The cases emphasize the opportunities associated with adopting a universal ownership perspective. They also point to more sustainable business models which could be adopted by larger investee organizations. Finally, these examples represent a foundation for developing best practice for institutional investors to implement a universal ownership perspective.

2.10.2 BNP Paribas Group

This case study has a social and environmental focus. BNP Paribas Group (BNP) provides institutional and retail investors with targeted products which contribute to the SDGs through their savings. As a financial institution, BNP Paribas has incorporated impact investing into its business model by offering a range of products and services that align with sustainable development goals. According to Addis et al., (2018), Paribas achieve the ESG impacts through:

Green Bonds: BNP Paribas is a prominent player in the green bond market, facilitating the issuance and investment in bonds that fund environmentally friendly projects. These projects can be related to renewable energy, sustainable infrastructure, clean transportation, and more.

Social Impact Bonds: BNP Paribas has also been involved in social impact bonds, which are financial instruments designed to fund projects that address social issues such as education, healthcare, and poverty alleviation. Investors receive returns based on the achievement of predefined social outcomes.

Positive incentive loans: BNP Paribas has been actively involved in offering positive incentive loans as part of its commitment to sustainability and impact investing. Positive incentive loans are financial products designed to reward borrowers who meet predefined targets (Houston & Shan, 2022). The concept behind positive incentive loans is to encourage and incentivize businesses to adopt more sustainable practices. Companies that achieve certain sustainability milestones or demonstrate improvements in their environmental or social performance can benefit from better loan terms, reduced interest rates, or other favourable conditions.

Microfinance: BNP Paribas has supported microfinance institutions and initiatives that provide financial services to underserved populations, especially in developing countries. Microfinance is a powerful tool to promote financial inclusion and alleviate poverty.

Impact Investment Funds: BNP Paribas offers various impact investment funds that allow clients to invest in projects and companies with a strong commitment to sustainability and social responsibility including renewable energy. As of the end of 2022, BNP Paribas had structured 19.4 billion euros in sustainable thematic funds (BNP Paribas, 2023). All these bank-wide strategic approaches aim to provide products and services that are widely accessible to institutional investors, leading to a low carbon economy.

2.10.3 Patamar Capital

This case study has a societal and environmental impact focus. Patamar Capital provides better economic activities aimed at transforming lives, livelihood, and local economies of low-income communities in Indonesia, India, Vietnam, and the Philippines (Addis et al., 2018). The institutional investor support is through investment support across early-stage or growth-stage companies in sectors such as healthcare, education, financial inclusion, agriculture, affordable housing, and SME digitization. The impact investing strategy of Patamar Capital revolves around finding companies with scalable business models that can effectively address social and environmental issues in poor communities. According to Patamar Capital (2023), this impact investment strategy results in;

- High investments (US$ 200,000–300,000) for 6–8 highly scalable women's small and medium-sized enterprises.
- Training and mentoring for 24 women's SMEs in Indonesia, in partnership with Kinara Indonesia.
- Early-stage investments (about US$ 25,000) as part of the acceleration program.
- Co-investments facilitated from investors within Patamar Capital's network.
- 2–3 women trained as members of Patamar Capital's team to work in the Southeast Asian venture capital and impact investing space.

This case study creates a positive social impact to underserved communities through improving financial health, increasing gender equality, improving rural economies via financial inclusion, improving access to and use of responsible financial services, and improving earnings and wealth creation via entrepreneurship and employment.

2.11 Conclusion

The concept of universal ownership provides a framework for institutional investors to engage with ESG investing. Universal owners are large investors with significantly diversified portfolios of investments and represent a wide diversity of society. There is an inherent connection between their investment choices and their eventual responsibilities. The concept of universal ownership therefore recognizes the interconnectedness of environmental, societal, and economic systems. In a technical sense, universal owners have both the opportunity and responsibility to reduce market wide systemic risk. This gives them a motivation to engage with investee organizations to manage and reduce externalities rather than misguidedly divest from those organizations and hope any eventual externalities won't affect their investment portfolios.

Managing externalities by investee organizations is key to successfully deliver on the universal ownership concept. The most direct mechanisms for managing externalities are impact investing and ESG metrics. Impact investing directly targets the key societal and environmental issues. ESG metrics are the tools of assurance by which impact can be delivered. Therefore, ESG factors have become an important consideration alongside financial considerations when institutional investors assess and select impact investments.

This chapter demonstrates how impact investments across a range of important societal and environmental dimensions can be evaluated by ESG metrics and potentially mitigate systematic risk. The cases provide explicit demonstration of how institutional investors can better incorporate externalities and sustainable finance in their portfolio choice. They illustrate how institutional investors can align their investment strategies with the goals of a sustainable and equitable global economy. By understanding the implications of universal ownership, externalities, impact investing, and ESG metrics, we can develop best practice and successfully continue to advance ESG issues and promote positive social and environmental outcomes.

References

Addis, R., Michaux, F., & McCutchan, S. (2018). *Scaling impact: Blueprint for collective action to scale impact investment in and from Australia.*

Bhutta, U.S., Tariq, A., Farrukh, M., Raza, A., & Iqbal, M.K., (2022). Green bonds for sustainable development: Review of literature on development and impact of green bonds. *Technological Forecasting and Social Change, 175,* 121378.

BNP Paribas (2023). *Responsible savings and investments.* https://group.bnpparibas/en/our-commitments/transitions/responsible-savings-and-investments#:~:text=As%20part%20of%20its%20own,local%20development%20and%20social%20impact

Bodie, Z., Kane, A., & Marcus, A. (2023). *Investments McGraw-Hill Irwin.*

Cardinale, B. J., Duffy, J. E., Gonzalez, A., Hooper, D. U., Perrings, C., Venail, P., Narwani, A., Mace, G. M., Tilman, D., Wardle, D. A. and Kinzig, A. P. (2012). Biodiversity loss and its impact on humanity. *Nature, 486*(7401), 59–67.

Darvas, Z., & Schoenmaker, D. (2018). *Institutional investors and development of europe's capital markets.*

Daugaard, D. (2020). Emerging new themes in environmental, social and governance investing: A systematic literature review. *Accounting & Finance, 60*(2), 1501–1530.

Dimson, E., Karakaş, O., & Li, X., (2015). Active ownership. *The Review of Financial Studies, 28*(12), 3225–3268.

Dorfleitner, G., Halbritter, G., & Nguyen, M. (2015). Measuring the level and risk of corporate responsibility–An empirical comparison of different ESG rating approaches. *Journal of Asset Management, 16,* 450–466.

Edmans, A., Levit, D., & Schneemeier, J. (2022). *Socially responsible divestment. European Corporate Governance Institute-Finance Working Paper (823).*

Eccles, R. G., Kastrapeli, M. D., & Potter, S. J. (2017). How to integrate ESG into investment decision making: Results of a global survey of institutional investors. *Journal of Applied Corporate Finance, 29*(4), 125–133.

EFAMA. (2021). *Asset management in Europe. An overview of the asset management industry. 13th annual review.*

Eidelwein, F., Collatto, D.C., Rodrigues, L.H., Lacerda, D.P., & Piran, F.S. (2018). Internalization of environmental externalities: Development of a method for elaborating the statement of economic and environmental results. *Journal of Cleaner Production, 170*, 1316–1327.

Global Impact Investing Network (GIIN) (2017). *Annual impact investor survey.*

Hawley, J., & Williams, A. (1997). The emergence of fiduciary capitalism. *Corporate Governance: An International Review, 5*(4), 206–213.

Houston, J. F., & Shan, H. (2022). Corporate ESG profiles and banking relationships. *The Review of Financial Studies, 35*(7), 3373–3417.

Kim, S. & Li, Z. (2021). Understanding the impact of ESG practices in corporate finance. *Sustainability, 13*(7), 3746.

Lukomnik, J., & Hawley, J. P. (2021). *Moving beyond modern portfolio theory: Investing that matters.* Routledge.

Markowitz, H. (1952). The utility of wealth. *Journal of political Economy, 60*(2), 151–158.

Matos, P. (2020). *ESG and responsible institutional investing around the world: A critical review.*

Monks, R. A. G., & Minow, N. (2004). *Corporate governance* (3rd ed.). Blackwell Publishing Ltd.

Monks, R. A., & Minow, N. (2011). *Corporate governance.* John Wiley & Sons.

Nemes, N., Scanlan, S. J., Smith, P., Smith, T., Aronczyk, M., Hill, S., Lewis, S. L., Montgomery, A. W., Tubiello, F. N. and Stabinsky, D., (2022). An integrated framework to assess greenwashing. *Sustainability, 14*(8), 4431.

Patamar Capital (2023). *Patamar Capital annual report 2022.* https://patamar.com/annual-report-2022/

Quigley, E. (2019). *Universal ownership in the Anthropocene.* SSRN 3457205.

Schoenmaker, D. (2017). Investing for the common good: A sustainable finance framework. Bruegel.

Schoenmaker, D., & Schramade, W. (2018). *Principles of sustainable finance.* Oxford University Press.

Schoenmaker, D., & Schramade, W., 2019. Investing for long-term value creation. *Journal of Sustainable Finance & Investment, 9*(4), 356–377.

Thompson, S. (2021). *Green and sustainable finance: Principles and practice* (Vol. 6). Kogan Page Publishers.

UN PRI (2018). *What is ESG integration?* https://www.unpri.org/investment-tools/what-is-esg-integration/3052.article

Van Duuren, E., Plantinga, A., & Scholtens, B. (2016). ESG integration and the investment management process: Fundamental investing reinvented. *Journal of Business Ethics, 138*, 525–533.

Ziolo, M., Filipiak, B. Z., Bąk, I., Cheba, K., Tîrca, D. M., & Novo-Corti, I. (2019). Finance, sustainability and negative externalities. An overview of the European context. *Sustainability, 11*(15), 42–49.

Chapter Three: **ESG Measurement and Ratings**

Introduction

In their chapter "A Review of ESG Measurements and Ratings," Albrecht, Ananthara-man, and Zhao provide a thorough review of how ESG factors are measured and how the plethora of ESG Ratings are determined. They review the publicly available data sources, the stated methodologies, and shortcomings of ESG ratings.

A disturbing criticism of ESG investing is that many of the investment products marketed as ESG or Sustainable have turned out to be misleadingly or fraudulently misrepresented. Some have been found to contain companies that have either en-gaged in greenwashing or have been rated inaccurately by one or more of the ESG rating services.

Seeking to understand the details of ESG ratings, many sustainable investors have taken a deeper dive into the specifics of their investments, asking if evaluations of in-vestee companies are accurate and if these companies are truly performing in ways that are consistent with the aims of investors. An investor might start with the goal of having her money invested in a manner which will support activities which she be-lieves will further ESG issues she considers most important to her. The investor is not taking direct action herself in, for example, improving corporate diversity, equity, and inclusion. These activities are carried out by the companies in whose assets she has invested. For most investors, even some of the larger, more sophisticated institu-tional investors, it is difficult or prohibitively expensive to determine which compa-nies are furthering the desired ESG goals. The fact that many companies make claims of superior ESG qualities only clouds the issue. "Greenwashing" has become a popular marketing tactic for many companies. Claims are made that the company has insti-tuted policies to, for example, manufacture and/or sell clothing that contains "sustain-able" or "eco-friendly" fibers. These claims are easy to make but the reality is all too often something different. They can be misleading or fraudulent and demonstrate the difficulty in relying on company advertising campaigns.

If the investor understandably mistrusts the claims of individual companies they might then look at industry ratings. But in the past some industry ratings have also been questioned. Some organizations which represent that they are providing over-sight or validation of those claims have been found not to be doing so. An investor who is aware of these issues may also turn to a "trusted" investment advisor for their assistance. In fact, one could argue that a fundamental economic justification for the existence of financial institutions is that they are able to provide this sort of expertise in assessing investment choices. Yet, several investment firms have been fined by the United States Securities and Exchange Commission (SEC) for misrepresenting their ESG portfolio construction processes. These SEC findings point to the difficulty for an investor to know if their investments are going into the kinds of assets that sell-side firms are representing to them.

So, if an investor cannot verify ESG claims on their own, if some companies mis-represent their ESG worthiness, if industry associations are not reliable, and financial

https://doi.org/10.1515/9783111178608-005

intermediaries misrepresent their processes, how can ESG worthy investments be identified? It should not be surprising that a plethora of firms have rushed to fill this information gap by providing ESG ratings, although there is perhaps only a dozen or so that are used most commonly by the majority of investors and asset managers. The proliferation of raters and ratings points to the fact that there is no one methodology which is superior to the others. The complexity of the process results in a wide range of solutions with varying degrees of arbitrary and ambiguous steps. First, the rater has to decide which factors to include as indicative of matters of concern for each broad category of Environmental, Social, or Governance. Secondly, how are these factors measured and compared across industries? Some factors lend themselves to objective or third-party quantitative measures but many are self-reported. Some are measured by inputs versus outputs. For example, how do we think about measuring diversity, equity, and inclusion by reported budget for this corporate function (inputs) as opposed to employee data (outputs)? And thirdly, there are the matters of scaling and weighting: do all factors get an equal weight and, if not, how to justify subjective weights? How do we weigh carbon emissions versus board governance issues? And how do we get all of these factors resolved into a single metric? When we look at the full range of complexity and judgement required it should come as no surprise that these questions are answered in many different ways, allowing for a broad array of competitors to offer their solutions.

In their chapter the authors provide a thorough review of the publicly available data sources and the methodologies used by various sources to evaluate and weigh that data into ESG metrics. They highlight the critical importance of understanding the various measurement methodologies and how different methodologies lead to different conclusions. For example, one rating methodology leads to including ExxonMobil and excluding Tesla in an ESG index, while an alternative methodology leads to the opposite result. The authors go on to analyze the key issue of the difficulties in measuring ESG performance, identifying the many unsettled questions about ESG disclosure and measurement. They conclude by pointing out several directions for future research.

Disen Huang Albrecht, Divya Anantharaman, Keyi Zhao

3 A Review of ESG Measurements and Ratings

3.1 Introduction

It is impossible nowadays to open *The Wall Street Journal, Financial Times*, or *Harvard Business Review* without coming across the ubiquitous acronym "ESG": non-financial corporate activities grouped under the catch-all name of "Environmental, Social, and Governance." The explosive growth of discussion on ESG reflects the burgeoning interest taken by many walks of society—investors, regulators, employees, media, consumers, advocates—in the impact, and especially the externalities, of corporations on everyone else. Debates have proliferated on the role of corporations in climate change, environmental pollution, human rights, and political processes, to name a few (Lee, 2021; US SIF, 2018). To what extent are corporations contributing to societal problems, and to what extent can they contribute to the solutions? To answer these questions, we need theories and opinions but, equally or more importantly, empirical data and statistical analysis. Correspondingly, high demand has risen for reliable and understandable measurement of ESG performance.

Buyers in the marketplace for ESG information will easily find over 150 purveyors of ratings, rankings, and indices (Douglas et al., 2017). Why and how are they similar or different? What makes an ESG performance measurement product high-quality? Are some more authoritative than others? Which one is most suitable to my informational needs? In this chapter, we aim to equip financial professionals, academic researchers, and business students with the ability to think through such questions and formulate informed answers. We provide an in-depth analysis of several of the most prominent ESG ratings products in the U.S.: their data, their methodologies, their strengths, and their weaknesses. We explain the underlying difficulties of measuring ESG performance, some of which are improvable, some of which require trade-offs, and some of which may be insurmountable. To address some of these difficulties, researchers from the fields of accounting, finance, management, and economics have published suggestions for specific commercial ESG ratings accompanied by empirical validations; we review their innovations as well. At the end, we compile a list of related research questions that are open for investigation.

Before we move on, we first lay out the definition and terminology we use throughout this chapter. The definition of ESG we use is a commonly accepted one: the voluntary integration of economic, social, and environmental concerns into business practices in ways that go beyond legal requirements (European Commission, 2001; McWilliams & Siegel, 2001). It is less obvious whether the third letter, G for Governance, belongs here at all. Usually, good governance is legally required for the busi-

https://doi.org/10.1515/9783111178608-006

ness. It is conducted with the goal of maximizing returns to shareholders, not addressing externalities on non-shareholders. Therefore, the majority of ESG researchers tend to include only the social and environmental dimensions in ESG, even while keeping the acronym intact for ease of communication (Berg et al., 2021). Accordingly, we also confine this review on ESG to the environmental and social dimensions, which represent the impact of corporations on the planet and on human beings, respectively. "E" encompasses topics such as climate change, energy consumption, pollution, and biodiversity. "S" refers to individuals or organizations that have a stake in the decisions made by a company, such as employees, customers, local communities, supply chain partners, and, of course, shareholders—collectively termed stakeholders (Freeman, 1994; Goodpaster, 1991).

Several terms and concepts are precursors to ESG and have largely been superseded in recent discourse, e.g., "sustainability," "corporate citizenship," and "corporate social responsibility." Participants largely use these earlier terms and ESG interchangeably, although their definitions vary slightly (Valor, 2005). For example, "sustainability" originally places emphasis on the environmental dimension and later extends toward the social dimension, while "corporate citizenship" and "corporate social responsibility" fold environmental responsibility into the company's social relationships. Financial professionals traditionally take a narrower view of corporate ESG. The CFA Institute (Institute of Charter Financial Analysts) defines ESG as non-financial information that is still relevant in making investment decisions (CFA Institute, n.d.). This view prioritizes investment returns and evaluates ESG as contributing or detracting from financial performance. More recently developed, the concept of "socially responsible investing" (SRI) or "sustainable finance" goes farther still to consider supporting ESG developments, e.g., green energy, in conjunction with pursuing financial returns. The SRI movement has gathered such impetus that it has given rise to opposition: starting in 2022, many Republican-led states introduced bills forbidding asset managers of state pension funds and insurance funds from considering ESG factors (Rives, 2023). The ESG reporting and investing landscape is ever-changing and any review is timely.

The rest of this review is structured as follows. The second section catalogues the sources of publicly available ESG information: corporate disclosures (classified into mandatory disclosures, mandatory disclosures with managerial judgment, and voluntary disclosures) and external sources. The third section reviews methodologies for measuring ESG performance and uses one rating product with a long history, MSCI ESG KLD STATS, to illustrate areas for improvement. The fourth section analyzes the difficulties inherent in measuring ESG performance. The fifth section lists open questions arising from the previous analyses. The sixth section concludes the review. With this systematic review, we hope to help readers think critically about the construction and limitations of ESG performance measures, analyze the potential consequences of choosing different ESG ratings products, and refine third-party ESG assessments for their own informational needs.

3.2 Sources of Publicly Available ESG Data

We see a major distinction in publicly available ESG information: much of it is self-reported by the firm (hereafter, firm "disclosure") and some is externally reported by other parties. In Section 3.2.1, we go over three types of self-reported information: mandatory disclosures, mandatory disclosures with managerial judgment, and voluntary disclosures. These distinctions have important implications for information content, format, and quality. In Section 3.2.2, we briefly touch on external sources of ESG information such as news articles and lawsuits which tend to be scattered and difficult to process on a large scale. There are a handful of databases that aggregate external ESG information with varying degrees of usability, to which we point readers.

3.2.1 Corporate Disclosures

Based on different levels of regulation or discretion, we classify ESG disclosures into three categories: mandatory, mandatory with managerial judgment, and voluntary.

Mandatory disclosure refers to information that firms are legally required to reveal. It is typically overseen by a government agency that administers filings and enforces compliance. When it comes to corporate ESG issues, mandates often concern non-financial topics that are important to citizens, such as workplace injuries or water pollution. This type of reporting can be highly granular, down to the level of the manufacturing plant. Each piece of mandatory disclosure is standardized regarding content and format. However, because each regulator devises its own standards and presentation. Anyone who needs to compile this scattered information into machine-readable forms for large-scale statistical analysis faces an intensive task.

At the other extreme, voluntary disclosure is not regulated or enforced. Every aspect is at the discretion of the company. Unless companies also voluntarily seek assurance, voluntary disclosure has no third-party certification. The most consolidated form of voluntary ESG disclosure is the standalone ESG report which proliferated during the last two decades (KPMG, 2013). Now the trend is to integrate ESG reporting as a section in the annual report (KPMG, 2017). Company websites are another major repository of voluntary ESG disclosures. Voluntary ESG disclosures also appear piecemeal in marketing campaigns, in press releases, and on social media (e.g., LinkedIn posts).

At the intersection of mandatory and voluntary disclosure lies a type of disclosure that contains elements of both, which we label "mandatory with managerial judgment." Financial regulators like the Securities and Exchange Commission (SEC) and the Financial Accounting Standards Board (FASB) require publicly held corporations to disclose financially material information, i.e., information that 1) is relevant enough and 2) concerns large enough amounts of money, relative to the size of each company, to affect investor decisions (SEC, 1999). However, who decides what is financially material and needs to be disclosed? Corporate managers do, using professional judgment. There is a margin for reasonable managers to make different reporting choices. Thus, this type of disclosure is more regulated and accountable than voluntary ESG disclosure but less so than mandatory ESG disclosure. It can also be labor intensive to compile, scattered across various SEC filings over an indeterminate period—8-Ks, 10-Qs, 10-Ks, etc.

Table 3.1 summarizes the previous three types of ESG disclosure: to what domain the regulator belongs, who is required to report, how granular is the information, what are the content requirements, and what are the format requirements.

Table 3.1: Types of Corporate ESG Disclosures.

Disclosure Type	Regulator Domain	Reporting Entity	Reporting Level	Content Requirements	Format Requirements
Mandatory	Non-financial	All entities that meet specific criteria	Company or facility level	Highly specific to regulations	Standardized and uniform format
Mandatory with Managerial Judgment	Financial	All publicly held entities	Company level	Financially material information only	Broad guidelines
Voluntary	None	All willing entities	Usually at company level	At discretion of reporting entity	At discretion of reporting entity

Next, in Sections 3.2.1.1 and 3.2.1.2, we provide detailed and concrete examples of ESG-related mandatory disclosure and mandatory disclosure with judgment. In Section 3.2.1.3, we discuss the credibility of voluntary ESG disclosures. In Section 3.2.1.4, we review voluntary disclosure guidelines available for use that improve credibility.

3.2.1.1 Examples of Mandatory ESG Disclosures

The White House at one time discussed comprehensive standards for ESG reporting (White House, 2021). In March 2024, this discussion resulted in new rules mandating climate-related disclosures to accompany the annual financial statements (SEC, 2024). In the meantime, Table 3.2 lists several important extant mandates on ESG disclosures, along with their focus, regulations, regulators, and data sources.

While our review is U.S.-focused, mandatory ESG reporting has recently become more sweeping in the European Union (EU), with the (i) European Union's Directive 2014/95 requiring large listed EU firms to publish nonfinancial reports covering environmental matters, social and employee factors, respect for human rights, anti-

Table 3.2: Examples of Mandatory Corporate ESG Disclosures.

Topic	Sub-Topic	Reporting Entity	Regulator	Regulation	Data Repository
Environmental	Greenhouse gas emissions	Facilities in certain industries and over a certain size	U.S. Environmental Protection Agency (EPA)	Final Rule for Mandatory Reporting of Greenhouse Gases, effective 2010	EPA website
	Toxic emissions	Facilities in certain industries and over a certain size	EPA	Section 313 of the Emergency Planning and Community Right-to-Know Act (EPCRA) and Section 6607 of the Pollution Prevention Act (PPA)	EPA website
Social – employees	Mine safety and health data, including violations, citations, fatalities	Publicly held mining companies	Securities and Exchange Commission	Dodd-Frank Act, effective 2012	Quarterly and annual financial statements of individual companies
	Injury rates, severe injuries, and fatalities	Entities that meet certain criteria (e.g., industry or size)	Occupational Safety and Health Administration (OSHA)	OSHA Data Initiative 1996–2011	OSHA website
	Employee benefit plan	Employers	U.S. Department of Labor (DOL) Employee Benefits Security Administration (US Department of Labor, 2017)	Employee Retirement Income Security Act of 1974 (ERISA)	DOL website (Disclosures required to participants, not the public)
Social – supply chain	Efforts to reduce forced labor and human trafficking in supply chain	Retailers and manufacturers doing business in California with annual worldwide gross revenues over 100 million USD	California Department of Justice Office of the Attorney General	California Transparency in Supply Chains Act of 2010	None (Reported individually on company websites or in written disclosures)

corruption issues, and board diversity, and (ii) the European Commission's issuance of the European Sustainability Reporting Standards in 2023 (European Commission, 2023; Pike, 2023). The International Sustainability Standards Board (ISSB) has also issued Global Sustainability Standards (IFRS, 2023) which affects all companies who follow International Financial Reporting Standards (IFRS) inside and outside the EU. We point readers to Haji et al. (2023) for a global perspective on ESG reporting regulations.

3.2.1.2 Examples of Mandatory Disclosures with Managerial Judgment

1) *Environment-Related Disclosure*
   Since 1982, Regulation S-K has required public companies to disclose material contingent liabilities related to environmental laws (Ching & Diglio, 2011).
2) *Social-and-Governance-Related Disclosure*
   Regulation S-K also requires disclosure on board diversity. While board composition generally falls under Governance, the personal characteristics of board members arguably fall under Social as well. The SEC issued new compliance interpretations in 2019, urging companies to give a short description of factors that affect the nomination of board members. Companies are also expected to disclose if and how self-identified characteristics, such as race, gender, and religion, affect the nominees (SEC, 2019).
3) *Human Capital-Related Disclosure*
   The SEC introduced new disclosure requirements in August 2020 designed to provide stakeholders with an understanding of firms' human capital resources – including the number of employees and any measures or objectives that the firm focuses on in managing its business, including those related to the development, attraction, safety, engagement, and retention of employees (SEC, 2020).

3.2.1.3 Credibility of Voluntary ESG Disclosures

Disclosure without accountability could be meaningless at best or deceptive at worst. For example, more than half of sustainability disclosures in the Form 10-K are boilerplate, meaning they apply to most peers in the industry and provide little distinguishing information (Rodriguez et al., 2017). "Greenwashing," the practice of falsifying or exaggerating an organization's ESG engagement and performance, is a major issue facing stakeholders (Gingrich et al, 2019; Reilly, 2020). Since ESG disclosure first appeared in the 1970s and 80s, many have questioned whether it is more performative than substantive—a tool for marketing or public relations (Frankental, 2001). In general, the quantity and quality of voluntary ESG disclosure varies with firm characteristics, business activities, and external events (Gamerschlag et al., 2011; Hahn & Kühnen, 2013; Patten, 1992). Please see Christensen et al. (2021) for an extensive literature review.

3.2.1.4 Voluntary Disclosure Guidelines

Even though companies are free not to impose any standards on voluntary ESG disclosures, many appreciate the benefits of committing to established frameworks. These frameworks market themselves as carefully constructed and high quality, meaning companies who adopt them signal commitment to transparency and accountability to the public. As more and more companies share common guidelines, the comparability of ESG information increases across companies and information processing costs decrease for ESG report readers. Below are examples of several prominent sets of voluntary ESG reporting guidelines:

- The Global Reporting Initiative (GRI) Guidelines had been adopted by 75% of the largest 250 companies globally and referenced by over 60% of the S&P 500 in 2018 (IRRC, 2018). The GRI organization cooperates closely with the United Nations Global Compact, a voluntary initiative for CEOs to implement sustainable goals. The European Commission used the GRI Guidelines as a starting point to develop the 2023 European Sustainability Reporting Standards (European Commission, 2023).
- The Sustainability Accounting Standards Board (SASB) Standards focus on helping companies communicate financially material ESG information. To that end, the SASB has created a materiality map with critical topics for each industry (SASB, 2023).
- The Carbon Disclosure Project (CDP) organization offers a global disclosure system for companies, cities, and other organizations to measure and communicate their impacts on the environment. The CDP collects climate change, forest, and water data from companies using questionnaires (CDP, n.d.).
- The Task Force on Climate-related Financial Disclosures (TCFD) provides guidelines for disclosing climate-related risks without adding excessive new reporting burdens. It recommends that financial and nonfinancial organizations include material climate risk-related "governance, strategy, risk management, and metrics and targets" in annual SEC filings (TCFD, n.d.).

3.2.2 External Sources

Scattered ESG information appears from non-corporate sources in many places: from government agencies on fines and penalties, from journalistic investigations on TV and in newspapers, from whistleblowers like Hemanth Kappanna (against Volkswagen for emissions fraud; Ewing, 2019), and from advocates like Erin Brockovich (against PSEG for groundwater contamination; Dorian et al., 2021). The availability of external ESG information is ad hoc and unpredictable. Some companies are large, conspicuous, and likely to draw attention; some are not. Some topics make for dramatic reporting; some do not.

In recent years, several databases have begun compiling this kind of information. Violation Tracker by the nonprofit Corporate Research Project of Good Jobs First can be found at https://violationtracker.goodjobsfirst.org/. It covers corporate misconduct since 2000, including fines and penalties, civil and criminal cases, and some class action lawsuits. Stanford Law School hosts a database of class action lawsuits against corporations at https://securities.stanford.edu/. The commercial database RavenPack gathers tens of thousands of news articles and other kinds of textual data at https://www.ravenpack.com/.

All the internal and external sources of ESG information reviewed in Section 3.2 provide a rich basis for constructing assessments of ESG performance, which we discuss in Section 3.3.

3.3 Tools for ESG Measurement

In Section 3.3.1, we review ESG performance measures constructed by academic researchers using publicly available data. Interested readers can refer to the relevant research publications to learn how to replicate these measures, extend the measures to more recent periods, or use the data shared by the authors. In Section 3.3.2, we review several leading commercially available ESG ratings products. Each product costs tens to hundreds of thousands of dollars. Their main consumers are institutional investors such as mutual funds and pension funds (SustainAbility, 2023).

3.3.1 ESG Measurements Constructed from Databases

In Table 3.3, we list measures for various aspects of corporate environmental and social performance by topic, along with the research publication and data sources from which they originate.

Not everyone has the time or skills to construct and validate their own ESG performance measures. Third-party rating agencies provide buyers with processed ESG information, which they use their touted research and expertise to make machine-readable, easily digestible, and (more or less) comparable across large numbers of firms. Next, we will discuss their constructions, achievements, and limits.

3.3.2 ESG Measurements Constructed by Rating Agencies

In the most recent annual survey by the SustainAbility Institute on the marketplace for ESG information, 53% of investors ranked commercial ESG ratings among their top three most consulted sources (SustainAbility, 2023). Yet, only 37% percent of re-

Table 3.3: Common Measurements for Environmental and Social Performance.

Topic	Subtopic	Measure	Publication	Data Sources
Environmental	Climate change	Greenhouse gas (GHG) emissions	Matsumura et al. (2013); Griffin et al. (2017)	Carbon Disclosure Project (CDP); corporate ESG reports
	Pollution	Toxic chemical emissions: pounds of chemical emissions; weighted toxic chemical emissions; total pounds of toxic chemicals scaled by firm revenue	Chatterji et al. (2009); Berrone and Gomez-Mejia (2009); Konar and Cohen (2001); Hertwich et al. (2001)	Toxic Release Inventory (TRI) on the EPA website; facility-level data from the TRI aggregated to parent companies in the S&P 1500 from the Corporate Environmental Profiles Directory (CEPD)
		Major spills reported to Emergency Response Notification System	Chatterji et al. (2009)	Same as above
	Compliance	Value of penalties and number of penalties related with violations of major federal environmental statues	Chatterji et al. (2009)	Same as above
		Permit denials associated with Resource Conservation and Recovery Act (RCRA)	Chatterji et al. (2009)	Same as above
		Shut-ins by Minerals Management Service (MMS)	Chatterji et al. (2009)	Same as above
	Innovation	Number of successful patent applications relating to air and water pollution, hazardous waste management, and alternative energy	Carrión-Flores and Innes (2010)	US Patent and Trademark Office
	Lawsuits and liabilities	Number of pending environmental lawsuits against the firm	Konar and Cohen (2001)	SEC 10-K filings
		Number of notice letters; settlement amounts; capital costs, operating and monitoring costs from the Record of Decision	Graham et al. (2001)	EPA

(continued)

Table 3.3 (continued)

Topic	Subtopic	Measure	Publication	Data Sources
Social	Labor practices	Employee lawsuits	Unsal (2019)	U.S. National Labor Relations Board
		Wage and Hour Compliance Action data	Unsal (2019)	U.S. Department of Labor
		Employee violations	Unsal (2019)	U.S. Department of Labor
		Discrimination	Unsal (2019)	Lawsuit press releases
		Injury rates	Cohn & Wardlaw (2016)	OSHA and U.S. Bureau of Labor Statistics
		Employee satisfaction	Edmans (2011)	Fortune's list of 100 Best Companies to Work for in America
	Community	Political contributions to federal election campaigns	Cooper et al. (2010)	Federal Election Commission
		Anti-corruption	Weismann (2009)	Department of Justice (DOJ), SEC enforcement actions and cases
	Product responsibility	Product recalls	Ni et al. (2016)	U.S. Consumer Product Safety Commission (CPSC)

spondents agreed that "ESG ratings are a credible/quality source of information on corporate ESG performance" (SustainAbility, 2023, p. 18). It appears that investors routinely reference third-party ESG ratings while also being concerned about their limitations. At the same time, institutional investors are devoting more resources to creating in-house ratings based on customized needs (SustainAbility, 2023). This is an emerging area of employment and consulting opportunities. However, all ESG raters face similar challenges regarding choosing methodologies and integrating information. Consumers of ESG ratings face the challenge of interpreting and comparing the end results, which is impossible without understanding the original data and transformation process.

First, in Section 3.3.2.1, we provide a high-level comparison of nine leading ESG rating products and their methodologies. Second, in Section 3.3.2.2, we discuss the reasons for and implications of ESG rating agencies having such disparate methodologies. Last, in Section 3.3.2.3, we dig deeper into the characteristics of one of the longest-running and most researched ESG ratings, MSCI ESG KLD STATS (KLD ratings, for short).

3.3.2.1 Overview of Leading Ratings Products

Rating agencies typically begin by gathering information that they consider relevant to corporate ESG, assign scores to multitudes of aspects, and then aggregate these scores into some semblance of an overall assessment. In the process, they need to make a litany of decisions: what are the relevant topics, where to locate credible information, whether to create absolute scores or relative scores compared to peers, whether to assign binary or categorical or continuous scores, how to define comparison groups (which is extra important for the agencies producing relative performance measures), how to weight different aspects of ESG including negative events, and whether they engage and communicate with the companies they scrutinize or stay distant observers. Each rating agency operates by its own beliefs and models. We gather publicly available documentation on the methodologies of nine leading ESG rating products and list their approaches to seven key decisions in Table 3.4, in alphabetical order. Please note that MSCI ESG KLD STATS and MSCI ESG Ratings are distinct products; many rating agencies offer multiple rating products, which is often the result of changing ownership. Please see a history of mergers and acquisitions among ESG rating agencies in Larcker et al. (2022). Information that we could not determine from documentation is marked with "N/A."

The decisions summarized in Table 3.4 involve trade-offs, with no objectively and universally superior choice in many cases. For example, choosing between absolute and relative performance is one of the fundamental presentation choices in ESG ratings. On the one hand, absolute performance scores can be meaningless—in a vacuum, is an ESG Score of 7 good or bad? How about 4? Instead, we need to compare across peers and across time so that we assess how each firm is doing relative to benchmarks. On the other hand, changes in relative scores over time are far less interpretable than changes in absolute scores over time. A company can have no change in underlying ESG performance but experience a change in ESG scores simply because one or more industry peers have improved ESG performance, experienced a major negative event, or even experienced a peer group reclassification. A firm can also experience no apparent change in ESG scores while underlying ESG performance changes over time, so long as those changes align with its peer group. Thus, while assessing firm performance relative to peers produces valuable information, knowing only relative performance can hinder understanding.

Several leading ESG rating products are not included in this table but warrant honorable mentions. Bloomberg produces an array of ESG related datasets but we are unable to obtain documentation on their methodologies without subscriptions. Morningstar Sustainalytics does not only rate companies but also portfolios in the Morningstar Sustainability Rating for Funds (Sustainalytics, 2023). Also, Morningstar incorporates ESG risks into credit risk in its DBRS credit ratings (DBRS Morningstar, 2023).

3.3.2.2 Credibility of ESG Rating Products

1) Ratings Disagreement
In the previous section, we saw that reasonable rating agencies disagree. Anecdotally, the same company can receive vastly different scores in different rating systems. As *The Wall Street Journal* reported in 2018, Tesla received a 0 environmental score from FTSE Russell but a near-perfect environmental score from MSCI (Mackintosh, 2018). The divergence in ratings resulted from the agencies prioritizing different topics: FTSE Russell based their rating on factory emissions while MSCI offset current emissions against future emission reductions resulting from Tesla's products and technologies (Mackintosh, 2018).

While most cases of rating disagreement are less extreme, statistical analyses demonstrate that correlations among different agencies' ratings are surprisingly low. Chatterji et al. (2016) analyze six ESG rating products and find that correlations between them range from −0.12 to 0.67. There is even a negative correlation between two of the six ratings, which indicates that firms regarded as socially responsible in one rating were systematically less likely to be regarded as socially responsible in the other rating. The gap still exists after the researchers adjust for differences in underlying approaches to the extent possible.

Is one rating more reliable than another? Is one approach more credible than another? So unanswerable are these questions that a group of researchers at the MIT Sloan of Management organized a research agenda around the meaning of ESG ratings and named it the Aggregate Confusion Project (MIT Sloan School of Management, 2023). The lack of comparability across ESG ratings is a major concern; it could mislead

Table 3.4: Overview of Methodology in Most Popular ESG Rating Products.

Ratings Product	Absolute/ Relative Performance	Industry Classification	Score Scale	Score Weights	Materiality	Treatment of Negative ESG	Company Engagement
1 CSRHub CSR Ratings	N/A	Proprietary but provides map to NAICS codes	0–100	By credibility and value of data source	N/A	Consideration of special issues	N/A
2 FTSE Russell ESG Scores	N/A	N/A	N/A	By materiality	Based on exposure	N/A	Appeals process
3 ISS ESG Ratings	Absolute	Proprietary	D– – A+	By multiple factors	Based on long-term value creation	N/A	N/A
4 MSCI ESG KLD STATS	Absolute	N/A	0–1	None	Based on industry key issues	Negative performance indicators	Companies invited to review collected data
5 MSCI ESG Ratings	Relative	Global Industry Classification Standard (GICS) developed by MSCI and S&P	CCC–AAA	By subindustry contributions to and realization horizon of negative externalities	Based on industry key issues	Review of controversies	Yes
6 S&P Global (formerly RobecoSAM) ESG Ratings	Relative	Proprietary	0–100	By materiality	Based on likelihood and magnitude of impact	Analysis of media and stakeholders	Yes

(continued)

Table 3.4 (continued)

Ratings Product	Absolute/ Relative Performance	Industry Classification	Score Scale	Score Weights	Materiality	Treatment of Negative ESG	Company Engagement
7 **Morningstar Sustainalytics Company ESG Risk Ratings**	Absolute	Proprietary	0–100	Dynamic weighting	Yes	Idiosyncratic issues	Yes
8 **LSEG (formerly Refinitiv, Thomson Reuters, ASSET4) ESG Scores**	Relative	Thomson Reuters Business Classifications (TRBC)	0–100	Based on relative importance of each category	None	ESG Controversies Score	N/A
9 **RepRisk Index**	Absolute	N/A	0–100	None	By materiality of risk	N/A	N/A

users, cause spurious research conclusions, and lead to suboptimal decisions (Bouten et al., 2017; Chatterji et al., 2016).

Researchers have uncovered preliminary explanations for the divergence in ESG ratings. Bouten et al. (2017) and Chatterji et al. (2016) find that disagreement arises from different models of ESG as well as different measures used for the same components of the model. Berg et al. (2022) find that divergence in ESG ratings comes primarily from differences in scope and differences in measurement while differences in weighting schemes are less critical. Voluntary ESG disclosure itself contributes to disagreement among ESG rating agencies (Christensen et al., 2021; Berg et al., 2023). When companies disclose more information, disagreement among ESG ratings actually increases (Christensen et al., 2021). Berg et al. (2023) argue that standardizing and regulating disclosure, thus freeing the rating agencies to compete on accuracy, will naturally improve the validity and credibility of ratings.

An opposing view suggests that disagreement is rational. Gibson et al. (2020) find that disagreement on environmental ratings is positively associated with future stock returns and hypothesize that disagreement reflects differences in risk. Interestingly, they also find that disagreement on social and governance ratings is negatively associated with future stock returns and attribute this result to optimistic bias on social and governance issues.

However, it is not necessarily desirable or beneficial to eliminate ratings disagreement. After all, different stakeholders assign different weights to the same issues. Investors are more likely to care about financial materiality while local communities are more likely to care about environmental impact and employees are more likely to care about benefits, training, and advancement opportunities. Rating agencies themselves may not be bothered by ratings disagreement; how else can they differentiate their products from one another (Bouten et al., 2017)? Rating agencies may even believe that their clients want second, third, fourth opinions on ESG (Bouten et al., 2017). The issue is not the disagreement itself or whether disagreement is a symptom of noise and lack of meaningful information. If ratings become high-quality representations of underlying performance then users only need to decide which methodology is the best one for their needs.

2) Rating Bias

Sometimes, companies receive systematically different ratings due to characteristics that have little to do with ESG performance. In an analysis of over 4,000 companies rated by Sustainalytics, Doyle (2018) finds that larger companies receive higher ratings than small and medium-sized companies and argues that some of these accolades are unwarranted. Large companies may have better ESG performance or large companies may issue higher quality ESG disclosure, or both (Doyle, 2018). When rating agencies evaluate disclosure quality as part of their criteria, larger companies that have more resources to devote to disclosure have an advantage. What's more, a large company that has a few high-profile negative ESG events can still receive a higher than average rating due to offsetting while a small company that is committed to ESG goals can receive an average rating due to lack of disclosure (Doyle, 2018). Smaller companies are less likely to receive high scores even if they are innovative and perform well in ESG. Fortunately, there is evidence that size bias is on the wane, thanks to increased disclosure by mid-size companies and improvements in rating methodologies by agencies such as MSCI (Guillermo, 2019).

Doyle (2018) also finds that companies operating in countries with stricter disclosure regulation and enforcement receive higher ratings. European companies on average receive higher ratings than North American companies in Sustainalytics ratings. Again, we see that ESG disclosure quality is contributing to ESG ratings (Doyle, 2018; Trevor, 2019). While this should be the case some of the time, it should not be the case all the time.

Not only do ratings exhibit patterns, rating disagreement also exhibits patterns that may reflect bias: companies in the S&P 500, companies that do not have credit ratings, and companies that are less profitable have higher disagreement (Gibson et al., 2020).

3) Rating Oversimplification

Many companies operate complex business lines spanning several industries. Companies that are classified into the same industry may not face the same risks, meaning imposing the same measurements and weights across one arbitrarily defined industry may be inappropriate (Doyle, 2018). With messy industry classification, company-specific risks can be obscured by industry-adjusted scores (Trevor, 2019).

4) Rating Obfuscation

Bouten et al. (2017) point out that the more convoluted and inscrutable are rating agencies' methods, the less capable potential customers become of rejecting their ratings as inappropriate for specific informational needs.

Rating agencies do not seem to be concerned with replicability. For example, LSEG ESG scores (formerly known as Refinitiv, Thomson Reuters, or ASSET4 ESG scores under successive past ownership) use a proprietary industry classification method, the Refinitiv Business Classification (TRBC) system, to create peer groups benchmarks. This makes unraveling LSEG's relative performance scores into each company's original scores impossible. As a result, LSEG's relative performance scores are not comparable with other rating agencies' absolute scores. While this keeps LSEG scores highly proprietary, it also diminishes the comparability of LSEG scores outside the family of Refinitiv industry classification products.

3.3.2.3 Suggestions for Improvement: The Case of KLD Ratings

Over more than two decades, researchers have been refining the measurement of ESG performance using the KLD database. It is one of the most used ratings in ESG research and, consequently, researchers have thoughtfully identified many issues with its construction and application. Many of these weaknesses and suggestions apply to other rating agencies as well. We use the particularities of the KLD database to illustrate the most important improvements that rating agencies can consider, depending on the goals they prioritize.

For example, KLD ratings assign a value of 0 or 1 to each preset subtopic and then add these indicators together into the count of KLD strengths and the count of KLD concerns. This transformation is transparent and easy to implement but results in a loss of variation and nuances. Users of KLD ratings and any other rating product need to understand the trade-offs involved in the designs of rating systems.

As another example, the earliest analyses using KLD ratings use the net KLD Score as the proxy for ESG performance, which is similar to the ESG Combined Score in LSEG. For KLD, the net score requires subtracting the total number of KLD concerns from the total number of KLD strengths. For LSEG, this means using the net score which is a weighted combination of the ESG Score, produced from corporate ESG disclosures, and the ESG Controversies Score, produced from negative ESG news in the media; the weighting scheme is proprietary and not replicable. Researchers have made insightful critiques on the loss of heterogeneity and loss of variation resulting from netting the positive and negative aspects of KLD ratings. Suggested improvements including disaggregating KLD strengths and weaknesses and disaggregating either into components by topic as needed. If we carry this insight into the use of Refinitiv products then, we need to see more separate explorations and validations of the LSEG ESG Score and ESG Controversies Score. We need to decide in every instance of application which disaggregated score from which topic may be more relevant than the aggregated score. We need to remain highly aware of the heterogeneity and variation that is lost when we use any aggregated score and of our ability (or lack thereof) to analyze and quantify those losses. Please see additional critiques and suggestions side by side in Table 3.5.

Researchers continue to advance improvements that we can execute on different rating products, from which we take inspiration to improve unexamined rating products or create our own rating systems. However, other weaknesses in ratings are harder to address because they reflect difficulties inherent in measuring ESG performance. We cover these in Section 3.4 below.

Table 3.5: Limitations of the KLD Ratings Methodology and Suggestions for Improvement.

Nature of Limitation	Description of Limitation	Suggestions for Improvement

Scope	– Some categories do not fit the definition of ESG:
	  – Governance (Gao et al., 2014; Kim et al., 2012)
	  – Some product elements such as product quality (Lins et al., 2017).
		– Exclude less relevant categories (Gao et al., 2014; Lins et al., 2017)

Range	– Net score ranges from −12 to 15. Negative scores are unsuitable for statistical models that require non-negative numbers (Barnett & Salomon, 2012; Cohen et al., 2014).	– Add 12 to each net score so that it is non-negative (Barnett & Salomon, 2012; Cohen et al., 2014).

Consistency	– Total number of items changes from year to year.
	  – Human rights data not available before 2002 (Kim et al., 2012).
	  – RiskMetrics acquired KLD in 2009 and substantially changed items (Gupta et al., 2017).
		– Exclude
		  – Human rights indicators (Kim et al., 2012).
		  – Data after 2008 (Gupta et al., 2017).
		  – Data before 2009.
		– Standardize
		  – Normalize the number of strengths and concerns in each category into z-score equivalents (Koh et al., 2014; Mattingly & Berman, 2006).
		  – Scale the number of strengths (concerns) for each firm in each category by the maximum number of strengths (concerns) across all firms in that category that year (Lins et al., 2017).

Comparability	– Comparability is low across industries.	– Use industry fixed effects. – Transform the net score to indicate where it fits between the SIC 2-digit industry minimum and industry maximum (Erhemjamts et al., 2013; Hasan & Habib, 2017) – Subtract industry mean (Wong et al., 2011) or industry median (Dhaliwal et al., 2011) from firm score.

Table 3.5 (continued)

Nature of Limitation	Description of Limitation	Suggestions for Improvement
Stakeholder Differences	– Does not distinguish between stakeholder issues of varying importance (Godfrey et al., 2009; Luo et al., 2015; Mattingly & Berman, 2006).	– Distinguish between issues related to primary and secondary stakeholders, based on which groups have power over the firm (Luo et al., 2015). – Primary stakeholders' ESG topics: – Governance – Employee – Product – Secondary stakeholders' ESG topics: – Environment – Community – Diversity – Human rights
Materiality	– Does not consider materiality (Khan et al., 2016).	– Develop materiality assessments – Map KLD categories to SASB material topics for each industry – Construct Material Index = Material Strengths – Material Concerns (Khan et al., 2016)
Offsetting and Loss of Heterogeneity	– Companies can intentionally or unintentionally offset negative ESG issues by engaging in good ESG activities; as a result, net score does not reflect ESG risks (Kotchen & Moon, 2012). – Firms receiving the same net score may have different underlying performances. A firm with ten strengths and ten concerns and a firm with one strength and one concern both have net scores of 0 (Erhemjamts et al., 2013). – KLD concerns are better than KLD Strengths at capturing past performance and predicting future performance in environmental issues (Chatterji et al., 2009).	– Analyze strengths and concerns separately and/or by category as needed (Chatterji et al., 2009; Erhemjamts et al., 2013).

Table 3.5 (continued)

Nature of Limitation		Description of Limitation		Suggestions for Improvement
Loss of Variation	–	Binary indicators do not contain as much information as continuous variables such as emissions or injury rates (Chatterji et al., 2009).	–	Use underlying information instead of processed information.
Comprehensiveness	–	Does not reflect all publicly available information (Chatterji et al., 2009).	–	Use multiple data sources and ratings products as appropriate (Chatterji et al., 2009).

3.4 Difficulties in ESG Measurement

3.4.1 Empirical Proxy Versus Underlying Construct

The underlying construct we are interested in – "true" ESG performance – is not observable; raters instead use various observable instruments to represent or act as proxies for ESG performance (Bouten et al., 2017). The unavoidable, fundamental quality of empirical proxies is that they will never perfectly match their theoretical concepts. Each proxy faces choices, trade-offs, and limitations. Construct validity, which refers to whether the measurement of a concept captures what it is supposed to measure, is frequently (and rightly so) debated in ESG research (Chatterji & Levine, 2006).

3.4.2 Broad Versus Narrow Scope

Moreover, ESG is an umbrella construct, meaning that it rolls and compresses numerous theoretical concepts together into one empirical representation (Bouten et al., 2017; Gond and Crane, 2010). An umbrella construct is ambiguous and imprecise by nature.

3.4.3 Easy Versus Difficult Targets

Gjølberg (2009) points out that ESG rating systems do not distinguish between performance targets that are easy to achieve from those that are difficult to achieve. This allows firms to intentionally or unintentionally offset easy targets against hard targets. A firm that achieves three hard ESG targets receives the same overall ESG score as a firm that achieves three easy ESG targets. Theoretically, most people would probably agree that weighting ESG performance by the scope and difficulty of the activity involved is intuitive. Empirically, however, assigning difficulty levels and weights to various ESG targets is far from a clear, objective, or systematic exercise.

3.4.4 Process-Oriented Versus Results-Oriented

Gjølberg (2009) also proposes differentiating between process-oriented and results-oriented ESG initiatives. Process-oriented initiatives focus on "participation, continuous improvement, and learning processes" (Gjølberg, 2009, n.p.). Thus, they increase automatically with ESG involvement regardless of outcome. Issuing ESG-consistent corporate policies, implementing ESG management systems, and adopting GRI Guidelines are examples of process-oriented initiatives. On the other hand, winning awards like the Global 100 Most Sustainable Corporates by Corporate Knights is an example of a results-oriented initiative (Gjølberg, 2009).

Some ESG ratings incorporate both process- and results-oriented considerations (Delmas, Etzion, & Nairn-Birch, 2013). Process-oriented measures, such as codes of conduct, can obscure good and bad ESG results (Chatterji & Levine, 2006). If users need to invest extra time to investigate the impact and credibility of process-oriented measures, then the presence of process-oriented measures can increase information-processing costs (Chatterji & Levine, 2006). Delmas and Blass (2010) argue that process-oriented indicators are more subject to "window-dressing" due to their non-quantifiable nature. However, process-oriented initiatives may lead to socially responsible outcomes in the future (Gjølberg, 2009). Weighting achieved results and potential results would be an ambiguous and contentious exercise.

Concerns have even been expressed that ESG ratings predominantly incorporate process-oriented considerations over outcomes. Grewal and Serafeim (2020, n.p.) argue that most components that make up ESG ratings reflect "intentions, efforts, and investments that organizations make to achieve an intended outcome rather than the outcome itself." They give the example that most Social scores would reflect, say, investments made into diversity and inclusion programs but not whether and the extent to which diversity has actually improved within the firm's ranks.

3.4.5 Hard Requirements Versus Soft Requirements

Gjølberg (2009) suggests that we distinguish between ESG initiatives with hard requirements and ESG initiatives with soft requirements. Initiatives with hard requirements stipulate that firms should achieve certain ESG outcomes to claim membership while initiatives with soft requirements impose no performance standards. Initiatives such as the GRI Guidelines or the United Nations Global Compact (UNGC) require no past or current demonstrated record for companies to join. Other initiatives, such as the World Business Council for Sustainable Development (WBCSD), consider company ESG commitment and achievements as prerequisites to membership (Gjølberg, 2009).

Correspondingly, Gjølberg (2009) proposes categorizing ESG measurements into hard and soft requirements based on whether minimum standards are imposed. ESG measures with soft requirements have comparability issues. For example, carbon emissions policies can range from loose to strict. Therefore, whether a firm has a carbon emission policy is a soft requirement. Other measures, such as greenhouse gas emissions, use more concrete standards and are more comparable across different companies. Hard requirements are usually more reliable measures of ESG performance. Various qualities can also interact; results-oriented initiatives that have hard requirements can better reflect ESG achievements than process-oriented initiatives with soft requirements (Gjølberg, 2009).

3.4.6 Disclosure Versus Performance

Large amounts of the information available about corporate ESG performance come from voluntary disclosures and are thus susceptible to opportunistic reporting. Companies do not disclose corporate ESG performance randomly. A company can increase transparency strategically in response to pressure from the media or consumers for poor ESG performance. Thus, we need to keep companies' disclosure motivations in mind. Earlier, we also discussed the issue that larger and older companies disclose more while small and growing firms may be resource-constrained and disclose less (Doyle, 2018). Overall, better disclosure does not necessarily mean better performance but better disclosures and better performance are often correlated with the same underlying qualities, such as commitment to ESG.

Attempts to assess ESG performance often mix easy and difficult targets, process-oriented and results-oriented processes, hard requirements and soft requirements, and disclosure and performance into one evaluation. However, this method weakens the construct validity of the ESG performance measure, as the chair of the SEC warns (Mirchandani, 2020). When a rating system consolidates criteria belonging to many different dimensions it may obscure true performance among assessments of varying validity. In Table 3.6 we use KLD ratings again to illustrate the mixing of various criteria.

3.4.7 Materiality

Various stakeholder groups have different material concerns and materiality thresholds, and material topics between different stakeholder groups sometimes overlap (Khan et al., 2016). Whose materiality to prioritize poses a significant challenge to presenting unified ratings. The SASB takes an investor viewpoint and its materiality clas-

Table 3.6: Examples of mixed criteria in KLD ratings.

Disclosure	Performance
Communications (ENV-STR-E). STATS-1996 through STATS-2004 "The company is a signatory to the CERES Principles, publishes a notably substantive environmental report, or has notably effective internal communications systems in place for environmental best practices."	**HUMAN CAPITAL – OTHER STRENGTHS (EMP-STR-X)** "This indicator is designed to capture best-in-class management performance in the area of human capital that is not covered by other MSCI ESG Research human capital indicators. Metrics include recognition by reputable third-party sources for excellent workforce management."
Process-oriented	**Results-oriented**
ENVIRONMENTAL MANAGEMENT SYSTEMS (ENV-STR-G) "This indicator measures whether a firm has an environmental management system (EMS) in place, and whether it is certified to a third-party standard, such as ISO 1400."	**TOXIC EMISSIONS AND WASTE (ENV-CON-D)** "This indicator is designed to assess the severity of controversies related to a firm's non-GHG emissions. Factors affecting this evaluation include, but are not limited to, a history of involvement in land or air emissions-related legal cases, widespread or egregious impacts due to hazardous emissions, resistance to improved practices, and criticism by NGOs and/or other third-party observers."
Soft requirements	**Hard requirements**
ENVIRONMENTAL OPPORTUNITIES – RENEWABLE ENERGY (ENV-STR-M) "This indicator is designed to evaluate the extent to which companies are taking advantage of opportunities linked to the development of renewable power production. Companies that proactively invest in renewable power generation and related services score higher."	**Hazardous Waste (ENV-CON-A). STATS-1991 through STATS-2009 Definition:** "The company's liabilities for hazardous waste sites exceed $50 million, or the company has recently paid substantial fines or civil penalties for waste management violations. Before 1996 the threshold for liabilities was $30 million."

Source: MSCI ESG KLD STATS: 1991–2014 DATASETS methodology.

sifications are based primarily on each financial impact of each ESG issue; in contrast, the GRI has a multi-stakeholder focus and does not define materiality in reference to firm value or financials. Instead, the GRI defines materiality as 1) the importance of companies' economic, social, and environmental impacts and 2) the usefulness of information for all stakeholders in making decisions. Companies reporting under GRI Guidelines also report their own materiality assessment process.

We use a simple example to illustrate how materiality affects the assessment of ESG performance in Table 3.7. Company A is a commercial bank while B is an oil refining company. Each is scored on the same issues on a 0–5 scale, with 5 being the score for best performance. Let us assume that they receive the same scores on all issues. In a scenario where we derive the overall ESG score by averaging all the issue-specific scores, A receives the same score as B. However, following the SASB Materiality Map, some of those ESG issues are financially material for commercial banking while others are material for oil refining. If we give a weight of 1 to financially material topics and a weight of 0 to financially immaterial topics, we can derive a weighted ESG score. After this operation, A's score is lower than in the unweighted scenario, and B's is higher. While A and B exhibit approximately the same performance in overall ESG, B has better performance in financially material ESG. Thus, from the viewpoint of return-oriented investors B is a better investment. In the end, what constitutes accurate and high-quality ESG performance measurement, depends on the viewpoint of the stakeholder.

Table 3.7: An illustration of materiality-weighted ESG ratings.

Issue	A (Commercial Bank)			B (Oil Refining)		
	Score	Materiality	Weight	Score	Materiality	Weight
Data Security	2	Yes	1	2	No	0
Access and Affordability	1	Yes	1	1	No	0
Product Design and Lifecycle management	3	Yes	1	3	No	0
Systematic Risk Management	3	Yes	1	3	No	0
Business Ethics	3	Yes	1	3	Yes	1
GHG Emission	3	No	0	3	Yes	1
Air Quality	4	No	0	4	Yes	1
Water and Wastewater Management	5	No	0	5	Yes	1
Ecological Impacts	4	No	0	4	Yes	1
Human Rights and Community Relations	5	No	0	5	Yes	1
Employee Health and Safety	4	No	0	4	Yes	1
Business Model Resilience	3	No	0	3	Yes	1
Management of Legal and Regulatory Environment	5	No	0	5	Yes	1
Critical Incident Risk Management	4	No	0	4	Yes	1
Unweighted Average ESG Score	3.50			3.50		
Materiality-Weighted ESG Score	(2+1+3+3+3)/5 = 2.40			(3+3+4+5+4+5+4+3+5+4)/10 = 4.00		

3.5 Questions for Future Research

As we saw throughout this review, the development of ESG performance measurement has advanced simultaneously along numerous dimensions and research has produced many tools and considerations for further improvement. However, it is still unclear how ESG ratings should ideally be compiled and what they truly reveal. We collect the following list of open questions as avenues for future research:

1) How should diversified firms operating in multiple industries apply the SASB industry-specific standards for ESG reporting?
2) How should a company choose between GRI and SASB and other reporting guidelines?
3) Which stakeholder group(s) should companies and raters prioritize when defining materiality? Can the benefits of producing information tailored to the information needs of each group meet or exceed the costs?
4) How can producers and users of ESG ratings disentangle ESG disclosure quality from ESG performance evaluations?
5) How should measures of ESG performance weight and quantify the value of different types of ESG activities, such as process-oriented and results-oriented initiatives, soft requirements and hard requirements?
6) What conditions and factors contribute to realizing positive outcomes from process-oriented initiatives such as systems, strategies, and policies?
7) Given the divergence in ESG rating products, are any ESG ratings more accurate than others and in what ways? Do divergent ratings convey unique information or mostly noise?
8) Does communication between rating agencies and rated companies reduce information asymmetry and make ratings more accurate or distort incentives and make ratings more biased?

3.6 Conclusion

This review provides a synopsis of recent developments and unresolved challenges in measuring ESG performance. In the process, we have explored sources of variation in ESG reporting such as the degree of regulation and enforcement. We have amalgamated publicly and commercially available data sources as a guide to information users. Throughout, we highlight the critical importance of understanding and assessing ESG measurement methodologies, as methodological choices will likely lead to different conclusions and decisions. The causes and consequences of differences among ESG rating systems remain inadequately understood. Aside from empirical investigations, we could benefit from theoretical guidance on when ESG ratings should converge and when they should diverge.

We recommend, for further reading, the following literature reviews published in the last three years listed in reverse chronological order: Tsang et al. (2023), Starks (2023), Andrew and Baker (2022), Coelho et al. (2002), Gillian et al. (2021), and Christensen et al. (2021).

References

Archer, J. G., McMahon, T. M., & Crough, M. M. (1990). *SEC reporting of environmental liabilities*. https://elr.info/sites/default/files/articles/20.10105.htm

Andrew, J., & Baker., M. (2020). Corporate social responsibility reporting: The last 40 years and a path to sharing future insights. *Abacus*, 56(1), 35–65.

Barnett, M. L., & Salomon, R. M. (2012). Does it pay to be really good? Addressing the shape of the relationship between social and financial performance. *Strategic Management Journal*, 33(11), 1304–1320.

Berg, F., Jay, J., Kölbel, J., & Rigobon, R. (2023). The signal in the noise. *EconPol Forum*, 24 (1), 23–27.

Berg, F., Fabisik, K., & Sautner, Z. (2021). Is history repeating itself? The (un)predictable past of ESG ratings. SSRN 3722087.

Berg, F., Koelbel, J. F., & Rigobon, R. (2022). Aggregate confusion: The divergence of ESG ratings. SSRN 3438533.

Berrone, P., & Gomez-Mejia, L. R. (2009). Environmental performance and executive compensation: An integrated agency-institutional perspective. *Academy of Management Journal*, 52(1), 103–126.

Bouten, L., Cho, C. H., Michelon, G., & Roberts, R. W. (2017). ESG performance proxies in large-sample studies: 'umbrella advocates', construct clarity and the 'validity police'. *Construct Clarity and the 'Validity Police'* (August 2017).

Carrión-Flores, C. E., & Innes, R. (2010). Environmental innovation and environmental performance. *Journal of Environmental Economics and Management*, 59(1), 27–42.

CDP. (n.d.). *About us*. https://www.cdp.net/en/info/about-us

CFA Institute. (n.d.). *ESG investing and analysis*. https://www.cfainstitute.org/en/research/esg-investing

Chatterji, A., & Levine, D. (2006). Breaking down the wall of codes: Evaluating non-financial performance measurement. *California Management Review*, 48(2), 29–51.

Chatterji, A. K., Durand, R., Levine, D. I., & Touboul, S. (2016). Do ratings of firms converge? Implications for managers, investors and strategy researchers. *Strategic Management Journal*, 37(8), 1597–1614.

Chatterji, A. K., Levine, D. I., & Toffel, M. W. (2009). How well do social ratings actually measure environmental, social, and governance? *Journal of Economics & Management Strategy*, 18(1), 125–169.

Ching, P. N., & Diglio, B. M. (2011). Staff accounting bulletin 92: A paradigmatic shift in disclosure standards. *Fordham Environmental Law Review*, 7(1), 75–110.

Christensen, D., Serafeim, G., & Sikochi, A. (2019). *Why is corporate virtue in the eye of the beholder? The case of ESG ratings*.

Christensen, H., Hail, L., & Leuz, C. 2021. Mandatory CSR and sustainability reporting: Economic analysis and literature review. *Review of Accounting Studies*, 26, 1176–1248.

Coelho, R., Jayantilal, S., & Ferreira, J.J. (2022). The impact of social responsibility on corporate financial performance: A systematic literature review. *Corporate Social Responsibility and Environmental Management*, 30(4), 1535–1560.

Cohen, P., West, S. G., & Aiken, L. S. (2014). *Applied multiple regression/correlation analysis for the behavioral sciences*. Psychology Press.

Cohn, J. B., & Wardlaw, M. I. (2016). Financing constraints and workplace safety. *The Journal of Finance*, 71(5), 2017–2058.

Cooper, M. J., Gulen, H., & Ovtchinnikov, A. V. (2010). Corporate political contributions and stock returns. *The Journal of Finance*, 65(2), 687–724.

CSRHub. *The CSRHub ratings methodology*. https://www.csrhub.com/csrhub-esg-ratings-methodology

DBRS Morningstar. 2023. *DBRS Morningstar brings ESG into focus*. https://www.dbrsmorningstar.com/esg

Delmas, M., & Blass, V. D. (2010). Measuring corporate environmental performance: The trade-offs of sustainability ratings. *Business Strategy and the Environment*, 19(4), 245–260. doi:10.1002/bse.676

Delmas, M. A., Etzion, D., & Nairn-Birch, N. (2013). Triangulating environmental performance: What Do environmental, social, and governance ratings really capture? *Academy of Management Perspectives*, *27*(3), 255–267. doi:10.5465/amp.2012.0123

Dhaliwal, D. S., Li, O. Z., Tsang, A., & Yang, Y. G. (2011). Voluntary nonfinancial disclosure and the cost of equity capital: The initiation of environmental, social, and governance reporting. *The accounting review*, *86*(1), 59–100.

Dorian, M., Gorin, T., Yamada, H., & Yang, A. June 10, 2021. ABC News. Erin Brockovich: the real story of the town three decades later. https://abcnews.go.com/US/erin-brockovich-real-story-town-decades/story?id=78180219

Douglas, E., Van Holt, T., & Whelan, T. (2017). Responsible investing: Guide to esg data providers and relevant trends. *Journal of Environmental Investing*, *8*(1), 91–114.

Doyle, T. M. (2018). *Ratings that don't rate the subjective world of ESG ratings agencies.* accf.org/2018/07/19/ratings-that-dont-rate-the-subjective-world-of-esg-ratings-agencies/

Edmans, A. (2011). Does the stock market fully value intangibles? Employee satisfaction and equity prices. *Journal of Financial economics*, *101*(3), 621–640.

EPA. U.S. *EPA releases greenhouse gas reporting rules.* https://afdc.energy.gov/laws/425

EPA. (2001). *Enforcement response policy for section 313 of the Emergency Planning Community Right-to-know Act (1986) and section 6607 of the Pollution Prevention Act (1990) [amended].* https://www.epa.gov/sites/production/files/2017-03/documents/epcra313erpamendments2017.pdf

Erhemjamts, O., Li, Q., & Venkateswaran, A. (2013). Environmental, social, and governance and its impact on firms' investment policy, organizational structure, and performance. *Journal of Business Ethics*, *118*(2), 395–412.

European Commission. (2023). *Questions and answers on the adoption of European sustainability reporting standards.* https://ec.europa.eu/commission/presscorner/detail/en/qanda_23_4043

European Commission. (2001). *Promoting a European framework for environmental, social, and governance.* https://ec.europa.eu/transparency/regdoc/rep/1/2001/EN/1-2001-366-EN-1-0.Pdf

Ewing, J. (2019, May 6). *New York Times.* Six years ago, he helped expose VW's diesel fraud. This year, G.M. let him go. https://www.nytimes.com/2019/05/06/business/hermanth-kappanna-vw-emissions-gm.html

Frankental, P. (2001). Corporate social responsibility – A PR invention? *Corporate Communications*, *6*(1), 18–23.

Freeman, R. E. (1994). The politics of stakeholder theory: Some future directions. *Business ethics quarterly*, 409–442.

FTSE Russell. (2023). *ESG Scores and data model.* https://www.lseg.com/content/dam/ftse-russell/en_us/documents/other/ftse-esg-scores-overview-2023.pdf

FTSE Russell. (n.d.) *ESG scores.* https://www.lseg.com/en/ftse-russell/esg-scores#:~:text=FTSE%20Russell's%20ESG%20Scores%20and,and,and%20Theme%20Exposures%20and%20Scores

Gamerschlag, R., Möller, K., & Verbeeten, F. (2011). Determinants of voluntary ESG disclosure: Empirical evidence from Germany. *Review of Managerial Science*, *5*(2–3), 233–262.

Gao, F., Lisic, L. L., & Zhang, I. X. (2014). Commitment to social good and insider trading. *Journal of Accounting and Economics*, *57*(2–3), 149–175.

Garz, H., Volk, C., & Morrow, D. (2018). *ESG risk ratings.* https://www.sustainalytics.com/esg-research/thematic-reports/esg-risk-ratings-innovation/

Gibson, R., Krueger, P., Riand, N., & Schmidt, P. S. (2020). ESG rating disagreement and stock returns. SSRN 3433728.

Gillian, S. L, Koch, A., & Starks, L.T. (2021). Firms and social responsibility: A review of ESG and CSR research in corporate finance. *Journal of Corporate Finance*, *66*, 1–16.

Gingrich, B., Chopra, R., & Hsu, A. March 1, 2019. *Nudging the needle on environmental regulation. University of Pennsylvania Wharton School of Business Public Policy Initiative Blog.* https://publicpolicy.wharton.upenn. edu/live/news/2872-nudging-the-needle-on-environmental-regulation/for-students/blog/news

Gjølberg, M. (2009). Measuring the immeasurable?: Constructing an index of ESG practices and ESG performance in 20 countries. *Scandinavian journal of management, 25*(1), 10–22.

Godfrey, P. C., Merrill, C. B., & Hansen, J. M. (2009). The relationship between environmental, social, and governance and shareholder value: An empirical test of the risk management hypothesis. *Strategic Management Journal, 30*(4), 425–445.

Gond J.-P., Crane A. (2010). Corporate social performance disoriented: Saving the lost paradigm? *Business & Society,* 49, 677–703.

Goodpaster, K. E. (1991). Business ethics and stakeholder analysis. *Business ethics quarterly,* 53–73.

Graham, A., Maher, J. J., & Northcut, W. D. (2001). Environmental liability information and bond ratings. *Journal of Accounting, Auditing & Finance, 16*(2), 93–116.

Grewal, J., Serafeim, G., & Yoon, A. (2016). Shareholder activism on sustainability issues. SSRN 2805512.

Grewal, J., & Serafeim, G. (2020). Research on corporate sustainability: Review and directions for future research. *Foundations and Trends in Accounting, 14*(2), 73–127.

GRI. *About GRI.* https://www.globalreporting.org/Information/about-gri/Pages/default.aspx

Griffin, P. A., Lont, D. H., & Sun, E. Y. (2017). The relevance to investors of greenhouse gas emission disclosures. *Contemporary Accounting Research, 34*(2), 1265–1297.

Guillermo, C. (2019). *Factors and ESG: The truth behind three myths.* www.msci.com/www/blog-posts/factors-and-esg-the-truth/01291000034

Gupta, A., Briscoe, F., & Hambrick, D. C. (2017). Red, blue, and purple firms: Organizational political ideology and environmental, social, and governance. *Strategic Management Journal, 38*(5), 1018–1040.

Hahn, R., & Kühnen, M. (2013). Determinants of sustainability reporting: A review of results, trends, theory, and opportunities in an expanding field of research. *Journal of Cleaner Production, 59,* 5–21. doi:10.1016/j.jclepro.2013.07.005

Haji, A.A., Coram, P., & Troshani, I. (2023). Consequences of CSR reporting regulations worldwide: A review and research agenda. *Accounting, Auditing & Accountability Journal,* 36(1), 177–208.

Harris, K. D. (2015). *The California Transparency in Supply Chains Act: A resource guide.* https://oag.ca.gov/sites/all/files/agweb/pdfs/sb657/resource-guide.pdf

Hasan, M. M., & Habib, A. (2017). Corporate life cycle, organizational financial resources and Environmental, Social, and Governance. *Journal of Contemporary Accounting & Economics, 13*(1), 20–36. doi:https://doi.org/10.1016/j.jcae.2017.0002

Hertwich, E. G., Mateles, S. F., Pease, W. S., & McKone, T. E. (2001). Human toxicity potentials for life-cycle assessment and toxics release inventory risk screening. *Environmental Toxicology and Chemistry: An International Journal, 20*(4), 928–939.

IFRS. (2023). *ISSB issues inaugural global sustainability disclosure standards.* https://www.ifrs.org/news-and-events/news/2023/06/issb-issues-ifrs-s1-ifrs-s2/

IRRC. (2018). *State of sustainability and integrated reporting 2018.* https://www.weinberg.udel.edu/IIRCiRe searchDocuments/2018/11/2018-SP-500-Integrated-Reporting-FINAL-November-2018-pdf

ISS. (2023). *ESG Corporate rating methodology and research process.* https://www.issgovernance.com/file/products/iss-esg-corporate-rating-methodology.pdf

Khan, M., Serafeim, G., & Yoon, A. (2016). Corporate sustainability: First evidence on materiality. *The accounting review, 91*(6), 1697–1724.

Kim, Y., Park, M. S., & Wier, B. (2012). Is earnings quality associated with environmental, social, and governance? *The accounting review, 87*(3), 761–796.

KPMG International Cooperative. (2017). *KPMG survey of corporate responsibility reporting 2017.* https://assets.kpmg/content/dam/kpmg/xx/pdf/2017/10/kpmg-survey-of-corporate-responsibility-reporting-2017.pdf KPMG International Cooperative. 2015.

KPMG International Cooperative. (2013). *KPMG survey of corporate responsibility reporting 2013.* https://assets.kpmg/content/dam/kpmg/pdf/2015/08/kpmg-survey-of-corporate-responsibility-reporting-2013.pdf

Koh, P. S., Qian, C., & Wang, H. (2014). Firm litigation risk and the insurance value of corporate social performance. *Strategic Management Journal, 35*(10), 1464–1482.

Konar, S., & Cohen, M. A. (2001). Does the market value environmental performance? *Review of economics and statistics, 83*(2), 281–289.

Kotchen, M., & Moon, J. J. (2012). Environmental, social, and governance for irresponsibility. *The BE Journal of Economic Analysis & Policy, 12*(1).

Larcker, D. F., Pomorski, L., Tayan, B., & Watts, E. (2022). *ESG ratings: A compass without direction. Rock Center for Corporate Governance at Stanford University Working Paper.* https://ssrn.com/abstract=4179647

Lee, A. H. (2021). *A climate for change: Meeting investor demand for climate and esg information at the SEC.* https://www.sec.gov/news/speech/lee-climate-change

Lins, K. V., Servaes, H., & Tamayo, A. (2017). Social capital, trust, and firm performance: The value of environmental, social, and governance during the financial crisis. *The Journal of Finance, 72*(4), 1785–1824.

Luo, X., Wang, H., Raithel, S., & Zheng, Q. (2015). Corporate social performance, analyst stock recommendations, and firm future returns. *Strategic Management Journal, 36*(1), 123–136.

Mackintosh, J. (2018). Is Tesla or Exxon more sustainable? It depends whom you ask. *Wall Street Journal.*

Matsumura, E. M., Prakash, R., & Vera-Muñoz, S. C. (2013). Firm-value effects of carbon emissions and carbon disclosures. *The accounting review, 89*(2), 695–724.

Mattingly, J. E., & Berman, S. L. (2006). Measurement of corporate social action: Discovering taxonomy in the Kinder Lydenburg Domini ratings data. *Business & Society, 45*(1), 20–46.

McWilliams, A., & Siegel, D. S. 2001. Corporate social responsibility: A theory of the firm perspective. *Academy of Management Review, 26*(1), 117–127.

Mirchandani, B. (2020). *What to make of the sec's warnings and recommendations for ESG Investing.* https://www.forbes.com/sites/bhaktimirchandani/2020/05/29/what-to-make-of-the-secs-warnings-on-esg-ratings-and-recommendations-for-esg-disclosures/#532f7b9f3184

MIT Sloan School of Management. (2023). *The aggregate confusion project.* https://mitsloan.mit.edu/sustainability-initiative/aggregate-confusion-project.

MSCI. (2023). *MSCI ESG Ratings methodology.* https://www.msci.com/documents/1296102/34424357/MSCI+ESG+Ratings+Methodology.pdf

MSCI. (2019). *MSCI ESG KLD STATS: 1991–2018 DATA SETS methodology.* https://wrds-www.wharton.upenn.edu/documents/1454/MSCI_ESG_KLD_STATS_2018_Data_Set_Methodology_Final.pdf

Ni, J., Flynn, B. B., & Jacobs, F. R. (2016). The effect of a toy industry product recall announcement on shareholder wealth. *International Journal of Production Research, 54*(18), 5404–5415.

OSHA. *Updates to OSHA's recordkeeping rule: Reporting fatalities and severe injuries.* https://www.osha.gov/laws-regs/federalregister/2001-01-19

OSHA. (2001). *Occupational injury and illness recording and reporting requirements.* https://www.osha.gov/laws-regs/federalregister/2001-01-19

Patten, D. M. (1992). Intra-industry environmental disclosures in response to the Alaskan oil spill: A note on legitimacy theory. *Accounting, Organizations and Society, 17*(5), 471–475.

Pike, O. (2023). *Thomson Reuters. What companies within and outside of the EU can expect of new European ESG regulations.* https://www.thomsonreuters.com/en-us/posts/esg/csrd-esg-regulations/

Refinitiv. (2022). *ESG score methodology.* https://www.refinitiv.com/content/dam/marketing/en_us/documents/methodology/refinitiv-esg-scores-methodology.pdf

Reilly, C. February 6, 2020. *Defined contribution pensions left behind*. University of Pennsylvania Wharton School of Business Pension Research Council Blog. https://pensionresearchcouncil.wharton.upenn.edu/blog/defined-contribution-pensions-left-behind/

RepRisk. (2023). *Reprisk methodology overview*. https://www.reprisk.com/news-research/resources/methodology#a-what-is-the-reprisk-rating

Rives, K. (2023). *Half of anti-ESG bills in red states have failed in 2023 as campaign pushes on*. https://www.spglobal.com/marketintelligence/en/news-insights/latest-news-headlines/half-of-anti-esg-bills-in-red-states-have-failed-in-2023-as-campaign-pushes-on-76276575

Rodriguez, A., Cotran, H., & Stewart, L. S. (2017). Evaluating the effectiveness of sustainability disclosure: findings from a recent SASB study. *Journal of Applied Corporate Finance, 29*(2), 100–108. doi:10.1111/jacf.12237

SASB. (2023). *SASB materiality map*. https://materiality.sasb.org/

SEC. (1999). *SEC staff accounting bulletin: no. 99 – materiality*. https://www.sec.gov/interps/account/sab99.htm

SEC. (2011). *SEC adopts dodd-frank mine safety disclosure requirements*. https://www.sec.gov/news/press/2011/2011-273.htm

SEC. (2019). *Questions and answers of general applicability*. https://www.sec.gov/divisions/corpfin/guidance/regs-kinterp.htm

SEC. (2020). *Modernization of regulation S-K Items 101, 103, 105*. https://www.sec.gov/files/rules/final/2020/33-10825.pdf

SEC. 2024. SEC Adopts Rules to Enhance and Standardize Climate-Related Disclosures for Investors. March 6, 2024. https://www.sec.gov/newsroom/press-releases/2024-31. Accessed March 10, 2025.

Starks, L.T. (2023). Presidential address: Sustainable finance and ESG issues—value versus values. *The Journal of Finance,* 78(4), 1837–1872.

SustainAbility Institute. (2023). *Rate the raters 2023: ESG ratings at a crossroads*. https://www.sustainability.com/globalassets/sustainability.com/thinking/pdfs/2023/rate-the-raters-report-april-2023.pdf

SustainAbility Institute. (2019). *Rate the raters 2019*. https://www.sustainability.com/our-work/reports/rate-raters-2019/

S&P Global (2022). S&P Global ESG Scores. https://www.spglobal.com/esg/documents/sp-global-esg-scores-brochure-2022.pdf?utm_medium=cpc&utm_source=google&utm_campaign=Brand_ESG_Search&utm_term=s&p&global&esg&ratings&methodology&utm_content=534418150272&gclid=Cj0KCQjw4vKpBhCZARIsAOKHoWSuu7gB3PYmp8EgVIZdwhUuuN_h2MnfW_RZm93Ee_Kf8daxb_A-OvIaAnrkEALw_wcB

Sustainalytics. (2020). *The esg risk rating: frequently asked questions – for companies*. https://connect.sustainalytics.com/hubfs/SFS/Sustainalytics%20ESG%20Risk%20Rating%20-%20FAQs%20for%20Corporations.pdf

Sustainalytics. 2023. *Morningstar sustainability rating for funds*. https://www.sustainalytics.com/investor-solutions/analytic-reporting-solutions/morningstar-sustainability-rating-for-funds

Sustainalytics. (2021). *ESG Risk Ratings—Methodology Abstract*. https://connect.sustainalytics.com/hubfs/INV/Methodology/Sustainalytics_ESG%20Ratings_Methodology%20Abstract.pdf

TCFD. (n.d.). About. https://www.fsb-tcfd.org/about/.

Thomson Reuters. (2018). *Thomson Reuters ESG Scores*. Retrieved from https://www.refinitiv.com/content/dam/marketing/en_us/documents/methodology/esg-scores-methodology.pdf

Trevor, D. (2019). *ESG ratings: A rebuttal of prevailing criticisms*. www.sustainalytics.com/esg-blog/esg-ratings-rebuttal-of-prevailing-criticisms/

Tsang, A., Frost, T., & Cao, H. 2023. Environmental, social, and governance (ESG) disclosure: A literature review. *The British Accounting Review,* 55, 1–21.

Unsal, O. (2019). Employee relations and firm risk: Evidence from court rooms. *Research in International Business and Finance,* 48, 1–16.

US Department of Labor. (2017). *Reporting and disclosure guide for employee benefit plans*. https://www.dol. gov/sites/dolgov/files/ebsa/about-ebsa/our-activities/resource-center/publications/reporting-and-disclosure-guide-for-employee-benefit-plans.pdf

US SIF. (2018). *Report on US sustainable, responsible and impact investing trends 2018*. https://www.ussif.org/files/Trends/Trends%202018%20executive%20summary%20FINAL.pdf

Valor, C. (2005). Environmental, social, and governance and corporate citizenship: Towards corporate accountability. *Business and society review, 110*(2), 191–212.

Weismann, M. F. (2009). The Foreign Corrupt Practices Act: The failure of the self-regulatory model of corporate governance in the global business environment. *Journal of Business Ethics, 88*(4), 615–66.

White House. (2021, May 20). Executive order on climate-related financial risk. https://www.whitehouse. gov/briefing-room/presidential-actions/2021/05/20/executive-order-on-climate-related-financial-risk/

Wong, E. M., Ormiston, M. E., & Tetlock, P. E. (2011). The effects of top management team integrative complexity and decentralized decision making on corporate social performance. *Academy of Management Journal, 54*(6), 1207–1228.

Chapter Four: **A Practical Guide to Sustainable Investing**

Introduction

A discussion of ESG investing necessarily entails an in-depth understanding of the investable assets available to the investor. In "A Practical Guide to Sustainable Investing by Asset Class" the authors Bhattacharji and Wong present the many different assets available, with a focus on ESG characteristics. The authors first identify several different approaches to sustainable investing: exclusionary screening; ESG integration, whereby the investor incorporates ESG factors into the investment process; thematic investing, which focuses on specific threads or topics; and impact investment. Each of these investing approaches have differences but each can generate measurable, positive social, or environmental impact. These alternative strategies are often confused by media commentators and even by otherwise sophisticated investors. For example, exclusionary screening is often done with little or no attention to its impact on financial performance of the portfolio. The negative performance of CalPERS is often cited as one of the worst examples of poor financial performance resulting from exclusionary screening. Exclusionary screening can be perfectly acceptable if financial performance is a distant secondary consideration. But some writers mistakenly conclude that ALL ESG investing has poor performance when returns are skewed negatively by the poor performance of exclusionary investments. In contrast to exclusionary, or negative screens, a more sophisticated approach to ESG investing involves the positive selection of companies whose ESG practices are superior, combined with a portfolio analysis designed to select investments which closely approximate conventional portfolios in terms of historical risk and return. The poor investment performance of the naïve exclusionary screening approach, when confused with the more sophisticated portfolio integration approach, can tarnish all forms of ESG investing. This is a recurring issue in coverage of ESG investing even in the more sophisticated financial news outlets.

One particularly useful distinction the authors make is that the investor or researcher should consider a company's impact from two different sources: the company's product and, separately, the company's conduct. It is then possible to assess a company on a "cradle to grave" basis, beginning with how the company sources its raw materials, the complete supply chain, its operations including fuel sources at each stage, its human resources practices, sales practices, impact on local communities, recycling and end of life disposals, and any other relevant factors.

An important section is the cautionary discussion of challenges to the investor pursuing a sustainable investing approach. These challenges include portfolio performance, politicization, greenwashing, and resource challenges involving not just financial commitment but also the time, effort, and other resources required to conduct holistic due diligence, monitoring, and corporate engagement.

The authors go on to provide a useful overview of sustainable investing by asset class for public equity, private equity, public debt, and private debt.

https://doi.org/10.1515/9783111178608-007

Preeti Bhattacharji and Patrick Wong

4 A Practical Guide to Sustainable Investing by Asset Class

4.1 Introduction

Sustainable investing, once a niche concept, has now firmly established itself as a mainstream investment strategy, growing to nearly $3 trillion in assets in 2023 (Morningstar, Inc, n.d.). As the world grapples with pressing environmental and social challenges, investors are increasingly recognizing the need to align their portfolios with sustainable practices and values, with the aim of driving change at scale while also realizing returns. The popularization of sustainable investing is a reflection of the growing awareness of how financial markets and broader societal and environmental issues are interconnected.

Despite growing popularity, the landscape of sustainable investing remains confusing and often opaque. As a result, persisting misconceptions continue to pervade the space. Does relying on a sustainable investing strategy mean sacrificing return? Is sustainable investing only about the climate and environmentalism? Compared to more "mainstream" strategies, is sustainable investing less predictable? These misperceptions can limit investors who may view sustainable investing as being uniquely risky or volatile.

This chapter explores—and debunks—the mythology surrounding sustainable investing and examines it through the lens of different asset classes, providing practical insights and guidance for those looking to gain a better understanding. As we will uncover, there are important roles that everyone plays when it comes to the sustainable investing ecosystem. In this chapter, you will better understand these roles and also better understand what role you're best suited to play.

4.2 What is Sustainable Investing?

Sustainable investing can be defined as a means of deploying capital with the intention of generating positive social and/or environmental impact alongside financial returns.

It is also important to understand what sustainable investing is not. For some, sustainable investing may be understood as only pertaining to environmental practi-

---

Note: This chapter is being provided for informational and educational purposes only. It contains the views of J.P. Morgan employees which may differ from the views of J.P. Morgan Chase & Co or its affiliates.

https://doi.org/10.1515/9783111178608-008

ces and climate activism. In actuality, sustainable investing is much more comprehensive. Affordable housing, access to education, human capital management, and plastic pollution are all themes (among others) that would be considered as sustainable investing. Consequently, the considerations for sustainable investors can be especially complex as investment decisions often require assessing (to the greatest extent possible) the full scale of a company's actions and impacts.

4.2.1 Different Approaches to Sustainable Investing

There are several approaches to assessing the sustainability practices of a business to determine if it is an appropriate fit for your portfolio.

Exclusionary Screening: Investors employing exclusionary screening avoid investments in companies or industries that do not align with their values or ethical beliefs. For example, an investor may choose to exclude tobacco or weapons manufacturers from their portfolio.

ESG Integration: This approach involves incorporating ESG factors into your investment process. Investors assess the impact of ESG risks and opportunities on the long-term financial performance of investments. ESG integration seeks to enhance risk management and identify companies that exhibit strong ESG characteristics.

Thematic Investing: Thematic investing focuses on selecting investments that actively align with specific sustainability themes or trends, such as renewable energy, clean technology, or healthcare innovation. Investors allocate capital to sectors aligned with their chosen themes.

Impact Investing: Impact investors intentionally seek investments that generate measurable positive social or environmental impact, in addition to financial returns. Impact measurement and reporting are integral to this approach.

No matter which approach you take, it is helpful to understand (to the greatest extent that you can) the holistic impact of the company that you are looking at. To understand that impact it is useful to think of the company in two parts: (1) the company's product (i.e., what it produces); and (2) the company's conduct (i.e., how it operates across its supply chain and operations). If you analyze the company's supply chain, operations, and product, then you can conduct a "cradle-to-grave" analysis of how the company's product and conduct holistically affect the world around it.

4.2.1.1 Evaluating a Company's Footprint with Cradle-to-Grave Analysis

"Cradle to Grave" refers to the entire lifecycle of a product or system, encompassing its creation (the "cradle" or beginning) to its disposal or end-of-life stage (the "grave" or end). This approach involves considering the environmental and social impacts associated with a product or system at every stage of its existence, from raw material extraction to manufacturing, distribution, use, and, ultimately, disposal or recycling.

–   Raw Material Extraction: The lifecycle begins with the extraction of raw materials from the environment, such as mining minerals, harvesting timber, or extracting oil. Sustainable practices at this stage may involve minimizing ecological damage and considering the social and health impacts on local communities where those materials are grown or harvested.

–   Manufacturing and Production: During the manufacturing and production phase, raw materials are transformed into finished products. Sustainable considerations include energy efficiency, waste reduction, emissions control, and worker safety and rights.

–   Distribution and Transportation: Efficient and sustainable transportation methods are crucial for reducing carbon emissions and minimizing the environmental footprint of goods as they move through the supply chain. If goods must travel a far distance, this may signal a negative impact on the environment given carbon emissions associated with many modes of transportation.

–   Product Use: Sustainable product design and consumer behavior during product use are critical factors. Energy efficiency, durability, and the minimization of harmful emissions during use contribute to a more sustainable approach.

–   End-of-Life Considerations: At the end of a product's life various options exist, such as recycling, reuse, or disposal. Sustainable practices involve designing products with recycling or reuse in mind, minimizing waste, and ensuring responsible disposal or recycling methods.

The end-of-life stage of a product is especially important as it can support a circular economy. For example, a jacket that can be repurchased by the original seller and resold to a different customer extends the life of the garment and avoids it landing in a landfill after just one season.

4.2.1.1.1 Why Cradle-to-Grave Analysis Matters

Assessing the cumulative impact of a product or process throughout its lifecycle is paramount. This analysis plays a key role in identifying areas where improvements can be made to reduce resource consumption, pollution, and waste generation.

–   Resource Efficiency: By considering the entire lifecycle, organizations can identify opportunities for resource conservation, such as using recycled materials, reducing energy consumption, and optimizing production processes for sustainability.

–   Waste Reduction: Minimizing waste generation and promoting recycling and reuse can lead to significant reductions in landfill waste and any associated environmental issues.

- Sustainability Goals: Many businesses and organizations set sustainability goals, such as achieving carbon neutrality or reducing water usage. The cradle-to-grave analysis helps measure progress toward these objectives.
- Regulatory Compliance: In some regions, environmental regulations require businesses to conduct lifecycle assessments and adhere to specific sustainability standards. Extended Producer Responsibility (EPR) laws are driving some of this activity.
- Working Standards: Proper working conditions and treatment of workers plays a key role in the product lifecycle. Assessing not only a company's environmental but also workforce impact gives investors a fuller picture of the company's impact.

By conducting cradle-to-grave analysis, investors have a holistic view into the inner workings of a business and how their products are made end-to-end—and if those internal processes are in line with practices that they as investors would like to support.

4.2.1.1.2 Examples of Cradle-to-Grave Analysis

- Automotive Industry: If you're investing in car manufacturers, you can assess the environmental impact of vehicles from the extraction of raw materials like metals and plastics to manufacturing, transportation, vehicle use, durability, and eventual disposal. This analysis can vary based on the company's approach to materials sourcing, fuel efficiency, and recycling programs.

  For instance, electrical vehicles have become increasingly popular, in part due to their lack of carbon emissions. However, electric car batteries are resource-intensive to create and can have negative environmental impacts when disposed. An investor in car manufacturers may use cradle-to-grave analysis to compare the holistic footprint of traditional vehicle producers and electric car producers and may push for more sustainable recycling and disposal initiatives for both.
- Consumer Electronics: An investor interested in consumer electronics may want to consider an additional layer of how those products reach customers. Sourcing raw materials is just part of the picture. A cradle-to-grave analysis can reveal how far those materials needed to travel before being put into production. It can also show if the packaging for these electronics is sustainably made.

  The findings from a cradle-to-grave analysis can help inform otherwise hard-to-decide tradeoffs across several components of a consumer product's entire lifecycle. Do the benefits of responsibly sourced raw materials outweigh the carbon emissions required to get those materials to the factory? Is the good of an energy-efficient design outdone by wasteful packaging?
- Food Industry: Sustainable food has become a popular theme among investors, in large part because of the large carbon footprint associated with factory meat pro-

duction. If you're a climate-minded investor, you may feel inclined to invest in vegetarian or "fake" meat alternatives that tout fewer greenhouse gas emissions. However, a cradle-to-grave analysis may find that the comparison may not be so clear-cut as alternative meats require much more energy-intensive processing than animal proteins. From harvesting crops to milling them down, to processing them to manufacture animal-like flavors and textures, you may find that an alternative meat investment isn't in line with your values.

4.2.1.1.3 Directionality and Momentum in Cradle-to-Grave Analysis

Directionality and momentum in sustainability analysis refer to the trend or trajectory of a particular sustainability aspect over time. They seek to answer, for example, if a company is improving its environmental practices or if the labor conditions within a specific industry are getting better or worse.

To illustrate the point, consider an established seafood supply giant. At first glance, it may appear to have a strong environmental record in terms of its supply chains and may receive positive scores—and press—for practices related to fisheries. However, a deeper analysis also considers directionality:

- Are the seafood supplier's environmental practices improving or deteriorating over time?
- Are there initiatives in place to address areas where the company lags, such as labor practices?

Understanding the directionality and momentum of sustainability factors can provide a more nuanced perspective on a company's commitment to sustainability. It allows investors and stakeholders to identify whether a company is making positive strides or falling short and facing challenges that need to be addressed.

4.2.1.1.4 Peer-Relative Analysis

To gain deeper insights into the sustainability landscape, it is essential to assess how a company's sustainability performance compares to its peers in the same industry or sector. Peer-relative analysis evaluates whether a company is a leader or laggard within specific contexts.

If the seafood supplier demonstrates strong environmental practices but falls behind its competitors in labor practices, understanding its relative standing is vital. Is the company performing better or worse than industry norms? Are there opportunities for the seafood supplier to learn from other leaders in its sector? And how would an investor value this seafood supplier knowing that it may lead in responsible seafood sourcing but provide subpar working conditions for its employees?

4.2.1.1.5 Leveraging Non-Traditional Data Sources

For comprehensive cradle-to-grave analysis, it is valuable to tap into non-traditional data sources as well as traditional ratings. These sources can provide unique and more timely insights that complement conventional ESG metrics and are increasingly incorporated into "sentiment analysis" for a company:

- Newspapers: Media reports often highlight recent sustainability-related issues, controversies, or initiatives that may not yet be captured by standard ESG data because it often takes time for this information to flow through the rating process.
- Community Meetings: Minutes from local community gatherings and discussions can shed light on a company's social impact, including its relationships with the communities in which it operates.
- Nonprofits and Watchdogs: NGOs, nonprofits, and watchdog organizations actively monitor corporate behavior and can provide valuable information on businesses' sustainability and ESG practices.

By incorporating data from these non-traditional sources, sustainable investors can make a more informed decision on where to allocate their capital.

4.2.2 The Downsides and Challenges of Sustainable Investing

While there is arguably a role to play for just about anyone in the sustainable investing ecosystem, it should be noted that sustainable investing is not without its challenges and downsides.

4.2.2.1 Volatility and Risk (Similar to Traditional Investing)

A common misconception is that sustainable investing is more susceptible to volatility and risks inherent in financial markets, partly because sustainable investing has a shorter history of study.

ESG-focused businesses, however, have demonstrated strong long-term returns (Quinson, 2023) and stability.

Just like all investments, however, sustainable investments are not immune to short-term flux and the impact of economic downturns. All investments can experience fluctuations in value and be subject to market dynamics.

It is important for investors to maintain a balanced perspective and understand that sustainable investing is often best suited for investors with a long-term investment horizon. The basic principles of portfolio construction and diversification still apply. After all, sustainable investing is still, at the end of the day, investing.

4.2.2.2 Politicization of Sustainable Investing

Sustainable investing intersects with a range of environmental, social, and political issues, including climate change, social justice, and corporate governance. Some investors may be uncomfortable with the idea of "weighing in" on these issues with their investment choices.

But certain types of investing (particularly ESG integration) are not about politics at all —they are about financial materiality. ESG investors simply acknowledge and price in the realities of a changing world, including shifting demographics, changing patterns of consumption, and an evolving regulatory environment. As an investor, you may or may not be in favor of these changes but you might still choose to acknowledge that the changes are real and material to your investments for better and for worse.

4.2.2.3 Greenwashing (Deliberate and Accidental)

Greenwashing is the practice of exaggerating or misrepresenting the environmental or social sustainability of a company or investment.

Some egregious companies and investors engage in greenwashing deliberately to attract assets, employees, or other benefits that they otherwise would not be able to get.

Other companies and investors engage in greenwashing accidentally by having good intentions but failing to invest the time and resources to properly vet and monitor investments. Similarly, some companies may pursue more sustainable practices for the sake of cost-cutting, though they may market these practices as only well-intentioned operational changes. The best way to prevent greenwashing is through robust due diligence, ongoing monitoring, and – if necessary – corporate engagement.

4.2.2.4 Resourcing Challenges

Sustainable investing often involves more than just financial commitment; it requires time, effort, and resources to conduct holistic due diligence, monitoring, and sometimes even corporate engagement. While this is not inherently a downside, it is necessary for investors to realistically assess their capacity to do this work.

As an investor, consider whether you have the necessary expertise, resources, and bandwidth to do the work directly. If not, alternative approaches (such as investing through sustainable fund managers or through a sustainable investing platform) may be more suitable. We will explore this later on in the chapter.

4.2.3 Sustainable Investing in Public Equities

Sustainable investing in public equities involves the selection and management of a portfolio of publicly traded stocks. As a sustainable investor in the public equity markets, you can decide whether you want to be passive, active, or a mix of the two.

Passive investors tend to be relatively hands off. You might buy and hold, for example, an ETF that automatically invests in renewable energy companies without the Portfolio Manager doing much bespoke portfolio construction. Passive investors tend to pay lower fees and argue that the market generally goes up, so the best thing to do is to ride the wave rather than spend time and energy tinkering with an individual portfolio. From a sustainability perspective, passive investors usually just want to make sure that their investments align with their objectives and that they are not investing in anything that runs afoul of their values.

In contrast, active investors tend to be more hands-on. As an active investor, you might evaluate companies, select individual stocks, and even engage directly with companies (or invest in managers who do that for you, often for a higher fee).

Active sustainable investors argue that buying a stock on the secondary market does not have any real impact – you have to actively own and engage as an investor to influence the market and a company's behavior. A key piece of active investing is therefore corporate engagement.

4.2.3.1 The Importance of Corporate Engagement in Sustainable Investing

Corporate engagement is a vital aspect of sustainable investing. It offers investors a unique opportunity to influence corporate behavior and promote responsible and sustainable business practices. Businesses similarly are motivated to engage with their shareholders to foster loyalty and maintain—particularly among larger shareholders —a strong relationship.

While the principles listed here are filtered through public equities, these same or similar principles can generally be applied to the asset classes that we'll be discussing later on in this chapter: private equities, public debt, and private debt.

4.2.3.1.1 The Power of Shareholder Voting
When you buy a share of a publicly traded company, you are not just acquiring a financial stake; you are also gaining a voice in the company's decision-making process. Every public company holds an annual meeting where shareholders have the opportunity to vote using ballots on various matters, similar to participating in an election.

Shareholder voting is one of the fundamental aspects of corporate governance, and it allows investors to express their preferences and values in an accessible and convenient method. This process can take several forms, including voting on the company's board of directors, executive compensation plans, and proposed corporate policies. While voting on these issues might seem like a minor action, it can carry significant weight in influencing corporate behavior, particularly in a direction that is in line with your beliefs and values.

4.2.3.1.2 Initiating Shareholder Ballots
Shareholder activism can go beyond casting votes during annual meetings. Investors have the power to initiate their own ballots on specific issues that concern them. This process involves submitting a proxy proposal which is then included on the company's official ballot. By doing so, shareholders can raise awareness of critical sustainability concerns and push for change at the corporate level.

Collaborative shareholder initiatives can be highly effective. Investors can work together to submit proxies and coordinate efforts to advocate for sustainable practices within a company. These coordinated actions amplify the collective voice of shareholders and increase the likelihood of influencing corporate decisions.

4.2.3.1.3 Engaging Directly with Companies
Active investors can take their commitment to corporate engagement a step further by engaging directly with company leadership, including C-suite executives and board members. These engagements can typically involve meetings, correspondence, or discussions aimed at addressing specific ESG concerns or sustainability-related issues.

Engaging with companies directly allows investors to communicate their expectations, share insights, and encourage specific business practices. While not an exact science, investors who have a larger stake in the business tend to carry more weight and influence at this level of engagement.

4.2.3.1.4 The Role of Faith-Based Investors and Interfaith Groups
Some investors and investment groups like churches and religious organizations carry more social and political cache and can often use that as leverage with company leadership.

Faith-based investors have led significant forays in corporate engagement related to sustainable investing. These investors often bring a strong moral authority to the table, emphasizing the ethical imperative of responsible business practices.

Interfaith groups like the Interfaith Center on Corporate Responsibility (ICCR) play a crucial role in facilitating corporate engagement efforts. ICCR and similar organizations bring together investors of various faiths to collaborate on sustainability initiatives and engage with companies collectively. Their combined influence and moral guidance can drive meaningful change within corporations.

4.2.3.1.5 Activist Takeovers and Changing Corporate Norms

In some cases, sustainable investors resort to activist takeovers to affect change within a company. This strategy involves pushing for the appointment of board members who are aligned with sustainability goals. An American impact-focused investment firm held a successful campaign to place climate activists on a large oil and gas corporation's board for instance, signaling a growing emphasis on environmental concerns in corporate governance (Sorkin et al., 2023).

4.2.3.2 Divesting as a Means of Activism

One of the key considerations in sustainable investing, particularly in public equities, is the choice between divestment and active engagement with companies. Divestment involves selling shares of companies that do not align with your sustainability goals. While it may seem like a straightforward approach to distance oneself from companies that engage in unsustainable practices, it comes with some important implications.

Divesting can be seen as relinquishing one's voting power as a shareholder. This means that investors lose the ability to influence corporate decisions and advocate for change from within. While it's challenging to argue that divestment alone directly changes corporate behavior, it can have indirect effects. By divesting from unsustainable companies, investors may signal to the market and other stakeholders that certain practices are unacceptable, potentially affecting the company's cost of capital.

The true power of divestment, however, may lie in its capacity to drive broader societal change by shifting norms. History provides numerous examples of practices that were once considered mainstream but are now widely seen as unacceptable. A common example that gets cited is slavery, which was once unfortunately ubiquitous but today is widely condemned. Sustainable investors recognize that by divesting from companies engaged in harmful practices they contribute to the delegitimization of these practices, potentially leading to broader changes in societal norms and consequently how businesses, communities, and institutions operate.

Ultimately, sustainable investors may choose divestment not only to protect their financial interests but also as a means of taking a stand against actions that they consider unethical or unsustainable. While divestment alone may not transform the corporate landscape overnight, it plays a role in the broader effort to reshape industries and create a more sustainable future.

4.2.3.3 Returns in Public Equities: Values-Based vs. ESG Approaches

When it comes to sustainable investing in public equities, investors may face the fundamental question of balancing financial returns with their ethical and environmental values. This results in two distinct approaches: the values-based approach (VBI) and the environmental, social, and governance (ESG) approach.

Values-Based Approach (VBI): In the values-based approach, investors prioritize their personal beliefs and values over financial returns. This stance is often seen when investors want to avoid investing in companies involved in activities that they find morally objectionable. For example, a cancer foundation might choose to divest from tobacco companies, regardless of the effect that divestment may have on its financial returns.

In a case such as this, the investors' commitment to their values takes precedence over potential returns. Some values-based investors are willing to accept higher tracking errors, even if it means their portfolio underperforms the broader market by a specific margin—as long as they remain true to their values.

ESG Approach: Investors adopting the ESG approach do not prioritize their values over their financial returns. While some ESG investors share a commitment to sustainability they generally believe that it is also possible to achieve competitive financial returns while simultaneously considering ESG factors sustainable practices. By incorporating ESG into their decision-making process, they seek to reduce risk (beta) and increase returns (alpha).

The choice between a values-based and ESG approach ultimately depends on investors' individual priorities and risk tolerance. While values-based investors prioritize their values, ESG investors aim to "do well by doing good," believing that they can achieve both objectives simultaneously.

4.2.3.4 Investing Indirectly through a Public Equities Manager

The most significant difference between direct and indirect investments in public equities is the involvement of a professional asset manager. While the overarching principles remain generally consistent between both methods, investing indirectly through managers introduces an added layer of complexity.

Just as you would scrutinize a company's sustainability footprint, you should also assess the suitability of an asset manager's sustainable investment strategy. In evaluating a potential sustainable asset manager, you want might to look at the following "4P" characteristics:

1. Principles and Philosophy: Understand the core values and guiding principles of the asset manager. Do their principles align with your sustainability objectives? The sustainable investment landscape is everchanging; it is essential to identify managers who share alignment with your objectives.

    Consider the challenge of divesting from coal, a non-sustainable energy source, while recognizing that this may have severe economic repercussions for a community that relies on the coal industry, such as the Appalachia region in the

United States. A well-rounded manager should be able to identify different trade-offs as they align with your values and principles.

2. People: Assess the diversity and breadth of the manager's background. Diversity considerations extend beyond gender and race; they could include where they grew up, how they currently choose to live, and what motivates them. The ability to leverage their lived experiences to add dimension to their advice and one's investment opportunities can be uniquely impactful.

   A manager who has lived, for example, in mixed income housing might be better positioned to run an affordable housing fund than a manager who has no such personal experience.

3. Process: Evaluate the manager's investment process. Does it involve a robust framework for incorporating sustainability at every step? Or does it merely involve slapping a "green" label on investments without a deeper commitment to sustainability? A well-defined process demonstrates a genuine dedication to sustainable investing, ensuring that sustainability factors are integrated systematically into the investment strategy.

4. Performance: Assess the manager's track record in sustainable investing. What is their historical performance in this space from a sustainability perspective? While traditional performance metrics include 1, 3, 5, and 10-year returns, it's important to also contextualize these metrics for minority managers who might not have as lengthy a track record. Consider the specific challenges faced by managers from historically marginalized groups, such as limited access to capital, and evaluate their performance within that context as well as understand how that experience could add to their partnership.

4.2.4 Sustainable Investing in Private Equity

Companies transition from private to public when they undergo an Initial Public Offering (IPO). As previously mentioned, once this occurs, their stock—or publicly traded equity—become available for public trading and anyone can buy or sell these stocks. The shift from private to public status comes with many regulatory requirements, transparency rules, and disclosure obligations, all aimed at ensuring fair and equitable participation in the wealth generated by these companies.

Before a company goes public, it exists in the realm of private equity. This stage typically occurs when a company is relatively young or not yet of a size where public trading is practical. Private companies have fewer disclosure obligations, operate with greater opacity, and provide less standardized information about their operations and inner workings. Additionally, unique to private equity is the requirement for investors to meet specific income or institutional thresholds to participate in private equity deals.

Accredited investors are those who can absorb the oftentimes higher risks associated with private equity investments and have the necessary resources to engage. Venture capital (VC) is a subset of private equity. VC investments are typically made in early-stage companies that the VC deems having significant growth potential. These investments may deliver substantial return or have a significant likelihood to result in a loss. In essence, private equity offers a high-risk, high-reward investment profile compared to publicly traded equity.

4.2.4.1 Evaluating Sustainable Investments in Private Equity

When deciding whether to make a sustainable investment in a privately held company, you can do much of the same "cradle-to-grave" analysis that you would use for a publicly traded company, with a few noteworthy distinctions:

1. Data Sources: It can be harder to find and gather data on privately held companies than publicly traded companies. Specialized, for-profit databases are usually required to get robust data sets in the private markets.

    Unlike their public counterparts, private companies often have fewer comprehensive data available. Private equity investments frequently involve companies at earlier stages of development. These startups and smaller enterprises may not have the extensive reporting mechanisms or capabilities in place that larger public companies do. As a result, evaluating their sustainability practices can be challenging.

2. Investment Channels: Investors interested in direct sustainable private equity often complain that it can be hard to find these opportunities. Some source deals through online platforms that were enabled by the JOBS Act or find investments through personal networks of family and friends. While some of these platforms have lower barriers to entry, others may require proof of significant assets.

4.2.4.2 Additionality in the Private Markets

Additionality is a cornerstone concept in impact investing more broadly; it suggests that private equity investments can facilitate actions, projects, and change that would not be feasible without this funding. This theoretically provides investors with an opportunity to have a more direct impact on a company's sustainability initiatives compared to investing in public equities.

Investors in private equity have the advantage of engaging with companies in their early stages of development, where they can potentially influence business practices more directly and help drive longer term positive changes. However, it is important to note that while the impact of these private equity investments can be more concentrated, they oftentimes may only affect smaller companies compared to the broader corporate governance impacts often associated with larger public companies. So, who ultimately has more impact? That is still hotly debated.

4.2.4.3 Challenges and Considerations of Direct Private Equity

1. Navigating Exits & Impact Lockstep: A significant challenge in sustainable private equity lies in what happens when a private company goes through an ownership transition (either getting acquired by another company or going through an IPO).

    When a company changes ownership, the company or the new owners might choose to shed some of their sustainability practices in the process. For example, a privately held company that donates to a local soup kitchen might be told after an IPO that such donations are an inappropriate use of shareholder capital.

    To address this issue, a concept known as "impact lockstep" has emerged. Impact lockstep ties a company's sustainable practices to its business model, ensuring that financial success is also correlated with positive environmental and social impacts. For example, a company that manufactures solar panels can demonstrate strong lockstep because the growth of their business is tied to selling solar panels which promote the use of a renewable and clean energy source.

    Benefit Corporations (Benefit Corps) tackle this same issue and are aimed at preserving sustainability and ESG commitments even as companies grow and face pressure from financial stakeholders to disengage from their sustainability practices. Benefit Corps are designed to protect a company's impact mission by recognizing the fiduciary responsibility to support multiple stakeholders rather than just shareholders.
2. Liquidity Lock-Up: Sustainable investing in private equity also requires the acceptance of a longer investment horizon. Investors must be prepared for illiquidity as private equity investments often involve lengthy lock-up periods, sometimes lasting 10 to 12 years.

4.2.4.4 Investing Indirectly through a Private Equity Manager

Sustainable investing in indirect private equity combines the principles of direct investing in private equities with the added layer of a fund manager. In this approach, investors channel their capital through their fund managers who then select and manage private equity investments on their behalf. Here's a closer look at this strategy and its key considerations:

Similar Foundations with a Managerial Layer: Building on the principles of sustainable investing in direct private equities, this strategy involves a significant addition—the role of fund managers. Instead of investing directly in private companies, investors allocate their capital to professional managers who specialize in identifying, nurturing, and monitoring private equity investments. These managers act as intermediaries, sourcing investments, representing the investors' interests, and leveraging and relying on their expertise to make informed decisions on the investors' behalf.

Choosing the Right Fund Managers: One of the critical tasks in sustainable investing in indirect private equity is selecting the appropriate fund managers. These individuals or teams play a pivotal role in shaping the sustainability performance of the underlying investments. Investors should assess several factors when choosing managers, including the "4Ps" outlined above. Managers who prioritize sustainable practices can help investors navigate complex decisions, especially when trade-offs between financial returns and sustainability goals arise.

Corporate Engagement Expertise: Private equity managers possess unique expertise in corporate engagement, allowing them to be a hands-on influence on the sustainability practices of the companies within their portfolios. They often have deep industry knowledge, experience, and networks, enabling them to work closely with portfolio companies to drive internal change and be comfortable going to bat for you.

Diversity, Equity, and Inclusion (DEI): The considerations related to diversity, equity, and inclusion that were discussed in the context of indirect public equities apply here as well. The lack of diversity in venture capital and early-stage funding has been a long-standing and persistent issue. Fund managers have a role to play in addressing this challenge by seeking out and supporting diverse entrepreneurs, businesses, and organizations. Initiatives like Halcyon, a nonprofit incubator in Washington, D.C., focus on minority and marginalized entrepreneurs and can help change the landscape by providing resources and opportunities for underrepresented founders.

Relationships Matter: In the world of private equity, the right relationships can make a substantial difference. Managers who have established connections within specific industries or regions may have access to unique investment opportunities and can exert greater influence on the companies that they invest in on your behalf. Building and nurturing these relationships can be a valuable asset for fund managers seeking to drive positive sustainability outcomes.

Fee Structures and Compensation: Sustainable private equity funds often adhere to standard fee structures common in the industry, such as the "2 and 20" model. This structure includes a 2% management fee and a 20% share of the profits, known as the "carried interest." However, some sustainable private equity funds are exploring innovative and novel compensation models that tie a portion of fees to sustainability metrics. This approach aligns the financial interests and motivations of fund managers with the achievement of sustainability goals.

Longer Investment Horizon: Like direct private equity investments, indirect private equity typically involves a longer investment horizon, often spanning a decade or more. Investors should be prepared for this extended lock-up period and consider the illiquid nature of these investments when building their portfolios.

4.2.5 Sustainable Investing in Public Debt

Public debt represents a significant component of the broader sustainable investing landscape, encompassing various types of bonds issued by governmental entities, nonprofits, and corporations. These bonds are instrumental in financing essential public projects and initiatives.

Understanding public debt and its role in sustainable investing requires a closer examination of its types, issuers, and sustainability considerations.

4.2.5.1 Types of Issuers and Issuing Authorities

Public debt includes a wide array of issuers, each with distinct purposes and priorities:
- Housing Finance Authorities (HFAs): These entities issue bonds to facilitate affordable housing initiatives and provide financing options for homebuyers among specific communities like teachers and firefighters, including programs like "Homes for Heroes."
- Development Financing Authorities (DFAs): DFAs issue bonds to support economic development projects, often in underserved communities, fostering job creation and community revitalization and infrastructure.
- State Bond Banks: These entities issue bonds to assist local governments and nonprofits in financing public infrastructure projects such as schools, hospitals, and public transportation systems.
- Nonprofits: Various nonprofit organizations issue bonds to fund their initiatives, aligning their mission with sustainable investing principles and other social impact programs.
- Community Development Financial Institutions (CDFIs): CDFIs issue bonds to support community development efforts, promote financial inclusion, and address economic disparities in underserved areas.
- Schools: Educational institutions, including public schools and universities, issue bonds to fund the building of facilities and creating or maintaining educational programs.

4.2.5.2 Corporate Engagement as a Bond Investor

When you think about corporate engagement, you likely think of public equities, but you can do corporate engagement as a bond investor as well.

Bondholders have the opportunity to influence the issuers' practices and commitments to sustainability and social impact. Monitoring bond issuers' activities, advocating for sustainable practices, and encouraging certain issuances can be effective methods to drive positive change and support the original goals and missions of the bonds. The Public Finance Initiative at Harvard University is an example of a group that does thoughtful engagement to improve racial justice through the bond markets.

4.2.5.3 Analyzing Bonds

When considering sustainable investing in public debt, it's important to analyze each specific type of bond:

– Corporate Bonds: Analyzing corporate bonds involves evaluating the issuer's environmental, social, and governance (ESG) performance, similar to the analysis of public equities. Assessing factors like supply chain sustainability, labor practices, and corporate governance can provide insights into the sustainability of specific corporate bonds.
– Mortgage Bonds: These bonds involve examining the dynamics of mortgages, understanding who benefits from them, and assessing whether the bonds align with responsible lending and homeownership practices.
– Municipal Bonds: Municipal bonds fund critical infrastructure projects such as sewer systems, affordable housing, and public transit. As a sustainable investor, you can try to ensure that these bonds align with your values and support priorities in a community that you care about.

Two common types of bonds are revenue bonds and general obligation bonds:

– Revenue Bonds: These bonds are tied to the revenue generated by specific projects or initiatives. For instance, a revenue bond might finance a tolled highway, with repayments coming from toll collections.
– General Obligation Bonds: These bonds are backed by the full faith and credit of the issuer. In essence, the issuer pledges its resources and reputation to ensure bond repayment.

In the event of a bond issuer facing financial distress or bankruptcy, sustainable investors should consider their rights and responsibilities. While bonds provide certain rights to bondholders, exercising these rights in a sustainable and responsible manner is sometimes a difficult consideration. For instance, while it may be in your legal right, would you as a sustainable investor be willing to repossess a community's solar panels or foreclose on an affordable housing complex? If not, how should you think about the relative risk of that investment?

4.2.5.4 Investing Indirectly through Public Debt Managers

Indirect investment in public debt involves entrusting one's capital to investment managers who, in turn, allocate those funds across a spectrum of bonds. While the principles of sustainable investing in indirect public debt closely mirror those of indirect public equities, there are some differences to consider within the bond market ecosystem specifically.

Investors in indirect public debt should be aware of the numerous intermediaries that play critical roles. Beyond investment managers, there are underwriters, syndicates, broker-dealers, and other participants who are actively involved in the issuance, distribution, and trading of bonds. To ensure that sustainable investing principles are upheld throughout the investment process, it's crucial to monitor and evaluate the actions and decisions of all stakeholders within this ecosystem.

While that may seem like a sizable undertaking, sustainable investors can leverage the expertise of their chosen investment managers who serve as stewards of their capital within the bond market. By partnering with reputable managers, investors can entrust them to navigate the intricacies of the bond market, assess bond issuers' sustainability practices and make investment decisions that reflect the investor's preferences.

4.2.6 Sustainable Investing in Private Debt

Private debt investments are a unique vehicle for sustainable investors to generate stable returns while supporting initiatives that align with their objectives.

4.2.7 Direct Private Debt

Direct private debt investments involve providing loans directly to organizations or entities in need of capital. Consider a local soup kitchen that relies on government reimbursements to maintain its operations. While it awaits reimbursement from the government, the soup kitchen may require a loan in the interim to purchase groceries and continue its charitable work.

In this scenario, a foundation dedicated to community development may step in to provide a loan to the soup kitchen. Once the government reimburses the soup kitchen it can repay the foundation with interest.

This interest rate can be determined based on whether the foundation wants to make the loan a market-rate Mission Related Investment (MRI) or a below-market-rate Program-Related Investment (PRI). A more detailed review of MRIs and PRIs is covered later in this chapter.

4.2.7.1 Investing Indirectly through Private Debt Managers

Investors who prefer a managed approach to private debt can turn to investment managers who specialize in this asset class. Many indirect private debt investments focus on areas like affordable housing, echoing the sustainability considerations applicable to private equity.

When assessing indirect private debt opportunities, sustainable investors should conduct thorough analyses of the underlying holdings, management teams, and the sustainability potential of their investments. Investment managers often provide investors with professional expertise and access to diversified private debt portfolios.

4.2.8 Exploring Mission-Related and Program-Related Investments

Some of the biggest sustainable investors are foundations, and they have two different tools in their sustainable investing toolkits: Mission-Related Investments (MRIs) and Program-Related Investments (PRIs).

Mission-Related Investments are market-rate investments made with the intention of achieving both financial returns and advancing their charitable mission. This approach challenges the notion that concessionary investments (where investors are willing to accept lower financial returns for higher social impact) are the only way to drive change. MRIs demonstrate that it is possible to generate competitive financial returns while contributing to positive social outcomes.

Examples of MRIs include investing in market-rate renewable energy projects and affordable housing projects.

Program-Related Investments are also designed to align with the organization's mission but they tend to be below-market-rate investments where the investor is taking uncompensated risk. PRIs offer foundations an alternative to traditional grant-making by allowing them to deploy their capital in ways that can potentially generate both social impact and financial returns, albeit with the expectation that there may be financial loss—in short, the impact of the capital is worth taking a loss.

Foundations, typically endowed with substantial assets, have a mandated requirement to distribute a certain percentage of their capital each year for charitable purposes. While grants have traditionally been the primary means of fulfilling this requirement, PRIs offer an innovative method to use their assets for social good. These investments can take various forms, with debt (both direct and indirect) being the most common.

Blended finance and hybrid capital structures often incorporate concessionary investments like PRIs into complex capital stacks. These approaches involve combining different types of capital, including grants, loans, and investments, to address complex social challenges.

4.2.9 Conclusion: Navigating Sustainable Investing Across Asset Classes

For many, the unknowns about sustainable investing give potential sustainable investors pause. As a multifaceted discipline with many types of roles, it is understandably daunting to know where you fit in and what space you want to—and should—occupy.

The tools and frameworks in this exploration have hopefully made the world of sustainable investing less mystifying and opaque. By understanding sustainable investing across each asset class, you can work toward a more sustainable economy.

References

Morningstar, Inc. "Global Sustainable Fund Flows: Q2 2023 in Review | Morningstar," n.d. https://www.morningstar.com/lp/global-esg-flows

Quinson, Tim. "Kroll's Message for Haters: ESG Makes Money for Investors." Bloomberg.Com, September 13, 2023. https://www.bloomberg.com/news/articles/2023-09-13/kroll-s-message-for-haters-esg-makes-money-for-investors#xj4y7vzkg.

Sorkin, Andrew Ross, Ravi Mattu, Bernhard Warner, Sarah Kessler, Michael J. De La Merced, Lauren Hirsch, Ephrat Livni, and Vivienne Walt. "Reassessing Engine No. 1's Fight against Exxon Mobil." The New York Times, May 31, 2023. https://www.nytimes.com/2023/05/31/business/dealbook/engine-no-1-exxon-mobil.html.

Chapter Five: **ESG in Private Equity**

Introduction

The Private Equity (PE) market represents a large and growing segment of the financial markets yet it is little understood by many investors. PE investing entails ownership of assets of companies which are not publicly traded. PE funds are managed by General Partners (GPs), with investing capital provided by Limited Partners (LPs) who may be institutional investors such as pension funds, insurance companies, university endowments, and corporate entities as well as high net worth individuals. The largest of the GPs will have several different funds, each of which may have billions of dollars in assets. The GP will invest in one or more of a range of assets: equity, bonds, structured investment products, etc., in a range of industries in accordance with the offering documents. The fund will hold the investments for a period of five to ten years or more, with the objective of selling the investments to yield the best return to investors. Historical outperformance by PE funds has raised their profile in recent years and forecasts of global assets under management in PE range upwards of $10 trillion by the late 2020s.

In their paper "ESG in Private Equity," Casazza and Herman investigate the large and growing role of ESG considerations in the private equity market. Historically, ESG issues were less central to PE participants due to two factors. First, the typical investment horizon of only five to ten years may be too short for many of the changes needed to affect GHG emissions, for example. Secondly, PE investments are more opaque than investments which are traded on public markets. Decision makers and investors may be less responsive to ESG concerns where it's more difficult for activists to identify the investors or the ESG issues. While some aspects of these two factors persist, in recent years there has been a substantial increase in focus and sensitivity of GPs, LPs, and activists generally in assessing and addressing ESG concerns in PE. This is especially true where European investors are involved and in cases where regulators have oversight. For many GPs, ESG has become a top strategic priority. The authors provide a detailed list of some of the important stakeholders who are instrumental in driving the ESG focus for many fund managers. In addition to investor involvement in advancing ESG interests, regulators in both the EU and the US have increasingly pushed forward pro-ESG agendas which are seen as key drivers in investment decisions in private markets, as they are in public markets. Casazza and Herman go on to discuss the impact ESG is having throughout the various stages of the PE Investment cycle: defining the fund's investment approach, fundraising, asset acquisition, managing portfolio investments, and, finally, investment exits.

Recent years have seen a backlash against some aspects of ESG investing but there is little doubt that there continues to be increased sensitivity to the risks posed by inattention to these issues. In their paper the authors conclude that "Holistic and sustained integration of ESG will depend ultimately upon whether GPs and their investors believe ESG actually results in better long-term returns in their portfolios."

https://doi.org/10.1515/9783111178608-009

Carol A. Casazza and Sarah J. Herman

5 Environmental, Social, and Governance in Private Equity

A growing number of asset managers continue to embrace ESG as a risk management tool to ensure long-term asset values despite pushback from vocal anti-ESG proponents, particularly in the US. ESG's resilience in the face of contemporary headwinds begs a deeper look at its application in private markets so we can better recognize the additive value that integrating ESG brings to investment transactions and business operations.

The intent of this article is to examine ESG in the context of the broadest portion of the private equity sector with common attributes. We will not include in our discussion several related asset classes, i.e., private debt, real estate, or infrastructure nor will we cover venture capital, whose immature business concept, early stage operations, and lack of revenue do not allow for meaningful comparisons with established businesses, no matter how big or small. Note that in this discussion of ESG we are explicitly excluding publicly traded companies because, by definition, private equity consists of equity not listed on a public exchange.

5.1 Private Equity Explained

Private equity (PE), simply put, is the investment of capital in private companies in return for equity or "ownership." Broadly interpreted, it can include all forms of investment in private companies along the maturity continuum, from early stage venture capital to growth equity, to leveraged buyouts of established enterprises, to turnaround investments of financially troubled companies. Additionally, it can mean ownership interest in not only operating businesses but also real estate and infrastructure.

The overall PE business model is to deploy capital, primarily from external sources, to acquire businesses with growth potential and then realize a return to investors upon later sale. Specifically, this starts with the solicitation of capital by the PE firm acting as a General Partner (GP) who creates a fund known as a Limited Partnership. The investors who have contributed the capital to the fund become Limited Partners (LPs). This fund capital is deployed through a series of investments where companies are acquired by the fund and become known as Portfolio Companies. The GP is now expected to facilitate the Portfolio Company's growth in value until it is sold or goes through another liquidity event (such as an IPO, merger, or recapitalization), returning proceeds to both the GP and LPs. Other than the broad parameters set out in the

https://doi.org/10.1515/9783111178608-010

limited partnership agreements which govern the relationship between the GP and the LPs, the LPs do not know the exact investments made with their capital that will ultimately constitute the fund. The funds themselves, which act as repositories of capital for investment, have finite terms of typically 7 to 10 years and the money invested in them is usually not available for subsequent withdrawals. We can view PE investments as illiquid investments with a comparatively long time horizon, though occasionally some funds may start to distribute partial profits after a number of years, perhaps after the sale of an individual Portfolio Company.

There are several ways to categorize the size of PE firms: the amount of assets under management (AUM), the amount of capital raised over a certain time period, the average size of the transactions size, etc. For our purposes, it is helpful to group PE firms by the size of the purchase price of the companies they target. Typically, large capital equity deals are $1 billion and above. There is some variation in what is thought to be the middle-market but an expansive definition would include transactions of between $50 million and $1 billion. Lower-middle market is often defined as companies valued at as low as $10 million. This metric is used here because the size and type of businesses that a firm acquires impacts the role ESG plays in the investment cycle, as we will explore below.

Table 5.1: Frequently Used Terms.[1]

Term	Definition
Fund	The pool of capital established for the purposes of private equity activity and investment. Often a PE firm will be responsible for several funds that may vary according to mandate or investment period.
General Partner (GP)	The managing partner in a PE firm who has unlimited personal liability for the debts and obligations of the limited partnership and the right to participate in its management. The General Partner is the intermediary between investors with capital and businesses seeking capital to grow.
Limited Partner (LP)	The investors in a limited partnership. Limited partners are not involved in the day-to-day management of the partnership and generally cannot lose more than their capital contribution.
Portfolio Company	A business entity that has been acquired by or secured at least one round of financing or capital from one or more PE funds.

---

1 These terms are based generally upon those found in the glossary developed by the International Limited Partners Association.

Table 5.1 (continued)

Term	Definition
Private Equity (PE)	Equity securities of companies that have not "gone public" (are not listed on a public exchange). Private equities are generally illiquid and thought of as a long-term investment. As they are not listed on an exchange, any investor wishing to sell securities in private companies must find a buyer in the absence of a marketplace. In addition, there are many transfer restrictions on private securities. Investors in private securities generally receive their return through one of three ways: an initial public offering, a sale or merger, or a recapitalization.
Private Equity Firm (Firm)	A firm that deploys capital for investment in private companies out of dedicated funds structured as limited partnerships in return for equity.

5.2 ESG in Private Equity, Generally

While there are several unique aspects of the PE sector that are particularly interesting in the context of ESG, there are two main attributes with significant importance.

First, Portfolio Companies are meant to be held for a relatively short and finite period of time, sometimes only five to six years. The decision calculus of making large capital investments or major shifts in operations, when the ultimate goal is to sell the company as soon as certain time or value criteria are met, is quite different from that of a public company where the board of directors and shareholders tend to be focused on value over a much longer, indefinite term. Thus a PE's "in and out" ethos may serve as a disincentive to making the changes necessary to lessen a Portfolio Company's ESG impact and operate more sustainably. For example, commitments to reduce greenhouse gases (GHGs) frequently extend over decades and require complex, expensive decarbonization plans for operations. Such timelines and expenditures may be at odds with a fund's investment strategy to increase value as soon as possible.

Second, because much of the information about these investments and even the funds themselves is private, it is difficult for those not part of the funds to access information about the ESG performance of the Portfolio Companies. This lack of transparency may be viewed as problematic for certain investors, especially those caring more about sustainability and social impact as we have seen with Millennials and Gen Z. Without the impetus of public scrutiny, GPs may not be as drawn to introducing ESG procedures or data collection.

Traditional investing has prioritized financial return solely and has not included much consideration of ESG risks. Over time, particularly with regard to investment in large, publicly held companies, ESG has become increasingly important in assessing value, as seen in shareholders' demands that ESG risks be routinely identified and managed. Both management and investors have begun to appreciate the other side of the ESG equation recognizing "opportunities" e.g., cost avoidance associated with energy efficiency or new markets such as solar power or recyclable plastics.

However, the waters become murkier when discussing impact investment in the private market context as a whole and ESG as a tool thereof. Marcie Frost, CEO of California Public Employees' Retirement System (CalPERS), was clear when she stated in March 2023,

> Applying the lens of ESG is not a mandate for how to invest nor is an endorsement of a political position or ideology. Those who say otherwise are actually advocating for investors like CalPERS to put on blinders, to ignore information and data that might otherwise help build on the retirement security of our two million members.

Impact investing, *writ large*, is the purposeful deployment of capital to solve a social and/or environmental problem and, consequently, create a positive and measurable impact. While embedding ESG risk management in any PE investment is likely to yield incidentally good outcomes, it is the purposeful deployment of capital to solve a social or environmental problem that distinguishes impact investment from merely considering ESG attributes.

5.3 ESG in Private Equity: Rising Expectations

Understanding the ESG playing field and its players is all the more important due to the rising expectations of civil society, investors, and government regulators (collectively, stakeholders) for how ESG drives the deployment of capital in private markets. Stakeholder interest and expectation is driven by a concern about the influence of the sector's outsized, accelerated growth over the past 10 years with AUM increasing from US $2 trillion in 2013 to US $4.4 trillion in 2022. As the PE asset class has grown and stakeholder considerations have developed, interested parties have demanded more disclosure in the areas of ESG risks and impacts and, increasingly, transparency as to the ESG performance of funds and their constituent companies.

We can see that investors especially have developed increased scrutiny regarding raising expectations for performance in ESG. In its annual 2023 Global Private Equity Survey, Ernst & Young (EY) found that ESG continues to be a key issue for LPs and their investment managers. Fund managers reported investor questions related to ESG governance and how GPs are assisting their portfolio companies with ESG-related concerns. According to EY, ESG was barely on the radar screen when EY began the survey 10 years ago but has now become a top strategic priority, especially for larger fund managers.

Stakeholders are more than just investors, though, and are diverse in mission, objective, and function. Within PE, they range from individual investors or investor groups, industry-led associations, and mission-driven advocacy organizations to global not-for-profits convening investor coalitions or initiatives. Who they are and their relationships with each other continue to evolve. Many have been increasingly influential in the PE ecosystem, advocating for the private markets to drive positive ESG performance by challenging firms and fund managers to utilize due diligence protocols, performance standards and targets, and/or reporting frameworks for their funds aimed at enabling those goals. Some of these stakeholders have even facilitated the development of PE-specific standards and serve as catalysts for a more robust integration of ESG into the sector as a whole. In practice, this means a GP or fund manager may face increased expectations of ESG reporting if one or more of their LPs is a member of any of these investor alliances.

Table 5.2 identifies selected stakeholders driving rising expectations for better ESG performance in the PE sector.

Table 5.2: Stakeholders driving rising expectations for better ESG performance.

I Organization
Civil Society
Ceres Investor Network https://www.ceres.org/networks/ceres-investor-network A global nonprofit working with capital market leaders to solve the world's greatest sustainability challenges. Utilizing networks and global collaborations of investors, companies, and nonprofits drives action and inspires equitable market-based and policy solutions. The Ceres Investor Network includes more than 220 institutional investors managing more than $60 trillion in assets. Ceres works with Network members to advance sustainable investment practices, engage with corporate leaders, and advocate for key policy and regulatory solutions to accelerate the transition to a just, sustainable, net zero emissions economy. Ceres global collaborations include Climate Action 100+, Net Zero Asset Managers Initiative, Paris Aligned Asset Owners, and The Investor Agenda.
Ceres Investor Network Private Equity Working Group https://www.ceres.org/networks/ceres-investor-network (private group) The largest PE ESG group based on collective assets under management. Ceres facilitates sessions that provide GPs and LPs with the latest climate-centric and sustainable investment practices, policies, frameworks, and tools to assess, manage, and mitigate ESG and climate risks, adopt investment practices in alignment with the *Net Zero Investment Framework*, align environmental and social impacts of investments to support sustainable development, and develop and implement investor climate action plans.
Asia Investor Group on Climate Change https://aigcc.net An initiative to create awareness and encourage action among Asia's asset owners and asset managers about the risks and opportunities associated with climate change and low-carbon investing.

Table 5.2 (continued)

Climate Action 100+

https://www.climateaction100.org

An investor-led initiative to ensure the world's largest corporate greenhouse gas emitters take necessary action on climate change. Over 700 investors, responsible for $68 trillion AUM, are engaging companies on improving climate change governance, cutting emissions, and strengthening climate-related financial disclosures in order to create long-term shareholder value. The work of the initiative is coordinated by five investor networks: Asia Investor Group on Climate Change, Ceres, Investor Group on Climate Change, Institutional Investors Group on Climate Change, and United Nations Principles for Responsible Investment.

Investors Group on Climate Change

https://igcc.org.au

An Australian and New Zealand network of investors with $30 trillion in global AUM and $3 trillion in local AUM which seeks to understand and respond to the risks and opportunities of climate change. International Investors Group on Climate Change

https://www.iigcc.org

A global group working closely with investors to provide guidance, frameworks, tools, and support with a goal of helping them respond to challenges and integrate management of climate-related risks and opportunities into their investment processes. Its mission focuses on bringing the investment community together to make significant progress towards a net zero and climate resilient future by 2030.

Net Zero Asset Managers Initiative

https://www.netzeroassetmanagers.org

An international group of asset managers committed to supporting the goal of net zero greenhouse gas emissions by 2050 or sooner, in line with global efforts to limit warming to 1.5 degrees Celsius; and to supporting investing aligned with net zero emissions by 2050 or sooner.

Paris Aligned Asset Owners

https://www.parisalignedassetowners.org

A global group of 56 asset owners with over $3.3 trillion in assets committed to transitioning their investments to achieve net zero portfolio greenhouse gas emissions by 2050 drawing on the *Net Zero Investment Framework* to deliver these commitments.

The Investor Agenda

https://theinvestoragenda.org

A policy advocacy organization founded by seven major groups working with investors: Asia Investor Group on Climate Change, CDP, Ceres, Investor Group on Climate Change, Institutional Investors Group on Climate Change, United Nations Principles for Responsible Investment, and United Nations Environmental Programme Finance Initiative. It advances a common leadership agenda on the climate crisis that is unifying, comprehensive, and focused on accelerating investor action for a net zero emissions economy.

Science Based Targets Initiative (SBTi)

https://sciencebasedtargets.org/resources/files/SBTi-Private-Equity-Sector-Guidance.pdf

Drives climate action in the private sector by enabling organizations to set science-based emissions reduction targets. SBTi proposed draft guidance for the PE sector in November, 2022.

Table 5.2 (continued)

United Nations Principles for Responsible Investment (UNPRI)
https://www.unpri.org/investment-tools/private-markets/private-equity
UN supported proponent of responsible investing, with
38 of the top 50 PE firms (by AUM) as signatories.

Initiative Climat International (iCI)
[The network's information and resources are hosted on the members-only UN PRI online
Collaboration Platform]
A global, practitioner-led community of PE firms and investors that seek to better understand and
manage the risks associated with climate change. The iCI was originally launched as the iC20 (Initiative
Climat 2020) in 2015 by a group of French PE firms to contribute to achieving the Paris Agreement's
objectives. The iCI has since expanded internationally and now counts some 212 firms representing
over US$3.4 trillion in AUM. iCI's members share a commitment to reduce carbon emissions of PE-
backed companies and secure sustainable investment performance by recognizing and incorporating
the materiality of climate risk.

United Nations Environment Programme Finance Initiative (UNEP FI)
https://www.unepfi.org
Brings together a large network of banks, insurers, and investors that collectively catalyzes action
across the financial system to deliver more sustainable global economies. Convened by a Geneva,
Switzerland-based secretariat, more than 500 banks and insurers with assets exceeding US$170 trillion
work together to facilitate the implementation of UNEP FI's Principles for Responsible Banking and
Principles for Sustainable Insurance, as well as three UN-convened net zero alliances. Founded in 1992,
UNEP FI was the first organization to engage the finance sector on sustainability and incubated the
UNPRI, now the world's leading proponent of responsible investment.

Net Zero Asset Owners Alliance (NZAOA)
https://www.unepfi.org/net-zero-alliance/
Convened by the UNEP FI, the NZAOA is a member-led initiative of institutional investors committed to
transitioning their investment portfolios to net-zero GHG emissions by 2050. Members are the finance
industry's first to set intermediate targets, which include CO_2 reduction ranges for 2025 (22–32%) and
for 2030 (40%–60%).

Sector Watch Dogs

Private Equity Stakeholder Project
https://pestakeholder.org
A nonprofit organization seeking to bring transparency and accountability to the PE industry and
empower impacted communities. Its mission is to identify, engage, and connect stakeholders affected
by PE with the goal of engaging investors and empowering communities, working families, and others
impacted by PE investments.

Private Equity Climate Risks
https://www.peclimaterisks.org
Investigates the role of the PE industry in the climate crisis and has issued the Private Equity Climate
Risks 2022 Scorecard & Report.

Industry Association

Table 5.2 (continued)

ESG Data Convergence Initiative (EDCI) https://www.esgdc.org An organization led by GPs and LPs with the mission of generating meaningful, performance-based, and comparable ESG data for the private equity industry. Interim benchmark covers 3,900 portfolio companies from 166 GPs. It was originally conceived by the Institutional Limited Partners Association (ILPA) https://ilpa.org, a group of over 500 LPs dedicated to advancing the interests of LPs and their members.
Academia
New York University Center for Sustainable Business https://www.stern.nyu.edu/experience-stern/about/departments-centers-initiatives/centers-of-re search/center-sustainable-business The CSB has developed the Responsible Investing Framework for Private Equity which lays out the criteria that investors, civil society, regulators, and others can explore to better assess a PE firm's performance through the lens of human capital management, financial engineering, strategy and innovation, and societal impact, amongst other categories. https://www.stern.nyu.edu/experience-stern/about/departments-centers-initiatives/centers-of-research/center-sustainable-business/research/value-drivers-private-equity-building-accountability-framework-positive-stakeholder

In response to this external pressure, PE has prioritized ESG by elevating its capacity in this area by incorporating ESG principles into investment policies and processes (e.g., due diligence), building ESG programs (e.g., waste reduction or occupational safety) to support Portfolio Company performance, gathering and reporting ESG data, articulating their ESG strategy and actions to investors, while using newly retained professional resources to do so. In 2021, KKR, one of the largest PE firms, formed a Sustainability Expert Advisory Council comprised of six leading independent experts across key ESG issues including climate; diversity, equity, and inclusion; labor and workforce; governance and transparency; and data responsibility, to augment its in-house expertise.

5.4 Dynamic Regulatory and Political Climate

Increasing stakeholder scrutiny has been joined by the increased scrutiny from regulators. The impact of the rapidly evolving ESG regulatory framework is by no means limited to the private markets. However, this body of emerging regulation is changing the environment in which private markets have operated without transparency to one with increased oversight.

The European Union (EU) along with its individual Member States are the global bellwethers of this policy dynamic, as seen through a steady progression of enacted ESG legislation and proposals both at the EU and Member State level. As the EU is changing the game, US regulators and ESG advocates are watching closely. There are already ripple effects caused by these European laws: they affect how US PE firms are soliciting investment funds in Europe, potentially affect how Portfolio Companies with European operations will be run, and may serve as a blueprint for legislation in other markets. Three EU laws warrant mention as they serve as examples of regulatory mandates for ESG-driven transparency, performance, and trade protectionism.

First, the EU's Sustainability Financial Disclosure Regulation (SFDR) now requires more fund transparency. This applies to all financial market participants (which includes PE firms) and financial advisors based in the EU and non-EU investment managers who market (or intend to market) their products to clients in the EU. It requires both firm level and "product" or fund-level disclosures related to the presence of ESG policies within the firm or fund. At its simplest, the rule requires that a manager label its fund to indicate whether the fund merely integrates sustainability risks (known as an Article 6 designation), promotes "environmental/ social characteristics" (Article 8), or has a "sustainable investment" objective (Article 9).

Second, the EU's Corporate Sustainability Reporting Directive (CSRD) requires in-scope entities to disclose certain ESG risks and to report publicly measures to address these risks. This new framework requires companies to include a large body of sustainability information in their annual reporting, in accordance with the detailed European Sustainability Reporting Standards (ESRS), and be accompanied by external "assurance" of the information provided. CSRD first takes effect in the financial year beginning January 1, 2024 and thereafter for any company with securities listed on an EU "regulated market." Although PE firms themselves are not listed on regulated markets, there will be major implications for their large portfolio companies. Additionally, larger private EU companies will be in scope in 2025, increasing the transparency requirements even outside of public companies.

Third, the EU has introduced the Carbon Border Adjustment Mechanism (CBAM) to protect those EU companies that already pay for their carbon emissions under the existing EU Emissions Trading System. This will now tax EU imports from certain industries such as cement, steel, and hydrogen, based on the GHG emitted during their production. Accordingly, funds containing Portfolio Companies in these sectors may be impacted.

Likewise, the US Securities and Exchange Commission proposed a rule to enhance and standardize climate-related disclosures for investors in March, 2022. The proposed rule sets out three levels of reporting GHG emissions. Generally, the first level, Scope 1, focuses on the direct GHG emissions of the company and Scope 2 reports GHG emissions of the energy providers used by the company. Scope 3 focuses on GHG emissions along the supply chain, including those of private companies who sell to publicly traded companies and of the end consumer. Scope 3 is legally and politically problematic because it requires publicly traded companies to seek out information from privately held companies. This creates an indirect regulation of privately held companies who are typically outside the SEC's regulatory authority. Until this and several other issues are resolved, issuance of a final rule is delayed to 2024 at the earliest and won't be effective until 2026.

While GHG reporting is delayed on the federal level, in October 2023 California enacted two expansive climate disclosure laws making California the first state in the US to impose requirements on GHG emissions disclosure and mandate reporting on climate-related financial risks, to begin in 2026. The reporting obligation applies to both public and private companies with annual revenues over $1 billion that operate in California and the requirement for biennial reporting on climate-related financial risks applies to companies with annual revenues over $500 million that operate in California.

This flurry of regulatory activity in the US and Europe has energized a counter-current of anti-ESG political activity. Opposition has included anti-boycott laws prohibiting the screening out of investments deemed to present a societal harm (e.g., Texas), revision of public pension investment policies to exclude ESG factors in investment considerations (e.g., Arizona and Florida), and laws blocking consideration of ESG in public contracting activities (e.g., Florida). As of this writing, various Congressional House committees have commenced hearings and inquiries related to ESG and investing.

ESG's oscillation in the US and steady, forward progress in Europe presents a dilemma for PE firms marketing to Europe-based LPs and/or with European operations. These firms are simultaneously encouraged to lessen their ESG efforts by the US anti-ESG movement while straining to comply with regulatory demands for transparency in Europe.

5.5 ESG through the Private Equity Investment Cycle

Given this dynamic environment, a helpful way to fully comprehend ESG as a tool for risk management and value creation and therefore judge its value in the PE context is to examine the application of ESG at each stage of the investment cycle.

5.5.1 Investment Approach

A US PE firm may choose to articulate how it sees ESG fitting into its overall investment approach. A specific ESG investment policy, where a firm has one, typically sets forth the firm's overall commitment to factor the assessment of ESG risks and opportunities into investment decisions and utilize good ESG management practices in operating the portfolio businesses. Further, an ESG investment policy may articulate more detailed commitments addressing, for example, the conduct of the firm's due diligence process or key operational risks like climate change impact. These commitments may be selectively applied to one or all of the funds the firm creates.

In addition to setting policies relating to its investments, the firm may also address particular ESG topics that apply to the firm as an operating company. For example, the firm may state that climate change risks be evaluated in all transactions while also requiring carbon offsets for air travel by employees on business. Similarly, its investment policy could require the assessment of labor practices as part of its transactional due diligence while having a diversity, equity, and inclusion policy for hiring and retention at the firm.

The ambition and scope of the firm's ESG investment policy should match the firm's capabilities. With size and scale comes the ability to adequately resource an ESG program and support the commitments made in the investment policy.

5.5.2 Fundraising

The first step in the investment cycle is to raise capital for the fund. Overwhelmingly, the capital comes from external sources such as institutional investors and wealthy individuals. This can include public and corporate pension plans, banks, insurance companies, sovereign investment funds, university endowments, other PE funds, and professionally managed family offices. Capital may also be contributed by individuals employed by the firm.

The potential investor's own opinions about ESG may affect the firm's fundraising strategy. If an investor is seeking to maximize social impact in their investment strategy they will be drawn to a potential fund with strong ESG attributes. Conversely, if an investor is resistant or hostile to ESG, seeing it as inhibiting potential financial returns, they will be less likely to invest in such a fund. Investors who are more neutral on the topic of ESG may be content with ESG as an incidental part of the firm's risk management approach. It is up to the firm to navigate the proclivities of individual investors as it searches for capital. Consequently, the firm may choose to solicit or market to only those investors that align with its approach to ESG.

As noted earlier, investors are increasingly doing their own ESG due diligence before choosing to invest with GPs so they may be more fully informed about the ESG risk, opportunity, and impact associated with their investment. PE-specific due diligence tools, such as questionnaires and technical guidance, have been developed by both the industry and stakeholders to facilitate the process. For instance, the United Nations Principles of Responsible Investment (UNPRI) has developed the *Limited Partners' Private Equity Responsible Investment Due Diligence Questionnaire* (UNPRI DDQ) to help investors understand and evaluate a GP's processes for incorporating material ESG risks and opportunities into their investment practices. The PE sector's professional association, Institutional Limited Partners Association (ILPA), has incorporated the UNPRI DDQ into its own broader set of due diligence questions intending to ease the administrative burden placed on both investors and GPs by standardizing the most frequent and important diligence questions. Widespread use of these tools is facilitating the integration of ESG topics into the standard slate of risks that are considered in investments.

There is an increasing desire by many stakeholders to assess the impact of investment decisions on human rights and to integrate human rights into the investment processes as part of a holistic approach to understanding the risks to society. Severe human rights impacts can often present reputational, operational, and financially material risks. Addressing this need for adequate information before investments are made, the UN PRI also developed Human Rights Due Diligence for Private Markets Investors.

Regardless of how an investor prioritizes ESG in its investment decision, it behooves the investor to understand the investment strategy of the fund before committing capital and to be informed about how the ESG is incorporated into investment practices so that it can be aligned with the investor's investment philosophy.

5.5.3 Acquisitions

With the investors' capital in hand, GPs seek to acquire companies across all sizes, sectors, and maturities in return for an equity stake. Many GPs may have specific strategies related to the target size they are looking for (e.g., revenue $75M, EBITDA $15M-$100M, transaction size no greater than $500M), sector (e.g., health care delivery only), or maturity (e.g., founder-owned companies seeking the first infusion of private capital).

Regardless of the size, sector, or maturity level of a target company, before the GP decides to invest in a company and bring it within their portfolio of investments they expend resources to assess the target's financial and operational health. Failure to uncover financial or operational gaps can ultimately result in poor investment outcomes. Consequently, ESG comes into play with due diligence at the acquisition stage.

The assessment of ESG risks is not unique to PE nor new to the public markets. The assessment of some of the attributes that make up ESG risks (e.g., environmental contamination liability, worker safety issues, fraud or corruption charges) is well-established. For instance, the conduct of environmental due diligence preceding the acquisition of real property or a company has been a routine practice for decades. The American Society for Testing and Materials developed professional standards for the conduct of environmental due diligence as a way for current or prospective property owners to gather information about potential environmental risks associated with a property; these standards have been in place since 1993 and have been revised periodically since then.

However, several new wrinkles have developed with the increased focus by stakeholders on ESG in the industry. First, these traditional but disparate due diligence work streams which were frequently done in isolation have been combined in the ESG "bucket." Assessment of individual risks that used to be assessed by separate teams are now being assessed together because these topics are seen to paint a holistic picture of risks that not only impact the financial condition of a business but potentially impact other stakeholders like customers and the community.

Second, and more importantly to many investors, the list of attributes has been expanded to include previously non-traditional topics such as climate change adaptation, supply chain work practices and human rights, cybersecurity and data privacy. This reorganized and expanded due diligence work stream is increasingly becoming part of a GP's commercial due diligence. Any due diligence is a systematic investigation or assessment to confirm the facts surrounding a target company's operation and the identification of risks associated with those operations and consists of the examination of information culled from due diligence questionnaires, management interviews, and caches of documents disclosed to virtual document rooms. In the ESG context, the output of the due diligence process is typically the ESG DD Questionnaire, ESG report(s) and/or a legal diligence memo. The ESG-related information that is reported gets included in materials that will be shared with investors and can affect the ultimate investment decision. This information can also be relevant once the company is acquired and have an impact on how it will be managed.

Many factors influence how ESG due diligence is conducted, such as the sector, size, and maturity level of the target company, which can all contribute to the orientation and extent of the ESG due diligence. For instance, if the target is a global chemical manufacturer the due diligence team will require specific types of technical subject matter expertise and environmental contamination may present a material risk to the transaction. In contrast, if the target is an apparel company with an extensive supply chain in developing countries, the due diligence team will require experts in labor rights and issues such as worker safety and child labor may present a material risk to the transaction.

5.5.4 Portfolio Management during the "Hold" Period

Since the goal of GPs and investors is to increase the value of the portfolio company, the GP provides strategic and operational support to help the company grow, thereby protecting the value of the investment. Typically, the GP will actively manage a portfolio company via a seat(s) on the board of directors and the deployment of operating partners, executives with specific sector expertise who are aligned with the business of the portfolio company.

Additional interventions by the GP in the portfolio company can vary. A large, newly-acquired, yet mature, portfolio company may already have in place a functioning enterprise risk management program which includes ESG risks. Middle market companies are typically well-established while remaining small enough to be flexible.

They are likely to be competently managed with developed products and services, along with predictable revenue streams. Yet to scale effectively, they require more operational enhancements compared to their larger peers. For instance, there may be room to deploy technologies that drive energy efficiency or waste reduction. Typically, lower middle market companies are less developed in the areas of management depth, software and systems, and robust planning and control processes. PE firms aimed at the lower middle market better understand the challenges and opportunities of these businesses, allowing them to provide more tailored financing and support. So for those middle- and lower middle-market portfolio companies which lack some or all institutional controls to manage ESG risk, the GP may install tools like compliance committees or quality management systems or enhancements like the hiring of professionally-certified occupational safety staff, the installation of a certified environmental management system, a diversity and equity program, fraud detection and compliance reporting system, etc.

Until now, we have focused on ESG risk identification and management. ESG is increasingly being used within PE as a tool to find value within a business, thereby making it a more lucrative opportunity for LPs. An initial step to creating value is cost avoidance. Operationalizing strong ESG programs has been shown to yield impactful cost savings. For instance, a well-managed worker safety program may result in the payment of fewer workers' compensation claims and reduced insurance premiums associated with occupational injuries over time. Similarly, reducing the amount of scrap material generated in a fabrication process reduces the cost of waste disposal and, in turn, lowers the cost of goods and increases profit margins.

Beyond cost avoidance, ESG can also be used by GPs as a lens through which to view a business to reveal new markets, expand a customer base, or yield a competitive advantage. For example, rethinking certain consumer products to see whether they can be converted from single-use to multi-use or made biodegradable (e.g., straws) to appeal to customers who prioritize sustainability. In certain sectors where the recruitment and retention of skilled employees is a critical success factor (e.g., health care delivery), having a strong ESG program within the portfolio company may attract new candidates and induce employees to stay, thus providing an edge in the market for talent.

Exit of the Investment: Sale of a Portfolio Company

The exit stage is crucial to the success of the fund as it is one of the ways investors receive their returns. PE firms will have a target return on investment that they aim to achieve upon the sale of the company. Funds can exit their investment via sale of the portfolio company to another company (sometimes a larger corporation known as a strategic buyer), a sale to another PE firm (sometimes known as a sponsor to sponsor transaction), an IPO (sale to the public of listed equity), or an Employee Stock Ownership Plan (sale to employees).

During the exit stage, ESG may be helpful in maximizing value in the market and be relevant to how the firm positions the company in the market. ESG public commitments, strong programs, and excellent performance may make a portfolio company more attractive to buyers with ESG impact strategies or when taking a company public through an IPO. In any case, it may be beneficial for the firm to highlight a strong ESG program with a track record of performance improvement backed by credible data, provide an explanation of how a business-focused ESG program provides a competitive advantage in the sector, or demonstrate the business value ESG has brought to customer and stakeholder relationships. Further, any buyer may view a business more favorably if it can demonstrate risks are well understood and managed. Capital investment in environmental controls, strong occupational safety performance, operational compliance committee, and high employee engagement scores are all indicators of lowered risk in the ESG area.

5.6 Conclusion

ESG as a tool for assessing risk and identifying opportunities is becoming more normalized in the PE sector. The incorporation of ESG into the diligence and investment process and portfolio company operations is propelled by an increasingly pervasive regulatory framework, especially in the European Union. While headwinds presented by anti-ESG policies continue to swirl in the US, it remains to be seen whether they can distract LPs from seeking the highest returns by ensuring that they are investing in businesses where every identifiable risk is managed and opportunity exploited. Holistic and sustained integration of ESG will depend ultimately upon whether GPs and their investors believe ESG actually results in better long-term returns in their portfolios.

References

ASTM. *E1528-22 Standard practice for limited environmental due diligence: Transaction screen process.* https://www.astm.org/e1528-22.html

Balakumar, U., & Whelan, T. (2023). *The road to responsible private equity a responsible investing framework, insights, and cases toward a positive pathway.* NYU Stern Center for Sustainable Business. https://www.stern.nyu.edu/sites/default/files/2023-03/Private%20Equity%20Whitepaper%203%2012%2023.pdf

Ceres, SustainAbility Institute. (2021). *The changing climate for private equity.* https://www.ceres.org/resources/reports/changing-climate-private-equity

Eccles, R. G., Shandal, V., Young, D., & Montgomery, B. (2022, July–August). Private equity should take the lead in sustainability. *Harvard Business Review*. https://hbr.org/2022/07/private-equity-should-take-the-lead-in-sustainability

Eccles, R. G., Streur, J., & Youmans, T. (2023, November 14). Let corporate purpose guide you through ESG turbulence. *Harvard Business Review*. https://hbr.org/2023/11/let-corporate-purpose-guide-you-through-esg-turbulence

EY. (n.d.). *2023 global private equity survey*. https://assets.ey.com/content/dam/ey-sites/ey-com/en_gl/topics/private-equity/ey-2023-private-equity-survey.pdf

Harrison, K. (2020, March 19). *ESG 2020: The transformation of financial services*. Russell Reynolds Associates. https://www.russellreynolds.com/en/insights/articles/esg-2020-the-transformation-of-financial-services

International Limited Partners Association. (n.d.). *Private equity glossary*. https://ilpa.org/private-equity-glossary/

KKR. (2001, December 1). *KKR announces formation of sustainability expert advisory council*. https://media.kkr.com/news-details/?news_id=e2d1304b-fdcb-48b7-8946-2f17138d53fb

Mauboussin, M. J., & Callahan, D. (2020). *Public to private equity in the United States: A long-term look*. Morgan Stanley. https://www.morganstanley.com/im/publication/insights/articles/articles_publicto privateequityintheusalongtermlook_us.pdf

Mitchenall, T. (2023, October 19). *After the political theatrics end, ESG will still be part of the private markets*. Private Equity International. https://www.privateequityinternational.com/after-the-political-theatrics-end-esg-will-still-be-part-of-private-markets/

Preqin. (n.d.). *ESG in alternatives in 2023*. https://www.preqin.com/esg/esg-in-alternatives#:~:text=ESG%20in%20Alternatives%202023&text=The%20report%20explores%20the%20potential,way%20to%20consider%20ESG%20risks.

Snow, D. (2007). *Private equity: A brief overview*. https://www.law.du.edu/documents/registrar/adv-assign/Yoost_PrivateEquity%20Seminar_PEI%20Media%27s%20Private%20Equity%20-%20A%20Brief%20Overview_318.pdf

United Nations Principles for Responsible Investing. (2023). *Human rights due diligence for private markets investors; Technical guide*. https://www.unpri.org/infrastructure-and-other-real-assets/human-rights-due-diligence-for-private-markets-investors-a-technical-guide/11383.article

Yan, C., Tatlock, M., Clare, T., Schenker, J., & Westling, H. (2021). *Private equity sector science based target guidance*. Science Based Targets, https://sciencebasedtargets.org/resources/files/SBTi-Private-Equity-Sector-Guidance.pdf

Zhang, H. *LPs navigate shifting tides in the ESG landscape*. (2023). Private Equity International. https://www.privateequityinternational.com/lps-navigate-shifting-tides-in-the-esg-landscape/

Chapter Six: **ESG—The Convergence of Social Justice and Value Creation**

Introduction

The focus of supporters of ESG investing has most often been on environmental risks and social justice issues which make the case for more environmentally friendly and equitable business practices. However, in "ESG – The Convergence of Social Justice and Value Creation" authors Darrisaw and Bolger point out that progress has been slow in convincing companies to focus more strategically on engaging the broadest possible cohort of customers, employees, distribution partners, and communities in their management practices.

They argue that, ironically, shareholder activists are increasingly succeeding not based on ethical or moral grounds but rather on compelling evidence that a corporation's focus on creating value for customers, employees, supply chain, and distribution partners, and local communities will produce more sustainable returns for investors.

This is the economic argument for a greater emphasis on stakeholder engagement in business and it comes precisely at a time when critics from the right[1] believe ESG issues are arbitrary nonpecuniary factors and a violation of management fiduciary responsibility to generate profits for investors.

By making the case that there is a direct link between having highly engaged, diverse stakeholders and more sustainable profitability, the argument shifts from a debate about just how much responsibility corporations have to society to one that focuses on the fiduciary responsibilities of leadership to find the best path to sustainable returns.

Superficial accounts of the returns generated by ESG strategies versus conventional investing often conclude that ESG portfolios underperform relative to conventional portfolios. This conclusion is often the result of including the investment performance of portfolios which have a heavy dose of divestment considerations in their construction. Divestment decisions are usually made with little or no consideration of investment performance or financial impact from a portfolio point of view. Generalizing the underperformance of divestment driven portfolios to the entire class of ESG portfolios is misleading at best and is counterfactual to many ESG investment performance studies and meta-analyses. In the modern era there are myriad ESG investment vehicles which are designed to mirror the risk and return profiles of conventional portfolios while still at a minimum tilting toward positive ESG performance. To confuse the financial performance of these latter ESG investments with simplistic divestment strategies can only result in spurious conclusions.

---

1 The Illusory Promise of Stakeholder Capitalism by A. Lucian Bebchuk, Harvard Law School, European Corporate Governance Institute (ECGI), National Bureau of Economic Research (NBER), and Roberto Tallarita, Harvard Law School.

https://doi.org/10.1515/9783111178608-011

Divestment as an ESG strategy has been frequently criticized in two dimensions: that it often results in subpar investment performance and, somewhat more controversially, it often does little to impact desired behavior by the target firm or industry. The authors spend some time discussing one dramatically successful case of divestment: the targeting of firms operating in South Africa in the 1970s. The Reverend Louis Sullivan became deeply concerned about the role of multinational corporations operating in South Africa during the era of apartheid. He believed that these companies had a responsibility to promote positive social change and improve the conditions of black South Africans. To address this issue, he developed a set of principles that corporations should follow to ensure ethical practices and respect for human rights.

In time, the Global Sullivan Principles, the NAACP Fair Share Model, and the European Union (EU) Sustainability Reporting Directive have converged to represent a shared commitment towards promoting corporate responsibility, social equity, and sustainable practices to benefit both shareholders and all stakeholders. Although these initiatives have distinct origins and contexts, they all contribute to the broader goal of fostering ethical business conduct and advancing societal well-being in a way that enhances long-term returns for both shareholders and society.

The authors discuss the convergence of the social responsibility movement with ESG, the rise of analytics demonstrating the return on investment of having highly engaged stakeholders, and the new European Union Corporate Sustainability Reporting Directive (CSRD), which may mark a watershed moment in the world of management in which racial equity is viewed as a source of value creation rather than a redress for past inequities.

Eric Darrisaw and Bruce Bolger

6 ESG—The Convergence of Social Justice and Value Creation

The concepts of ESG (Environmental, Social, Justice) and racial equity are making the shift from being viewed primarily as a social responsibility to becoming a fiduciary responsibility. This is because of the increasing ability to measure the impact of the customer, employee, distribution, supply chain, and community engagement on financial results and because of a new European Union law known as the Corporate Sustainability Reporting Directive (European Commission, 2024) that many legal scholars believe could do for stakeholder management what total quality management standards did for manufacturing: enhance efficiency and outcomes through a more strategic, systematic, and holistic approach to management.

Champions of equity in business and the broader issue of ESG (Environmental, Social, Governance) have long focused on the environmental impact and social justice issues to make the case for more environmentally friendly and equitable business practices. Despite decades making this argument, progress remains slow toward convincing organizations to focus more strategically on engaging the broadest possible cohort of customers, employees, distribution partners and communities in their organizational mission. Ironically, the arguments that may finally win the day are not based on ethical or moral grounds but rather on compelling evidence through analytics that inclusive practices produce more sustainable returns for investors.

This has become particularly important in light of the recent Supreme Court affirmative action decision (Arps et al., 2024).

The economic argument for a greater emphasis on stakeholder engagement in business comes precisely at a time when critics from the right (Heritage Foundation, 2024) decry what they believe is a diversion of profits to line the pockets of "disinterested" special interests from the left for what they are convinced is nothing more than social engineering and environmental sophistry. By making the case that there is a direct link between having highly engaged, diverse stakeholders and more sustainable profitability, the argument shifts from the debatable issue of just how much responsibility corporations have to society to one that focuses on the fiduciary responsibilities of leadership to find the best path to sustainable returns.

This chapter outlines the convergence of the social responsibility movement with ESG, the rise of analytics demonstrating the return on investment of having highly engaged stakeholders, and the new European Union CSRD, which may mark a watershed moment in the world of management in which racial equity is viewed as a source of value creation rather than a redress for past inequities.

Impact Shares, the manager of the NAACP (National Association for the Advancement of Colored People) minority empowerment ETF (exchange-traded fund) NACP

https://doi.org/10.1515/9783111178608-012

(NYSE: ARCA) is using the new European Union Corporate Sustainability Directive and related ISO 30414 human capital and ISO 10018 people engagement standards as scorecards for evaluating the actions of company stocks selected for its funds, according to its Corporate Engagement advisor, co-author of this article. The Impact Shares seeks to translate social values into sustainable returns. It is establishing a comprehensive evaluation framework for disclosures that address all stakeholders in a way that integrates rather than segregates DEI management practices. Investors and all stakeholders require detailed information to engage with portfolio companies.

6.1 DEI Value Creation Process

The focus on DEI as a source of value creation requires organizations to stop segregating Diversity, Equity, and Inclusion (DEI) into departments with little impact and to start integrating its principles into their stakeholder management and disclosure practices. Social activists in the investment community can help by focusing on the powerful economic case that DEI is simply better business rather than pursuing an adversarial approach that seeks to redress grievances.

The convergence of the Global Sullivan Principles, the NAACP Fair Share Model, and the European Union (EU) Sustainability Reporting Directive represents a shared commitment towards promoting corporate responsibility, social equity, and sustainable practices to benefit both shareholders and all stakeholders. Although these initiatives have distinct origins and contexts, they all contribute to the broader goal of fostering ethical business conduct and advancing societal well-being in a way that enhances long-term returns for both shareholders and society.

This convergence is significant because it demonstrates that DEI should not be segregated from an organization's overall business strategy as it often is today but rather fully integrated into its business processes to optimize access to talent, customers, distribution, and supply chain partners, as any great team does in athletics.

The traditional approach to DEI is to focus on inequality and social justice, and new research published in the National Library of Medicine provides a hint as to why. In their study, "The Business Case for Diversity Backfires," authors Oriane A. M. Georgeac and Aneeta Rattan (Georgeac & Rattan, 2024) find that "The use of the business case to justify diversity can result in underrepresented groups anticipating less belonging to organizations, which, in turn, makes them ultimately less likely to want to join the organization." This may also explain why many social activists in the investment sector focus on the social and moral argument rather than making the economic case.

Nonetheless, making the economic argument and baking DEI into all the processes of the organization is critical for success. While the business case for DEI may not be the best recruiting tactic for under-represented communities, it is critical to convincing companies to make DEI a part of their business process.

6.2 DEI Must be Integrated into Stakeholder Management Strategies

The economic case for DEI can only be fulfilled if integrated with human capital management and corporate governance processes and viewed as an investment in employees, customers, distribution and supply chain, and communities. Instead, DEI often focuses on anti-bias training and employee resource groups, which can actually divide people, when in fact it is most effective when made part of all engagements with customers, employees, supply chain and distribution partners, and communities. Chief diversity officers need more support from shareholders, boards of directors, and senior executives to implement DEI as an economic priority and systematic part of human capital and stakeholder management, which may explain why turnover in these positions (Weeks, Taylor, Birch, Bell, Nottingham, & Evans, 2024) is so high.

As noted in the recent research paper, "The Value of Diversity, Equity, and Inclusion,"(Edmans, Flammer, & Glossner, 2023) by Alex Edmans, Professor of Finance, London Business School, Caroline Flammer, Professor of International and Public affairs at Columbia University, and Simon Glossner, Federal Reserve Board, "companies can hit the target but miss the point – improve diversity statistics without improving DEI."

Shareholder activists often compound the issue by siloing DEI as a social or moral imperative without making an adequate investment case. This has only made matters worse by creating a backlash and accusations of social engineering. There is a growing cavalcade of DEI lawsuits and anti-ESG legislation on the basis that ESG in effect violates management's fiduciary responsibility to increase profitability, shareholder value, and investment returns.[1]

This is why the economic benefits of DEI and related human capital management practices are so important, even if not palatable to some social activists. The economic argument is simple: DEI is better business. The study by Alex Edmans et al. cited above does find a link between the financial results of DEI and future earnings surprises. The research suggests the market does not fully incorporate the performance benefits of DEI and the correlation with company earnings. This connection requires

---

[1] See SPC Global Report, *US state lawmakers have lined up more than 300 anti-ESG bills since 2021 – study,* https://www.spglobal.com/marketintelligence/en/news-insights/latest-news-headlines/us-state-lawmakers-have-lined-up-more-than-300-anti-esg-bills-since-2021-8211-study-80221263 Also: Lipton, Savarese, Shapiro, Schwartz, Bonnett, Yavitz, & Lu (2023).

additional examination to unlock potential opportunities for investment portfolio alpha generation.

Organizations with the broadest possible access to engaged customers, talent, supply chain and distribution partners, and supportive communities will perform better and be more resilient over the long term than those with a narrower community of engaged stakeholders. This is supported by multiple stock funds, research, and case studies.[2]

Racial equity audits need the active participation of business experts to not only assess demographic representation and DEI initiatives but also provide an auditable disclosure of an organization's actual management practices utilizing uniform global reporting standards to enable benchmarking and competitive analysis. DEI return on investment and financial materiality are key for investors and shareholders.[3]

6.3 Need for a Standardized Approach

As with climate issues, investors and other stakeholders need a measurable, standardized way of evaluating the impact of human capital management and diversity in public and private corporations, however, it must be in the context of overall good corporate governance, not only social equity but also financial equity for employees and stakeholders.

Ideas and opinions about diversity initiatives may vary but paying the bills doesn't. At the end of the day, business will be driven ultimately by economics and opportunity.

A standardized reporting framework to complement US Securities and Exchange Commission human capital SK disclosures rules is required that looks at how organizations address DEI across the enterprise. Otherwise, we are limited to "diversity snapshots" in time, with no understanding of how DEI is woven into business processes, measured, and improved.

The world's third largest economy has paved the way with a new international disclosure framework. The European Union apparently understands the need for a standardized approach to stakeholder management disclosures. Backed by the force of law and potential criminal penalties for noncompliance, the EU CSRD requires companies to provide detailed information on the practices and metrics related to workers, including metrics on turnover, pay equity, health, safety, discrimination claims, performance review practices, worker voice, work-life balance, and more. It is consid-

---

2 Enterprise Engagement Alliance library of research and stakeholder management performance.
3 Racial equity audits, a New ESG Initiative, Harvard Law School Forum, 2021; human capital transparency, the new competitive advantage; Financier worldwide, 2022, https://corpgov.law.harvard.edu/2021/10/30/racial-equity-audits-a-new-esg-initiative/

ered by many attorneys to be a game-changer in corporate disclosures, with far greater impact than the EU GDPR (General Data Protection Regulation) because it requires disclosures on over 80 specific metrics related to how an organization creates risks and opportunities for all stakeholders. Ironically, the European Union Corporate Sustainability Reporting Directive may provide the impetus for a more meaningful approach to DEI: the standardized disclosure of the actual practices used by organizations to manage and encourage diversity among all stakeholders, the metrics used to measure progress, and the steps taken over time to improve outcomes—all available on a free database in an easily comparable format. The law, which is expected to have far broader impact than the European Union GDPR (Global Data Privacy Regulation), will directly affect over 3,000 of the largest organizations in the US and up to 60,000 around the world starting in 2024.

6.4 Reverend Leon Sullivan and Global Corporate Responsibility Standards

The concepts of sustainability predate by decades the developments that led to the creation of the United Nations 2004 "Who Cares Wins" (United Nations, 2004). Reverend Leon Sullivan[4] was an influential American civil rights leader and Baptist minister in the twentieth century who made significant contributions to the advancement of human rights and economic equality. While he is most well-known for his involvement in the civil rights movement, Rev. Sullivan also played a crucial role in promoting ethical business practices through the establishment of the Global Sullivan Principles of Corporate Social Responsibility[5] which contains many of the principles of what today is known as Stakeholder Capitalism.

In the 1970s, Reverend Sullivan became deeply concerned about the role of multinational corporations operating in South Africa during the era of apartheid. He believed that these companies had a responsibility to promote positive social change and improve the conditions of black South Africans. To address this issue, he developed a set of principles that corporations should follow to ensure ethical practices and respect for human rights.

The Sullivan Principles gained widespread recognition and became an influential framework for corporate social responsibility. Many companies, particularly those with operations in South Africa, adopted these principles or developed their own similar codes of conduct. By advocating for ethical business practices and challenging the

---

4 Leon Sullivan Foundation, Biography of Reverend Leon H. Sullivan.
5 University of Minnesota Human Rights Library, *The global Sullivan principles*, http://hrlibrary.umn.edu/links/sullivanprinciples.html

status quo, Rev. Sullivan played a significant role in raising awareness about corporate responsibility on a global scale.

The Global Sullivan Principles, first published in 1977 and later revised in 1984, provided guidelines for corporations operating in South Africa, urging them to uphold certain standards, including:

Non-segregation: Companies should support the elimination of apartheid policies and work towards equal opportunities for all employees, regardless of race.

Worker rights: Corporations should promote fair employment practices, including fair wages, safe working conditions, and the right to unionize.

Education, training, and advancement: Companies should provide training and advancement opportunities to all employees, irrespective of race or background.

Community development: Corporations should contribute to the economic and social development of the communities in which they operate.

Equal treatment: All employees should be treated with dignity and respect, and discrimination based on race, religion, or gender should be eliminated.

The principles gained widespread recognition (Wikipedia) and support, both within the US and around the world. They influenced corporate behavior and encouraged dialogue between businesses, governments, and civil society organizations.

The goal of Global Sullivan Principles is combating discrimination, promoting human rights, and fostering economic development in the countries where they operated. Although the Global Sullivan Principles were initially focused on South Africa, their influence expanded beyond the apartheid context. They became a benchmark for corporate social responsibility globally and inspired the development of global standards and codes of conduct, such as the United Nations Global Compact which promotes corporate sustainability and responsible business practices worldwide (United Nations, 1999).

6.5 Sullivan Principles and European Union Sustainability Reporting Directive

The Sullivan Principles and the European Union's Corporate Sustainability Reporting Directive share a common goal of promoting responsible business practices and corporate accountability. While they are not directly connected, there are areas of convergence between the two frameworks.

The Sullivan Principles, as mentioned earlier, focused primarily on promoting ethical practices in companies operating in South Africa during the apartheid era.

They provided guidelines for multinational corporations to address issues related to racial discrimination, worker rights, and community development. The principles were not specific to sustainability reporting but aimed to improve overall corporate social responsibility.

6.6 NAACP Fair Share Model

The NAACP Fair Share Model, Corporate Scorecard, and Morningstar Minority Empowerment Index represent a collective effort to promote diversity, inclusion, and economic empowerment in the corporate world (NAACP, 2020). The NAACP Fair Share Model (Sims, 1993), originally developed by Reverend Benjamin Lawson Hooks and National Association for the Advancement of Colored People (NAACP), encourages companies to invest in minority-owned businesses, increase supplier diversity, create job opportunities, and support community development in underserved areas.

The Fair Share Model focuses on fostering economic inclusion for African Americans and other marginalized communities. The NAACP corporate scorecard evaluates and measures a company's performance in various areas, including social responsibility, workforce diversity, leadership representation, supplier diversity, and community engagement. The scorecard is a tool for evaluating and encouraging companies to improve their diversity and inclusion efforts.

The Morningstar Minority Empowerment Index (Morningstar) is a financial index developed by Morningstar, guided by the NAACP scorecard, which tracks the performance of companies that prioritize diversity, inclusion, and empowerment of minority groups. The index provides a means for investors to identify and support companies that demonstrate a commitment to diversity and inclusion.

6.7 Overlapping Principles

Corporate Responsibility: All three initiatives emphasize the importance of corporate responsibility. The Global Sullivan Principles, the NAACP Fair Share Model, and the EU Sustainability Reporting Directive urge companies to consider the social, environmental, and ethical impacts of their operations. They encourage organizations to adopt fair employment practices, support diversity and inclusion, and contribute positively to communities.

Human Rights and Social Justice: The Global Sullivan Principles and the NAACP Fair Share Model explicitly address issues of human rights and social justice. They promote equal opportunities, combat discrimination, and work towards creating a more inclusive society. By aligning their practices with these principles and programs, companies commit to upholding fundamental human rights and striving for social justice.

Stakeholder Engagement and Voice: The convergence of these initiatives recognizes the significance of engaging all stakeholders in decision-making processes. The Global Sullivan Principles and NAACP Fair Share Model emphasize collaboration with employees, customers, suppliers, and communities to foster dialogue and address social concerns. The EU Sustainability Reporting Directive highlights the need for companies to engage with all stakeholders and consider their interests in sustainability management and reporting.

Sustainability Reporting and Transparency: Both the EU Sustainability Reporting Directive and the Global Sullivan Principles emphasize transparency and reporting of non-financial information. The EU directive mandates certain companies to disclose environmental, social, and governance (ESG) information, enabling stakeholders to assess their sustainability performance. The Global Sullivan Principles advocated for companies to report on their progress in adhering to the principles, ensuring transparency and accountability.

Community Development: The Global Sullivan Principles and the NAACP Fair Share Model emphasize community development and investment. They encourage companies to contribute to the economic growth and well-being of underserved communities through initiatives such as job creation, education programs, and support for minority-owned businesses consistent with the purpose, goals, and objectives of the organization. The EU CSRD requires companies to report on how their management practices impact employees, supply chain, distribution partners and communities around the globe, including the risks and opportunities they create for all stakeholders and the environment. These initiatives recognize the importance of businesses actively participating in and benefiting local communities.

The convergence between the Sullivan Principles, NAACP Model, and the EU Corporate Sustainability Reporting Directive lies in their shared emphasis on corporate responsibility, transparency, and accountability as a means for sustainable value creation.

While these initiatives have distinct origins and may have different regional focuses, their convergence reflects a global shift towards recognizing the interconnection between business success and societal well-being. By aligning with the principles and programs set forth by the Global Sullivan Principles, the NAACP Fair Share Model, and the EU Sustainability Reporting Directive, companies can demonstrate their commitment to responsible and sustainable practices and contribute to social equity, shareholder returns, and the expectations of various global stakeholders.

The European Union has been actively working to enhance sustainability reporting and corporate transparency through EU CSRD law framework.

Based on the broad impact of GDPR privacy laws (IS Partners, 2020), this new law likely will become a legal standard for integrating DEI into business operating systems and disclosures and to help stop perpetuating a segregated approach that has produced unenviable results despite decades of well-intentioned efforts.

References

Arps S. et al., *Corporate DEI policies face scrutiny following SCOTUS affirmative action decision*, accessed August 3, 2024, https://www.skadden.com/insights/publications/2023/09/quarterly-insights/corporate-dei-polices-face-scrutiny.

Edmans A., Flammer C., & Glossner S. (2023), *The value of diversity, equity, and inclusion*, VOX EU, https://cepr.org/voxeu/columns/value-diversity-equity-and-inclusion

European Commission, *Corporate sustainability reporting*, accessed August 3, 2024, https://finance.ec.europa.eu/capital-markets-union-and-financial-markets/company-reporting-and-auditing/company-reporting/corporate-sustainability-reporting_en

Georgeac O. A. M. & Rattan A., *The business case for diversity backfires*, accessed August 3, 2024, https://pubmed.ncbi.nlm.nih.gov/35679195/

Heritage Foundation, *Project 2025*, accessed August 3, 2024, https://www.project2025.org/

IS Partners (2020), *GDPR three years later, what impact has it made?*, https://www.ispartnersllc.com/blog/gdpr-one-year-later-impact/

Lipton M., Savarese J. F., Shapiro A. J., Schwartz K. S., Bonnett E. E., Yavitz N. B., & Lu C. X. W., *Wachtell Lipton discusses mounting pressure on DEI initiatives*, https://clsbluesky.law.columbia.edu/2023/08/22/wachtell-lipton-discusses-mounting-pressure-on-dei-initiatives/?amp=1

Morningstar, *Morningstar minority empowerment TR USD*, https://indexes.morningstar.com/indexes/details/morningstar-minority-empowerment-FS0000DR2R?currency=USD&variant=TR&tab=overview

NAACP (2020), *NAACP issues statement on corporate social responsibility*, https://naacp.org/articles/naacp-issues-statement-on-corporate-social-responsibility

Sims C. (1993), NAACP Means Business, *New York Times*, https://www.nytimes.com/1993/08/31/business/the-naacp-means-business.html

United Nations (1999), GOOD corporate citizenship, business reputations, intimately tied, secretary-general tells corporation leaders, https://press.un.org/en/1999/19991102.sgsm7203.doc.html

United Nations (2004), Who cares wins, https://www.unepfi.org/fileadmin/events/2004/stocks/who_cares_wins_global_compact_2004.pdf

Weeks K. P., Taylor N., Birch A. H., Bell M. P., Nottingham A., & Evans L., (January 2024), Why DEI leaders are burning out, *Harvard Business Review*, https://hbr.org/2024/01/why-dei-leaders-are-burning-out-and-how-organizations-can-help#:~:text=Numerous%20organizations%20have%20also%20significantly,tenure%20of%20only%20three%20years

Wikipedia, *Sullivan principles*, https://en.wikipedia.org/wiki/Sullivan_principles#:~:text=The%20Sullivan%20principles,-Non%2Dsegregation%20of&text=Equal%20pay%20for%20all%20employees,%2C%20clerical%2C%20and%20technical%20jobs

Chapter Seven: **The Case Against Mandatory ESG Standards**

Introduction

In this chapter Morrison addresses the complications that have arisen due to the development of ESG investing in environmental and social activist circles, without a parallel evolution in legal and policy making arenas. This relative lack of attention paid to law and policy impacts is surprising and problematic. As U.S. government agencies have increasingly solidified voluntary ESG goals as mandatory standards, mostly on a partisan basis, the risks of potentially adverse economic and political impacts have increased. While there are obvious political motivations for much of the backlash to ESG investment, it would be reductionist to dismiss all objections as unfounded.

Morrison is concerned that regulatory proposals for ESG policymaking have had an overbroad scope, with the potential to impact virtually all aspects of the economy. And that impact is not immaterial. He quotes estimates of the 2022 burden of ESG-themed federal regulations as $2 trillion. He is also concerned about the risks of "regulatory capture" whereby regulation can be influenced by profit-seekers in opposition to the presumed regulatory goals of correcting anti-social behavior. In analyzing corporate behavior, one can find many instances of greenwashing where companies claim environmentally friendly practices but are found to be at best exaggerating any environmental benefits of their operations and in some cases making fraudulent claims. The case of ethanol is presented as just one example of a disappointing federally mandated environmental policy that has both negative economic and environmental effects.

He goes on to make the case that many ESG values are too subjective to be legally enforceable. For example, the UN Sustainable Development Goals include "Good Health and Well Being" and "Decent Work and Economic Growth." As desirable and aspirational as these goals may be, they open the door to abuse by being so vague that any business (or investment fund) can lay claim to promoting such goals while simply continuing business as usual. Fundamental to Morrison's concern is the lack of Congressional authority for U.S. executive actions promoting ESG goals. In 2024 the U.S. Supreme Court in several opinions gave substantial weight to those concerned with overreach by the agencies and the White House.

The author's solution is to trust in market signals favorable to ESG investments, emphasize voluntary corporate initiatives, and remove government mandates that too often have the perverse effect of masking price signals which would point the way to the most efficient ESG solutions. Modern companies have a great deal of flexibility to undertake ESG initiatives without the market-distorting impact of government mandates. Many states allow a board of directors to consider the interests of other stakeholders in addition to those of shareholders, and dozens of states have enacted benefit corporation statutes based on either the Model Benefit Corporation or the Public Benefit Corporation model.

Morrison's approach could be seen as putting the "private" into "private-public" partnerships, relying on the efficiency of pricing signals and believing in the ability of citizens to make informed choices.

https://doi.org/10.1515/9783111178608-013

Richard Morrison

7 The Case Against Mandatory ESG Standards

Environmental, social, and governance (ESG) investing has been widely analyzed from the standpoint of its constituent parts: E, S, and G. Much thought has been given over to specific environmental topics like climate change, social topics like workforce diversity, and how all of these factors could impact corporate returns on investment. However, ESG has been insufficiently scrutinized from a law and public policy perspective. This is an understandable development on the one hand, given that the decades-long history of corporate social responsibility and ethical investing theory has been a field dominated by social and environmental activists and business school theoreticians rather than political scientists. Yet, in the case of ESG itself, the relative lack of attention paid to law and policy impacts is more surprising. ESG *per se* was born in a world of public/private partnership and intentional harmonization of goals between large corporations and national and multilateral policymakers.[1]

As the conventional wisdom surrounding ESG policies has evolved from largely voluntary goals and strategies to ones that are expected to be mandatory and administered by government agencies,[2] this lack of focus on policy impacts has become more problematic. ESG advocates who attracted private sector support and enthusiasm with promises of low financial, regulatory, and reputational risk to affiliated firms have now, in effect, changed the terms of the contract without an equivalent negotiation among affected parties. Taking voluntary guidelines for ESG investing and management and rolling them into a mandatory set of regulations, as is currently envisioned by government agencies like the U.S. Securities and Exchange Commission,[3] will create an array of worrisome economic and political incentives rarely acknowledged by ESG advocates.

---

1 The origin of the phrase "environmental, social, and governance" and the acronym "ESG" was the 2004 report *Who cares wins*, which was a partnership between major international finance firms, the United Nations, and the Swiss Federal Department of Foreign Affairs. The influence of the UN and its various agencies and sponsored projects has been key to the development of ESG initiatives and frameworks, including the Sustainable Development Goals, the UN Environment Programme, and Principles for Responsible Investment, among others: https://www.unepfi.org/fileadmin/events/2004/stocks/who_cares_wins_global_compact_2004.pdf

2 *Get ready for the next wave of ESG reporting* (n.d.), KPMG, https://kpmg.com/xx/en/home/insights/2023/01/get-ready-for-the-next-wave-of-esg-reporting.html; see also a list of quotations from ESG professionals in Morrison (2021).

3 The proposed and final versions of the SEC's climate disclosure rule repeatedly cite existing voluntary reporting frameworks, including those from the Global Reporting Initiative, Sustainability Accounting Standards Board, and the Task Force on Climate-related Financial Disclosures as relevant models to emulate in mandatory form (Securities and Exchange Commission, 2002, 2004).

https://doi.org/10.1515/9783111178608-014

Moving from a hortatory and voluntary framework to one of required legal compliance – in particular, but not exclusively, in the context of U.S. legal and constitutional frameworks – produces a handful of particularly undesirable outcomes. Below we will explore the theoretical perils along with specific, real-world examples that have already been documented and that we are likely to see more of in an ESG-aligned world.

7.1 ESG as Regulatory Capture

Regulatory proposals advanced under the aegis of ESG policymaking have an extremely broad potential scope. Any human endeavor of non-trivial size will have some effect on the environment, some impact on society, and will require some sort of organizational governance. Even projects that are generally considered to have little in the way of physical impact on the world, like the creation of digital currencies, have come under significant ESG-related criticism for their energy use and related greenhouse gas emissions (Berlau, Broughel, & Patinkin, 2004). There is also a wider "green software movement" to decarbonize computing in general (Caballar, 2004). If digital computing tools with no material manifestation can become a high-profile target of environmental policymaking, it's difficult to imagine a corporate enterprise that would exist outside of ESG bounds. Thus, ESG policymaking is best understood as a way of orienting the full regulatory power of the state rather than, as it is sometimes considered, a niche subcategory of policymaking affecting only particular industries and topics. This is especially true in the current era of executive policymaking in the United States as the White House has pursued an all-of-government strategy toward issues like climate change and racial equity.[4]

As a form of regulation thus likely to significantly affect the entire economy and population, ESG-themed policy is subject to the same pitfalls and difficulties known to afflict all government regulation. The compliance burden of federal regulation in the United States, for example, is nearly 7.4 percent of U.S. gross domestic product, which was over $26 trillion in 2022 (Crews, 2023). That $1.9 billion and change weighs most heavily on large, public firms that are subject to the broadest range of both economy-wide and sector-specific rules. The price impact, however, is not simply limited to shareholders but impacts consumer prices and wages as well. Further, the full accounting of regulatory costs is a conceptually challenging undertaking. While the

---

4 Climate Policy Office, whitehouse.gov, https://www.whitehouse.gov/cpo/ Executive order on advancing racial equity and support for underserved communities through the federal government (2021), whitehouse.gov, https://www.whitehouse.gov/briefing-room/presidential-actions/2021/01/20/executive-order-advancing-racial-equity-and-support-for-underserved-communities-through-the-federal-government/

hard, direct costs are almost certainly in the neighborhood of $2 trillion per year, there are aspects of the regulatory state that are harder to quantify the effects of, meaning that the true impact may be much larger (Crews, 2017).

The burden of successive administrations adding, and rarely repealing, new regulations has significant negative consequences for economic growth and innovation. The accumulated burden of all regulatory mandates can have a darkly synergistic effect, by which the economic drag of the whole is greater than the estimated costs of each individual program added together. The long-term accumulation of regulatory compliance burdens has significant negative social and economic effects, raising inequality, causing distortions in the labor market, and hampering new business formation. That, in turn, means less innovation and economic growth overall (McLaughlin, Ghei, and Wilt, 2018, Coffey, McLaughlin, and Peretto, 2016).

Even more relevant in the case of ESG-themed policy, regulatory initiatives are often, and will likely continue to be, an instrument of rent-seeking and regulatory capture by private interests intent on obtaining market advantage via government mandates rather than value creation. Even in an environment of mostly voluntary ESG initiatives, corporations have been frequently accused of "greenwashing" their business-as-usual practices with a cynically insincere veneer of ESG virtue (Pears, Baines, and Williams, 2023). One can only imagine how much more motivated firms will be to engage in such public positioning when ESG guidelines are backed by the carrots and sticks of government agencies. Contrary to the hopes of ESG advocates, mandated compliance with a single set of government requirements is likely to make this problem worse, not better.

To the extent that future ESG regulations redirect significant flows of capital and change market outcomes, those regulations will be subject to the incentives described by the theories of regulatory capture and public choice. Both theories describe how economic ends subjected to political control are perverted in ways either inconsistent with or directly opposed to the aims of government policymakers. Some supporters of ESG policymaking assume these dangers will be minor or incidental. They should consider that it is entirely possible for the inefficiencies of political policymaking to erode the value of a theoretically advantageous policy so dramatically that no policy at all would have been preferable. This is especially the case when we consider the opportunity cost of both governmental and market actors.

The theory of regulatory capture was first advanced by University of Chicago economist George Stigler. It holds that economic regulation is often influenced by for-profit actors to their own benefit rather than existing to discipline their anti-social conduct, as is generally assumed (Stigler). Economic regulation often confers benefits to particular firms and industries while spreading costs throughout the entire economy. Any individual taxpayer or investor has little reason to expend effort opposing specific regulatory initiatives while the beneficiaries are highly motivated to lobby for the enactment and perpetuation of such policies.

The political economy of regulatory capture depends on incentives that are not respecters of causes. This renders the underlying rightness or goodness of the policy objective irrelevant. Even the most normatively praiseworthy goal can end up generating perverse incentives in the process of regulatory capture, and the policy goal need not be associated with corruption or self-dealing on its face. Indeed, many instances of economic rent-seeking via regulatory capture are initially proposed with a morally sympathetic cover story. The economist Bruce Yandle has theorized that this is more the norm than the exception, with his "Bootleggers and Baptists" analogy from alcohol prohibition. Major expansions of regulatory power are thus often supported surreptitiously by those who plan to profit by them (in Yandle's analogy, the bootleggers) and publicly by those making moral and ethical arguments explicitly in their favor (the Baptists) (Yandle, 1983, 1999).

The alleged win/win concept behind much ESG boosterism – that there will be net-positive outcomes from adding environmental and social requirements to the goal of profitability – makes it easy for any number of external stakeholders to demand that their own group goals be inserted into the mix. Efforts by labor unions, significantly augmented by executive policymaking in the Biden administration, are potent examples of this (U.S. Chamber of Commerce, 2023). Given the vague and flexible definitions by which ESG is regularly discussed, workers' rights are part of the "S" in ESG. And organized labor is considered to be the institutional stand-in for all workers, so anything that materially benefits labor unions is considered to be a pro-ESG policy. The national Teamsters union, for example, has informed members in its magazine that "ESG is enormously relevant to unionized companies and strong labor unions like the Teamsters [and therefore] is a critically important tool for advancing worker interests in the 21st century" (Adolphsen & Vernuccio, 2024).

Given their scope and ambition, efforts to enforce ESG-related goals into binding regulation must also reckon with the insights of public choice theory, which analyzes self-interest in the context of political decision making in the same way that economists have long done in the context of private life and market transactions (Shaw, n.d.). Developed by economists James Buchanan and Gordon Tullock, public choice reminds scholars to consider that policymakers are susceptible to the full range of human incentives when implementing government policy, and that the ostensible public-minded rationales for program implementation can often mask baser motives such as pride, vanity, greed, envy, and prejudice. The primary motivation of political actors, just like of individuals in any walk of life, is always going to be self-interest.

That self-interest, however, will not necessarily manifest itself as a desire for personal enrichment. A government policymaker may be more highly motivated to reward their friends and allies, provide advantages to institutions with which they are associated, or advance personal ideological preferences. A government official could, for example, approve a loan guarantee to a solar panel manufacturer in which they are a covert investor, thus securing a traditional financial benefit for themselves. But a highly motivated individual could also use their position to steer recognition and influence to a nonprofit institution for which they have been a board member, advisor, or award recipient. While applications of regulatory capture and public choice theories have often involved direct financial interest, policymaking in the context of ESG need not take that form in order to be problematic and unjust.

Unfortunately, this threat is only amplified by the traditional logic of ESG theory and its well-studied antecedents like corporate social responsibility which utilize a stakeholder approach to evaluating best practices. Stakeholderism, when combined with the legislative and regulatory process in a representative democracy, makes it even more likely that mandatory ESG policies will devolve into a trough of special interest benefits with any societal good being incidental to the process.[5] It's difficult to imagine many sectors of the economy that wouldn't potentially qualify for subsidies and preferential treatment under an ESG-informed future of government policymaking. Even politicians who frequently decry the ostensibly unfair subsidies to certain industries frequently endorse subsidies of equal or greater amounts for other for-profit corporations only slightly different from the supposedly undeserving ones (Edwards, 2024).

Take as one example the United States biofuels policy, long dominated by the production and mandated use of ethanol distilled from corn crops.[6,7] Despite being chemically useful for certain industrial purposes, ethanol has quite a few drawbacks. It is less energy dense than gasoline itself, meaning that vehicles powered with ethanol-added gasoline get worse mileage.[8] It can damage engines (Biobor Fuel Additives, 2023). More importantly, diverting arable land from human food production to biofuels increases food costs and threatens global food security (Tenenbaum, 2008). Popular biofuel inputs like palm oil also contribute to widespread deforestation and biodiversity loss (VanderWilde et al., 2023). And burning higher ethanol blends can increase the production of traditional air pollutants and their associated human health consequences (Jacobson, 2007).

---

5 For background on the development of stakeholder theory in the context research on corporate management, see Soukup (2021).

6 Some of the discussion of the EPA's biofuels program are adapted from a presentation given at the 2024 FIU Environment Forum on Climate Tech and Coastal Resilience at the campus of Florida International University in Miami, Florida on Friday, February 23, 2024, https://environment.fiu.edu/pro grams/environmental-finance-risk-management/environment-forum/

7 Dutch environmental consultancy Antea Group describe how increasing use of biofuels is consistent with ESG investing: *Emerging trends in biofuels: ESG and the energy transition*, July 13, 2022, Antea Group, https://us.anteagroup.com/news-events/blog/emerging-trends-in-biofuels-esg-and-the-energy-transition

8 According to the U.S. Department of Energy, "Ethanol contains about one-third less energy than gasoline. So, vehicles will typically go 3% to 4% fewer miles per gallon on E10 and 4% to 5% fewer on E15 than on 100% gasoline." U.S. Department of Energy (n.d.), *Ethanol*, fueleconomy.gov, https://www.fue leconomy.gov/feg/ethanol.shtml

Supporters of biofuel subsidies claim that they create environmental benefits, including a net reduction in greenhouse gas emissions. But full lifecycle analysis of how biofuels are created and used does not support that conclusion. Biofuel policies draw additional land into agricultural production and require use of more fertilizers, insecticides, and pesticides and fossil-fueled farm machinery. When those land-use changes are considered, carbon dioxide emissions are actually higher because of the use of ethanol as a fuel additive than they would be otherwise, in addition to the other problems it generates (DeCicco & Schlesinger, 2018).

So, we have a federally mandated environmental policy – subsidies for the production of and mandates for the use of biofuels – that has both negative economic and environmental effects. This result, while perverse, is nonetheless a textbook example of interest group politics. The dynamic combines rent-seeking by producers and logrolling by politicians with concentrated benefits and diffuse costs, yielding a policy status quo that has become politically unchallengeable but delivers terrible real-world results. The federal government's corn ethanol program, which disproportionately benefits agricultural interests in Midwest states like Iowa, has become a famous case study on interest group influence. Many political writers have declared it a "third rail" of American politics, meaning that opposing it would be fatal to the national ambitions of any prominent politician.[9]

This is, unfortunately, precisely the scenario we should expect from further ESG-themed regulation of the private sector. In the spirit of a stakeholder-focused approach, we would expect a collaboration between environmental advocates, private corporations, and government policymakers. To overcome complaints from corporate actors that they are being unfairly burdened, we would expect government policy that sweetens the deal with provisions like subsidies and purchase guarantees. We would expect to see supporters of such programs attempt to diminish and distract from the program's obvious deficiencies to protect the reputations of the individuals and institutions involved in creating it. We would also expect to see what has become the most ironic but most easily foreseeable result of the ethanol program, which is that the non-environmental stakeholders retain enough political clout to perpetuate and expand the program even when it has become clear that the net environmental benefit has become negative.

While this course of events is disappointing enough, there is yet another angle to the ethanol program which is a further warning to future ESG policymakers. To counter complaints about the then-current state of corn ethanol production, the Environmental Protection Agency (EPA) in the mid-2000s began promoting cellulosic ethanol, made from grasses and non-food plant stalks. It was hoped at the time that this would reduce the food security pressure created by using corn for traditional ethanol

---

9 "Despite a change in the fuel mix and concerns about ethanol's environmental cost, challenging U.S. farmers' share of what is sold at the pump is a political third rail" (Lauren Silva Laughlin, 2019).

products, in addition to providing other potential advantages. Pursuant to statutory requirements in the 2005 Energy Policy Act and then expanded by the 2007 Energy Independence and Security Act (EISA), the EPA established annual quotas for cellulosic biofuels production and blending (U.S. Environmental Protection Agency, 2024).

National policymakers confidently predicted that the fuel refining and blending industries would produce the necessary gallons of cellulosic ethanol to meet these ambitious targets.[10] Unfortunately, the production did not proceed as planned. Originally required by the EISA to scale up steeply from 100 million gallons per year in 2010 to 16 billion gallons by 2022, the EPA drastically reduced the sub-targets for cellulosic biofuels almost immediately (Lewis, 2016). They were cut to a mere 6 million gallons, for example, in 2013 (Yehle, 2013). The most recent EPA targets for cellulosic ethanol production were 840 million gallons for 2023 and just over 1 billion gallons in 2024, a dramatic shortfall from initial plans (Inbal & York, 2023).

Assessments of the cellulosic ethanol portion of the federal biofuels program by objective observers have not been kind. An analysis by environmental news website Climatewire in 2018 declared it to be a categorical failure. Veteran environmental reporter John Fialka wrote: "While the effort to produce cellulosic ethanol from wood and plant wastes was intended to reduce U.S. reliance on ethanol made from corn and other food sources, it has actually increased it" (Fialka, 2018). In a mandated 2018 report to Congress, the EPA tersely observed, among its major findings, that "Substantial volumes of cellulosic and advanced biofuels have not been produced as anticipated by EISA" (U.S. Environmental Protection Agency, 2018).

This desire by policymakers to mandate (or simply assume) future technological developments that will immanentize scenarios impossible today is also common in ESG goalsetting. Net-zero targets that assume a majority of future electrical supply being generated by wind and solar is an analogous example. Much like the planners who set targets for cellulosic ethanol and simply assumed that future technology and market conditions would appear to meet those requirements, many climate-focused ESG proponents today insist that the missing technology for a majority-renewable grid – in this case, utility-scale batter storage that is cost-competitive with conventional generation technologies – will simply appear magically sometime between 2030 and 2050. Much recent research has suggested that that assumption is at least as much wishful thinking as the predicted grass and corn-stalk ethanol volumes of almost 20 years ago.

There is major uncertainty over whether the mass battery storage part of a renewable grid future is possible, much less likely. Mark Mills of the Manhattan Institute, a prominent critic of the government-programmed rush to renewables and bat-

---

10 President George W. Bush predicted in 2006 that cellulosic ethanol would be "practical and competitive within six years." See the transcript of President Bush's 2006 State of the Union address to Congress as carried by CQ Transcripts Wire and republished by *The Washington Post*, January 31, 2006, http://www.washingtonpost.com/wp-dyn/content/article/2006/01/31/AR2006013101460.html/

tery storage, wrote in 2022 that "Two decades of aspirational policies and trillions of dollars in spending, most of it on [solar, wind, and battery] tech, have not yielded an 'energy transition' that eliminates hydrocarbons" (Mills, 2022). He also estimated in a 2019 study that "the cost to store energy in grid-scale batteries is . . . about 200-fold more than the cost to store natural gas to generate electricity when it's needed" (Mills, 2019).

Of course, the uncertain arrival of cost-competitive battery storage may not matter if the generating facilities themselves never get built. Advocates of renewable energy infrastructure – the kind of energy that it is generally taken for granted will need to be scaled up dramatically to achieve ESG goals for decarbonization – tend to downplay or wave away the difficulty of getting such facilities sited and built on a timeline consistent with frequently cited net-zero energy goals. In the United States especially, environmental protection laws like the National Environmental Policy Act are, ironically, the chief obstruction to such rapid upscaling of wind and solar capacity (Van Boom, 2023). Significant efforts to streamline environmental permitting in the Trump administration (Loyola, 2020) were rolled back by the Biden administration (Capito, 2022) and only in the Fiscal Responsibility Act of 2023 did Congress authorize some partial reform of the process (Loyola, 2023). Unfortunately, efforts by President Biden's White House Council on Environmental Quality on permitting reform threaten to roll back what little ground has been gained, with one regulatory policy expert writing that the new rule that was still under consideration in Spring of 2024 would "lead to longer approval times, increased litigation risk, and mounting uncertainty surrounding the steps to obtaining a permit, all while throwing in doubt the viability of America's ongoing clean energy transition" (Broughel, 2023).

Yet ESG goals and policymaking, whether at the international, federal, or state and local level, continue to assume the near-future emergence of such technology. The International Renewable Energy Agency, for example, estimates that 90 percent of the world's electricity can and should come from renewable energy by 2050 (United Nations, n.d.). The intermittency and low energy density of renewable sources would make even a far more modest goal impossible without the mass-storage battery capacity that, as yet, does not exist. One scenario for a net-zero emissions energy future published by the International Energy Agency (IEA) acknowledges that batteries will have little relevance to shipping and aviation emissions until "large improvements in battery energy density" are achieved, eventually scaling up to a 90-fold increase in battery demand by 2050 compared to 2020.

The IEA also notes that battery storage demand (assuming the necessary energy densities can be obtained) will create another environmental problem, that is, dramatically increased mining activity in order to extract the necessary minerals to manufacture the future volume of batteries required. Demand for lithium for use in batteries in their scenario analysis "grows 30-fold to 2030 and is more than 100-times higher in 2050 than in 2020" (International Energy Agency, 2021). Needless to say, increasing mining capacity to accommodate that demand would conflict with any number of "E"-adjacent ESG concerns, like water quality, wildlife habitat, and forestation in developing countries (Kimbrough, 2023).

Thus, even in a best-case scenario in which unlikely leaps are made in development of battery storage capacity and affordability, the expansion of battery manufacturing would leave future ESG policymakers with an extremely unpalatable choice: abandon efforts to force transportation markets away from an internal combustion model and toward an all-electric model or countenance the despoliation of ecologically sensitive tracts of land throughout the world in pursuit of increasingly large supplies of lithium, nickel, and cobalt ore and their eventual refined usable forms.

If ESG policymaking is, as seems described above, more about providing financial and reputational benefits to a heterogenous collection of stakeholders, however, there is no conflict at all. Whatever technological and environmental reality prevails, there will always be incentives to authorize more taxpayer-funded programs and subsidies for both EV production and production of critical minerals. But that will be very different from an actual focus on maximizing environmental quality, the supposed reason for all of these programs in the first place.

While expanding funding for established programs is generally the rule for federal budgets, reexamination and reform of existing programs is far less common. Market processes are famously responsive to changing availability of resources, prices of inputs, and consumer preferences. Government laws and regulations – whether they are focused on ESG concerns or anything else – are not. Entrenching today's understanding of social and environmental needs in a sticky framework of law threatens to undermine not just the efficient functioning of a consumer-driven economy but also the very environmental and social goals that advocates claim to prioritize.

ESG regulation is promoted as a win/win scenario in which corporate profits will complement the achievement of valuable public policy goals like climate mitigation. Yet any attempt to implement such a program will have the same pitfalls as other forms of economic regulation: cronyism, accumulated burden, slow growth and innovation, path dependency, inability to adapt to changing market conditions, and arbitrary government preferences for certain sectors and firms over others.

Over the long term, the incentive structure of the regulatory state, which stunts innovation and functions as a barrier to entry for new firms, will tend to strangle and enervate the creative-destructive energy that a market economy in known for, providing fewer options and less robust solutions to ESG challenges. Even if future ESG regulation manages to avoid such constricting impacts on future growth, it is likely that over time interest-group stakeholders and their goals will come to dominate any actual environmental and social policy improvements.

7.2 Many ESG Values are too Subjective to be Legally Enforceable

Many of the things that ESG standards purport to measure are too subjective to bear the weight of a legally enforceable definition. If we look at the UN Sustainable Development Goals, considered the basis for many ESG frameworks, we can see this quite clearly (Kretkowska, 2023).[11] While the first two goals, "No Poverty" and "Zero Hunger," are clear, ones like "Good Health and Well-Being," "Quality Education," and "Decent Work and Economic Growth" depend entirely on the perceptions on the individuals evaluating them.[12]

What level of healthcare outcomes is good enough? What educational standards exhibit sufficient quality, and when does work qualify as decent? Even among well-informed observers operating in good faith in the same society, answers to those questions will vary dramatically based on the values and priorities of whomever is doing the evaluation. What would be considered acceptable across the globe is even more contested.

Regulatory agencies in the United States has already begun to confront this reality. In March 2022, SEC chairman Gary Gensler released a short video describing the agency's new rule that would further regulate the naming of investment funds (Gensler, 2022). The proposed rule (since adopted in final form by the SEC in September 2023) (Securities and Exchange Commission, 2023) addressed allegations that ESG-themed investment funds were being named and marketed in misleading ways, necessitating amendments to the agency's existing rules on fund names, which were first issued in 2001 (Securities and Exchange Commission, 2001). Gensler's video explanation, and the analogy he used to justify the rule to a non-expert audience, demonstrate how ESG policymaking in general lies on an uncertain foundation.

Gensler explained his concerns about investment products that market themselves as "green" or "sustainable." Hundreds of funds managing trillions of dollars claim to be prioritizing some ESG goal in addition to generating financial benefit for their customers. These funds, Gensler argued, should be subjected to rules such that investors can be assured that those representations are accurate, but his own argument demonstrates how this will likely not be possible.[13]

---

11 For more background on the involvement of the United Nations with the origins on ESG, see Gramm & Keeley (2023).

12 United Nations Department of Economic and Social Affairs, *The 17 goals*, https://sdgs.un.org/goals

13 Some of the discussion of the SEC's amendments to the "Investment Company Names" rule is adapted from the author's comment letter to the SEC on the proposal: *Comments of the competitive enterprise institute in the matter of the proposed rule "investment company names" before the Securities and Exchange Commission, Release No. IC-34593; File No. S7-16–22, RIN 3235-AM72*, August 15, 2022, https://www.sec.gov/comments/s7-16-22/s71622-20137814-308138.pdf, and this article on the topic: Morrison (2022).

Gensler claims an impressive pedigree for this sort of regulation, noting his agency's history of regulating investment fund names, going back to the passage of the Investment Company Act of 1940, with the goals of the subsequent rules being that "when a fund company uses a name, you should be able to read that name and trust what it says." Then he makes a relatable comparison: investment funds should be like a carton of skim milk. When a customer goes to a supermarket and looks for a carton of milk they can trust that it is actually fat free because producers in the United States are required to accurately print the fat content directly on the carton and are subject to regulatory penalties for any inaccuracy.

The problem with this analogy, especially in the context of ESG criteria, is that the investment themes that people are most concerned with are not clear and quantifiable. The terms that Gensler focuses on in his explanation – "green" and "sustainable" – are inherently subjective and their definitions are hotly contested.[14] You can send a sample of milk to a chemistry lab for analysis and confirm its fat content but no high-tech process can adjudicate whether investing in, say, nuclear energy rather than wind power is "better for the environment." That's a subjective judgment. How heavily, in this example, should we weigh concerns about long-term storage of radioactive waste versus the number of birds killed by turbine blades each year? Should we prioritize infrastructure that can be built quickly or that will last the longest? No spreadsheet formula can answer these questions; only investors (and policymakers) weighing multiple competing values in the context of specific projects can make such a judgement.

Thus, there is no objective answer to which investment fund is the most sustainable or environmentally friendly, because different people disagree about how those things should be measured. It's perfectly reasonable for a finance regulator like Gensler to raise concerns about potential investor confusion but solving that confusion with an arbitrary government definition does not improve the situation. Conversely, claiming to guarantee reliable definitions of contested terms, but shrinking back from the challenge of actually doing so, is also not helpful to the investing public.

Investment firms can, of course, choose to create and market funds that track environmental characteristics that are easily definable and verifiable – such as whether

---

14 Arizona State University has an entire School of Sustainability, for example, and its website acknowledges the difficulty of defining the concept, describing the attempt to do so as "wondrously complicated." The proffered definitions from their academic experts may strike most objective observers as less wonderous than incoherent: https://schoolofsustainability.asu.edu/about/defining-sustainabil ity/. Even when attempting a single consistent explanation of sustainability in the realm of finance and investing, experts acknowledge that the concept is subjective and highly contextual, exactly the characteristics that would make it a poor choice for management via government regulation. See Alexandra Spiliakos writing for Harvard Business School's *Business Insights* blog in 2018: "Many successful organizations participate in sustainable business practices, however, no two strategies are exactly the same. Sustainable business strategies are unique to each organization as they tie into larger business goals and organizational values" (Spilliakos, 2018).

corporations are co-signers of the U.N.-sponsored Principles for Responsible Investment or have adopted the auditing methodology recommended by the Sustainability Accounting Standards Board. A fund may exclude equity holdings in oil and gas firms or only invest in renewable energy technology. Those are fairly straightforward distinctions. Customers who are motivated to pursue what they consider to be "sustainable" investment products can thus be encouraged to seek out the most specific – and thus easily falsifiable – claims when shopping for funds. In this case, though, no greater governmental oversight specific to ESG is necessary, simply the same anti-fraud protections that U.S. investors have always enjoyed.

In its final amendments to the fund name rule, the SEC insisted that "Funds that consider ESG factors in their investment strategies comprise a thematic area that entails unique considerations" but ultimately declined to actually adopt any unique or specific regulation of that investing theme (Securities and Exchange Commission, 2023). For now, the standard for ESG-themed investment funds is the same for all others, simply that a fund's holdings must be at least 80% related to the named theme of the fund. Anyone familiar with ESG theory and the notoriously flexible terminology like "socially responsible," however, can testify that requiring four-fifths fidelity to a phase with no agreed-upon definition is hardly a meaningful regulatory standard. In its fund-name-rule amendment the agency thus effectively dodged the question. That may have actually been the least bad outcome given the ambition of the original proposal, but there is no guarantee future decision makers at the SEC will continue to follow this path.

When it comes to inherently vague terminology, the SEC has the optional of an alternate framework – in this case the approach followed by the Federal Trade Commission (FTC) when it comes to subjective claims of consumer products. The FTC polices advertising claims that are outright lies but not ones that are recommendations, general characterizations, or what are sometimes called "puffery." As with the skim milk example, a company selling hot dogs can't claim that its product is 100 percent beef if it is actually 50 percent pork but they can claim that they are "the most delicious hot dogs in the world" – an inherently subjective designation. It's up to each consumer to weigh conflicting product claims and determine if, in their experience and by their own judgment, such subjective assertions are valid.

Many ESG and sustainability claims are like the allegedly delicious hot dog. It would be a mistake for a government regulator to even ask if they are "true" at all because different people have different opinions on what meets those definitions. The only way to do otherwise would be for regulators to arbitrarily designate one view as the correct one, simply for the purpose of legal clarity. This strategy of imposed legibility doesn't actually solve the problem of conflicting values, and creates additional downstream problems as well. This is especially the case when the terrain being regulated and defined is as broad and fast-changing as ESG theory itself.[15]

7.3 ESG Policymaking has a Democratic Deficit

Calls for mandatory ESG standards in the United States, whatever their ostensible strengths, must reckon with the nation's legal and constitutional structure and its limitations. Administrative agencies like the Securities and Exchange Commission, for example, aren't free to expand their own regulatory authority because Congress has allegedly "failed" to act on implementing more ambitious climate policy (Leber, 2022). Policy advocates can be expected to pivot from attempting to influence one branch to another if they perceive their efforts in that new direction will be more fruitful, but such tactical shifts by activists have no bearing on the respective powers and legal authority of the branches of the U.S. government itself. If Congress declines to enact ESG-adjacent policies, other branches of government cannot exceed their established authority to make up for this perceived deficit.

Despite attempts by numerous previous administrations, the president specifically is also not empowered to exercise additional authority if Congress declines to pass legislation he and his political allies consider necessary. In July 2022, for example, President Joe Biden said in a speech: "Let me be clear: Climate change is an emergency. In the coming weeks, I'm going to use my power to turn these words into formal, official government actions. When it comes to fighting climate change, I will not take 'no' for an answer" (Abutaleb, Romm, & Phillips, 2022). While Biden's rhetorical enthusiasm was no doubt welcomed by his allies in the environmental activist movement, refusing to take "no" for an answer it is not a constitutionally meaningful option open to the head of the executive branch of government.

Biden's impatience with Congress echoes that of his most recent Democratic predecessor, Barack Obama, who famously insisted in regards to his policy agenda that, "I am going to be working with Congress where I can to accomplish this, but I am also going to act on my own if Congress is deadlocked." He reminded Republicans in Congress frequently of his threat to act unilaterally in the absence of their approval, using the memorable phrase "I've got a pen, and I've got a phone" (Keith, 2014). One of the Obama administration's most ambitious and controversial environmental policies, the EPA's Clean Power Plan (CPP), was just such an attempt to get around a recalcitrant Congress when it came to regulating the energy sector in pursuit of reducing greenhouse gas emissions. And it is precisely the kind of climate-conscious regulation of private companies that we should expect from future ESG rulemaking.

---

15 For a discussion on the pitfalls of "imposed legibility" by regulators, see Chilson (2021). Chilson quotes several passages on the same topic from Scott (1998).

After many years of complex administrative procedure and legal challenges, however, the Clean Power Plan was eventually overturned, precisely because it was an attempt to unconstitutionally supersede congressional action on a major question of public policy. In the Supreme Court's opinion in *West Virginia v. EPA*, the lawsuit that directly challenged the legitimacy of CPP, the majority made clear that executive action which attempts to manufacture new legal authority is invalid. This is especially true when, as in the case of climate change, Congress has considered and rejected multiple such policies in the past. When the EPA claimed that it had authority under the Clean Air Act to implement the CPP, the Court wrote "the regulatory writ EPA newly uncovered in Section 111(d) conveniently enabled it to enact a program, namely, cap-and-trade for carbon, that Congress had already considered and rejected numerous times" (*West Virginia v. Environmental Protection Agency*, 2022).

The Court's placing the question of agency authority within the context of previous congressional action (or lack thereof) is key here to the defensibility of executive environmental policymaking and future mandatory ESG regimes, which would likely seek to accomplish similar purposes. In the years prior to promulgation of the CPP and the subsequent litigation over its legitimacy, many bills related to greenhouse gases, climate change, and regulation of energy use had been proposed and debated in Congress. Not approving those bills was not an omission or a passive dereliction, it was a conscious policy choice by the legislative branch of government. In fact, some recent congressional action on ESG policymaking has been an explicit rejection of it (Goldberg & Mann, 2023). It is thus not the place of the EPA (or the SEC) within the U.S. constitutional order to overrule Congress, no matter how pressing an executive agency's leaders believe a given issue to be (Vollmer, 2022). Someone who supports more aggressive federal policy on, say, climate change can and should acknowledge the statutory limits of such initiatives (Morrison et al., 2022).

The mismatch between ESG policymaking enthusiasm and statutory authority can also be seen in an institution like the Federal Reserve. Like its cousins the independent agencies, the Fed doesn't automatically have the authority to promulgate climate finance programs just because policy advocates are urging it to, even if other central banks around the world have done so already (Schröder Bosch, 2023). In September 2023, for example, several members of Congress wrote to Federal Reserve Chair Jerome Powell "urging him to consider climate-related financial risks and ensure the financial institutions they oversee do the same" (Markey & Pressley, 2023). One month later, Powell largely rejected these calls, saying in a public statement that "The Federal Reserve is not and will not be a 'climate policymaker.' Decisions about policies to address climate change must be made by the elected branches of government" (Powell, 2023).

Such a decision is in line with recent scholarship on the topic of monetary policymaking and the limits of the Federal Reserve's mission. Christina Skinner of the University of Pennsylvania, for example, recently wrote that "despite the substantive importance of climate change, the U.S. Federal Reserve presently has relatively limited legal authority to address that problem head-on . . . many aspects of climate change sit outside the Fed's legal remit today" (Skinner, 2021). As in similar cases noted above, the purported urgency of the topic in question does not supersede the statutory limits of the institutions being asked to respond.

This concern is a rule-of-law question rather than an ESG policy one and, as such, will apply differently in different national and multilateral contexts. Skinner points out that her former employer, the Bank of England, is in a different position than the U.S. Federal Reserve. Its former Governor Mark Carney as well as the European Central Bank's Christine Lagarde have pursued climate-themed central bank policies far more aggressively than the Fed, and the multilateral Network for Greening the Financial System (NGFS), composed of central bank representatives from nations around the world, has as well. But that is, at least in part, because they have different legal and jurisdictional powers at their disposal, not because their representatives care more about the issue (Skinner, 2021).

These statutory limitations suggest an obvious political remedy. Congress can amend statues like the Clean Air Act, the Securities Act of 1933, and the Federal Reserve Act to explicitly expand the ambit of the EPA, SEC, and Federal Reserve to include climate policy and risk. But that only brings us back to the original starting point, which is the inability of climate policy advocates to convince Congress to further regulate greenhouse gas emissions in the first place. Advocates are stuck, for now, between two problematic realities: they want to use executive policymaking to bypass a Congress that refuses to pass aggressive climate legislation, but federal courts won't allow them to administratively implement climate policy that has been rejected by Congress. Again, any mandatory ESG regulation on hot-button topics like climate change, and environmental protection more broadly, will face the same barriers.

This legal background is especially relevant to the potential for ESG rulemaking because one of the most aggressive rationales for implementing ESG-focused policy is that it is inevitable, meaning any private sector actor who ignores or opposes it is playing a foolish and financially risky game. According to this theory, it matters very little whether any given agency has the authority to implement any particular program since the future of public policy in every developed nation will be in the direction of greater ESG mandates eventually. Thus, companies, trade associations, non-profit advocacy organizations, and skeptical politicians should simply cease any public criticisms of ESG policy implementation and climb aboard the bandwagon since they're otherwise on the losing side of history.

This bold claim is very prominent among would-be ESG policymakers, including the United Nations-affiliated Principles for Responsible Investment (PRI), which describes itself as "the world's leading proponent of responsible investment." PRI has created a concept, which it has helped popularize in regards to climate policy in particular, called the "Inevitable Policy Response (IPR)" (Principles for Responsible Investment, n.d.). This theory states that "governments will be forced to act more decisively than they have thus far, leaving financial portfolios exposed to significant transition risk." So, whatever climate policy that private-sector entities might have thus far been subjected to, they should expect it to become stricter and more prescriptive over time. These near-future policy responses "will increasingly be forceful, abrupt, and disorderly leaving financial portfolios exposed to significant transition risk."

This line of thought was echoed in the Securities and Exchange Commission's proposed climate disclosure rule which claimed that climate risks were material to investors, citing, among other factors, "changes in regulation." The draft rule also cited previous research by the Financial Stability Oversight Council which predicted that a sharp fall in asset prices could be triggered by "risks associated with a transition towards a low-carbon economy, particularly if that transition is disorderly" (Securities and Exchange Commission, 2002). The draft rule also advised registrant firms to disclose "existing or likely regulatory requirements or policies, such as GHG emissions limits."[16]

Regulatory burdens and compliance costs are, of course, something public companies may very well want to disclose to current and potential shareholders, but the key phrase here is "likely." The rhetoric of organizations like PRI suggests that stricter GHG emissions are literally inevitable, such that it would be irrational not to price them into future corporate management decisions – something which, according to the same theory, can only be done fully under a mandatory reporting standard such as the SEC is currently seeking to implement. The logic of this argument is even more forceful if one expects future climate laws to be "abrupt and disorderly." This covers advocates of the Inevitable Policy Response from both ends. Observers are told that more aggressive climate regulation in inevitable, but even if it has been a long time coming, that allegedly only makes it more likely that when such regulation does arrive it will be abrupt and disorderly, so greater risk is tautologically always looming.

That arrival, however, is far from inevitable. Climate policy advocates have been demanding greenhouse gas emissions limits in the United States at least since President George H. W. Bush signed the 1992 United Nations Framework Convention on Climate Change, yet no significant legislation in that direction has even been passed. In 1997, when the Kyoto Protocol was being considered, concerns over the potential loss of U.S. jobs and other nations not being equally subjected to its requirements were so intense that the U.S. Senate voted 95–0 to preemptively reject it.[17] When Sens. John McCain (R-AZ) and Joe Lieberman (D-CT) introduced three successive "Climate Stewardship" bills in 2003, 2005, and 2007, they all failed to garner the necessary support of their elected colleagues, despite extensive debate, news coverage, and lobby-

---

16 SEC (2022), 101.
17 S. Res. 98, A resolution expressing the sense of the Senate regarding the conditions for the United States becoming a signatory to any international agreement on greenhouse gas emissions under the United Nations Framework Convention on Climate Change, 105th Congress, First Session, https://www.congress.gov/bill/105th-congress/senate-resolution/98

ing. A similar defeat greeted the Lieberman-Warner Climate Security Act in 2008 (Lavelle, 2018). The American Clean Energy and Security Act of 2009, co-sponsored by Reps. Henry Waxman (D-CA) and Edward Markey (D-MA), failed, as did the American Clean Energy Leadership Act of 2009, the Carbon Limits and Energy for America's Renewal Act, the Practical Energy and Climate Plan, and the Clean Energy Standard Act (Center for Climate and Energy Solutions, n.d.).

During that time there has been successful legislation related to renewable energy and various climate-adjacent topics but it has been overwhelmingly subsidies for industry rather than any mandate they stop using fossil fuels or reduced greenhouse gas emissions. In other words, Congress has been quite promiscuous with clean energy carrots but generally refused to produce the kind of climate policy sticks that entities like the PRI have long warned about. Moreover, the chances of the U.S. Congress enacting major climate legislation in the near term – whether a carbon tax, a national cap-and-trade program, or a national "clean electricity" standard – are extremely small. If anything, the chances for an expensive, disruptive program implemented by Congress are probably less now than during most of the last three decades.[18]

Moreover, in the past few years, both in the U.S. and around the world, popular political discontent has been mounting against climate-specific and ESG policymaking in general. This level of pushback makes the IPR theory look shakier than ever. ESG policies have become a flashpoint in Congress (Rives, 2023) and in state governments across the country (Dial & L'Hommedieu, 2023). UK Prime Minster Rishi Sunak has pulled back on his own government's previously announced net-zero policies (Crerar, Harvey, & Stacey, 2023). Protests by farmers throughout Europe in 2023 and 2024 against climate and associated land-use policies have become so widespread and politically disruptive they threaten to halt or permanently derail implementation of new environmental policy initiatives throughout the continent (Hughes, 2024). In February 2024 the EU decided to delay parts of its Corporate Sustainable Reporting Directive for two years (Council of the European Union, 2004) and in March 2024 the European Union failed to advance what was seen as key legislation on climate change and biodiversity (Casert, 2024). Financially, ESG investing in itself seems to have peaked, as global ESG funds began to see net global outflows in January 2024 amid "a major exodus by US investors from environmental, social and governance strategies" (Schwartzkopff, 2024). The exodus of major asset management firms from the organization Climate 100+ was also widely reported as a major blow to ESG activism and a win for U.S. critics in Congress (Gonzales, 2024).

Thus, advocates of ESG regulation are forced back into a familiar position. Congress will not adopt their preferred policies, and current administrative law and pre-

---

18 For more on the likelihood of future climate legislation in the United States, see Morrison et al. (2022).

cedent do not allow for executive agencies to implement significant expansions of regulatory authority without authorization from Congress. Attempts to evade that limitation will likely be greeted with years' worth of litigation and uncertainty followed by an awkward and expensive retreat from the original, overly aggressive policy. The inevitability of ESG policy advancing was supposed to be the lever needed to herd private-sector firms into supporting the movement, but now that the scenario is increasingly in doubt the entire edifice seems to be crumbling. News and commentary on the decline of the ESG movement is frequently to be found in U.S. outlets heading into the mid-2020s, from the inquiring headline "Is ESG Already Over?" in *Reason* magazine (Greene, 2024) to "Why ESG Investing Might Never Recover" in *The Wall Street Journal* (Sindreu, 2024) to "No, ESG and DEI don't just have a branding problem" in *Fortune* (Meadvin, 2024) to "ESG has lost its meaning. One advocate says let's throw it in the trash" on CNN.com (Goodkind, 2023).

This softening of support for and retreat from ESG practice, both among policymakers and multi-trillion-dollar asset managers, makes the democratic deficit of ESG theory even more concerning (Sadasivam, 2022). If ESG turns out to be an investing and political fad that is even now running its course, it is certainly the worst time for a handful of elite decision-makers to implement its premises via executive means.

7.4 Conclusion: Voluntary ESG Solves these Problems

Fortunately, advocates of ESG-aligned goals need not depend on the force of the state to advance their desired outcomes. The world of truly voluntarily corporate initiatives is a vibrant and dynamic one. As many ESG advocates have emphasized, there are market opportunities to be gained from catering to consumer demand for everything from a clean energy ETF (BlackRock, n.d.) to a climate-activist backpack (Gelles, 2022) to a pint of socially progressive ice cream (Gelles, 2021). But the viability of those ESG plays depends on feedback from customers and the wider universe of market participants. Government-enforced ESG standards would kill the market feedback that allows for price signals to efficiently communicate such demand.

Despite criticism from some ESG advocates that U.S. corporate law is too shareholder centered to allow for new models of enterprise and thus requires additional government intervention, modern companies have a great deal of flexibility to accommodate ESG initiatives. Innovations in corporate governance to allow for goals other than profit maximization for shareholders have quite a long history. Many states, for example, have laws known as constituency statutes that allow a board of directors to consider various other stakeholders or "constituencies" when making decisions on behalf of the corporation (Lockner, 2022). Pennsylvania was the first state to adopt such a law, in 1983, but a majority of states have since followed (Bisconti, 2009). Dozens of states have, more recently, adopted benefit corporation statues, based on either the

Model Benefit Corporation Legislation or the Public Benefit Corporation model, which also call for corporate boards to prioritize benefits to non-shareholder stakeholders. In addition, independent non-profit groups like B Lab exist to audit and evaluate firms that want to demonstrate that they have an ESG-informed approach.[19] None of these options involve a governmental mandate.

The cost and dysfunction involved in using government regulation to achieve one's environmental and social aims is underrated by many activists, including those promoting ESG investing theory. When and if ESG management guidelines are adopted by national governments and multilateral organizations, they will be subject to the same significant pathologies as all interest-group politics. Those mandatory policies, once enacted, will also become a roadblock to any additional improvements in the areas being regulated, even assuming that there was a net advantage to the enactment of the initial rules themselves. Mandatory ESG standards would likely become a ceiling rather than a floor, allowing firms to ignore calls for more ambitious targets by pointing to their compliance with whatever mandates managed to make it through the sausage-factory of political policymaking. Advocates for societal progress through ESG-informed business practices should be the ones demanding more than that.

References

Abutaleb Y., Romm T., & Phillips A. (2022, July 20), Biden vows to act on climate if Congress won't, *Washington Post*, https://www.washingtonpost.com/politics/2022/07/20/biden-issue-new-policy-climate-vowing-act-if-congress-doesnt/

Adolphsen S. & Vernuccio F. V. (2024), The next president will face an emerging ESG threat, Institute for the American Worker, https://i4aw.org/wp-content/uploads/2024/03/I4AW_ESG-Study.pdf

Anderson L. (2020, April 21), To decarbonize, let's rethink permitting for large infrastructure projects, Breakthrough Institute, https://thebreakthrough.org/issues/energy/large-infrastructure

Berlau J., Broughel J., & Patinkin A. (2004), *Don't depower crypto: Biden's electricity tax would harm conservation, innovation* (Competitive Enterprise Institute), pp. 1–2, https://cei.org/wp-content/uploads/2024/01/Crypto_Energy_Use_3.pdf

Bisconti A. (2009), The double bottom line: Can constituency statutes protect socially responsible corporations stuck in Revlon Land, *Loyola of Los Angeles Law Review*, *42*(3), 768, n. 13 and p. 781, https://digitalcommons.lmu.edu/cgi/viewcontent.cgi?article=2666&context=llr

BlackRock (n.d.), *iShares global clean energy index ETF*, blackrock.com, https://www.blackrock.com/ca/investors/en/products/327373/ishares-global-clean-energy-index-etf

Broughel J. (2023, September 1), White House environmental regulation undermines permitting progress, *Forbes*, https://www.forbes.com/sites/jamesbroughel/2023/09/01/white-house-environmental-regulation-undermines-permitting-progress/?sh=2ab9793432e1

Caballar R. D. (2004, March 23), *We need to decarbonize software*, IEEE Spectrum, https://spectrum.ieee.org/green-software

---

19 Morrison (2021), 72–77.

Casert R. (2024, March 25), A major European nature protection plan stumbles at the final hurdle, *Associated Press*, https://apnews.com/article/eu-climate-nature-protection-farmers-protests-7b222f346d4898e32766b230da781385

Chilson N. (2021), *Getting out of control: Emergent leadership in a complex world* (New Degree Press), 136–139

Coffey B., McLaughlin P., and Peretto P. (2016), *The cumulative cost of regulations*, (Mercatus Working Paper, Mercatus Center at George Mason University), pp. 38–39, https://www.mercatus.org/media/58256

Congress climate history, https://www.c2es.org/content/congress-climate-history/

Council of the European Union (2004, February 7), *Council and Parliament agree to delay sustainability reporting for certain sectors and third-country companies by two years*, europa.eu, https://www.consilium.europa.eu/en/press/press-releases/2024/02/07/council-and-parliament-agree-to-delay-sustainability-reporting-for-certain-sectors-and-third-country-companies-by-two-years/

Crerar P., Harvey F., & Stacey K. (2023, September 20), Rishi Sunak announces U-turn on key green targets, *The Guardian*, https://www.theguardian.com/environment/2023/sep/20/rishi-sunak-confirms-rollback-of-key-green-targets

Crews C. W. Jr. (2017), *Tip of the costberg: On the invalidity of all cost of regulation estimates and the need to compile them anyway, 2017 edition* (Competitive Enterprise Institute), 15–27, https://ssrn.com/abstract=2502883

Crews C. W. Jr. (2023, November), *Ten thousand commandments: An annual snapshot of the federal regulatory state, 2023 edition* (Competitive Enterprise Institute), 1–6, https://cei.org/studies/ten-thousand-commandments-2023/

D. Meadvin (2024, February 16), No, ESG and DEI don't just have a branding problem, *Fortune*, 2024, https://fortune.com/2024/02/16/esg-dei-branding-problem-diversity-inclusion-debate/

DeCicco J. M. & Schlesinger W. H. (2018), Reconsidering bioenergy given the urgency of climate protection, *Proceedings of the National Academy of Science*, *115*(39), 9642–45, https://www.pnas.org/doi/full/10.1073/pnas.1814120115

Dial L. C. & L'Hommedieu A. E. (2023, May 25), *The ESG debate heats up*, K&L Gates, https://www.klgates.com/The-ESG-Debate-Heats-Up-State-AGs-Investigating-Asset-Manager-Involvement-in-ESG-Initiatives-and-Related-Proxy-Voting-5-25-2023

Edwards C. (2024, March 27), *Biden's corporate welfare bonanza*, Cato at Liberty, https://www.cato.org/blog/bidens-corporate-welfare-bonanza

Fialka J. (2018, July 16), How a government program to get ethanol from plants failed, *Scientific American*, https://www.scientificamerican.com/article/how-a-government-program-to-get-ethanol-from-plants-failed/

Gelles D. (2021, August 15), How the social mission of Ben & Jerry's survived being gobbled up, *The New York Times*, https://www.nytimes.com/2015/08/23/business/how-ben-jerrys-social-mission-survived-being-gobbled-up.html

Gelles D. (2022, September 14), Billionaire no more: Patagonia founder gives away the company, *The New York Times*, https://www.nytimes.com/2022/09/14/climate/patagonia-climate-philanthropy-chouinard.html

Gelles D. (2024, February 19), More Wall Street firms are flip-flopping on climate. Here's why, *The New York Times*, https://www.nytimes.com/2024/02/19/business/climate-blackrock-state-street-jpmorgan-pimco.html

Gensler G. (2022, March 1), Twitter post, https://twitter.com/garygensler/status/1498708322677149700

Goldberg E. S. & Mann R. (2023, March 1), *ESG rule challenged in congress and courts*, Morgan Lewis, https://www.morganlewis.com/blogs/mlbenebits/2023/03/esg-rule-challenged-in-congress-and-courts

Goldberg E. S. & Mann R. (2023, March 1), *ESG rule challenged in congress and courts*, Morgan Lewis, https://www.morganlewis.com/blogs/mlbenebits/2023/03/esg-rule-challenged-in-congress-and-courts

Gonzales F. (2024, February 20), *Wall Street giants exit Climate Action 100+*, Wealth Professional, https://www.wealthprofessional.ca/news/industry-news/wall-street-giants-exit-climate-action-100/383781

Goodkind N. (2023, October 3), ESG has lost its meaning. One advocate says let's throw it in the trash, cnn.com, https://www.cnn.com/2023/10/03/investing/premarket-stocks-trading/index.html

Gramm P. & Keeley T. (2023, December 19), *Ending environmental, social, and governance investing and restoring the economic enlightenment*, American Enterprise Institute, 1–6, https://www.aei.org/wp-content/uploads/2023/12/Ending-Environmental-Social-and-Governance-Investing-and-Restoring-the-Economic-Enlightenment.pdf?x85095

Greene R. (2024), *Is ESG already over?* https://reason.com/2024/01/14/is-esg-already-over/

Hughes K. (2024, February 16), Will farm protests derail EU climate change plans?, *The Herald*, https://www.heraldscotland.com/politics/viewpoint/24122079.will-farm-protests-derail-eu-climate-change-plans

Inbal J. & York S. (2023, December 11), New renewable fuel standard volume targets facilitate renewable natural gas production, U.S. Energy Information Administration, https://www.eia.gov/todayinenergy/detail.php?id=61045

International Brotherhood of Teamsters (2023), Teamsters shareholder power, *Teamster: The Teamster Magazine*, International Brotherhood of Teamsters, 12–21, https://teamster.org/wp-content/uploads/2024/01/1924FINALMagTeamsterWINTER2023.pdf

International Energy Agency (2021), *Net Zero by 2050: A roadmap for the global energy sector*, iea.org, p. 71, https://www.iea.org/reports/net-zero-by-2050

J. Powell (2023, October 24), *Statement by Chair Jerome H. Powell on principles for climate-related financial risk management for large financial institutions*, Federal Reserve, https://www.federalreserve.gov/newsevents/pressreleases/powell-statement-20231024b.htm

Jessop S. & Kerber R. (2024, February 15), JPMorgan, State Street quit climate group, BlackRock steps back, *Reuters*, https://www.reuters.com/sustainability/sustainable-finance-reporting/jpmorgan-fund-arm-quits-climate-action-100-investor-group-2024-02-15/

Kimbrough L. (2023, September 8), Study: Tricky balancing act between EV scale-up and mining battery metals, *Mongabay*, https://news.mongabay.com/2023/09/study-tricky-balancing-act-between-ev-scale-up-and-mining-battery-metals/

Kretkowska A. (2023, November 24), *SDGs and ESG: Why the United Nations Sustainable Development Goals should top every boardroom agenda*, Morningstar Sustainalytics, https://www.sustainalytics.com/esg-research/resource/investors-esg-blog/sdgs-and-esg–why-the-united-nations-sustainable-development-goals-should-top-every-boardroom-agenda

Lavelle M. (2018, August 26), John McCain's climate change legacy, *Inside Climate News*, https://insideclimatenews.org/news/26082018/john-mccain-climate-change-leadership-senate-cap-tradebipartisan-lieberman-republican-campaign/

Leber R. (2022, July 20), Congress failed on climate. What can Biden do now?, *Vox*, https://www.vox.com/23270518/biden-climate-manchin-executive-action

Lewis M. (2016, July 25), Running drivers into the blend wall: Push to ratchet up renewable fuel standard rewards ethanol lobby at consumers' expense, Competitive Enterprise Institute, *OnPoint*, no. 219, pp. 1–2, https://cei.org/studies/running-drivers-into-the-blend-wall/

Lockner A. (2022), *Constituency statutes: The overlooked predecessor to the ESG movement*, Robins Kaplan, https://www.robinskaplan.com/resources/legal-updates/the-robins-kaplan-spotlight/2022/spotlight-september-2022/constituency-statutes. See also a discussion of constituency statues in Morrison (2021), 11–12.

Loyola M. (2020), *Modernizing Environmental Reviews under the National Environmental Policy Act* (Competitive Enterprise Institute), https://cei.org/wp-content/uploads/2020/12/Mario_Loyola_-_Mod ernizing_NEPA_Environmental_Reviews.pdf

Loyola M. (2023, June 13), Permitting reforms, finally: One bright spot in the debt-ceiling compromise, Competitive Enterprise Institute, *OnPoint*, no. 286, https://cei.org/wp-content/uploads/2023/06/On Point-Debt-Ceiling-Permitting-Reform-1.pdf

McLaughlin P., Ghei N. , and Wilt M. (2018), *Regulatory accumulation and its costs: An overview* (Mercatus Policy Brief, Mercatus Center at George Mason University), https://www.mercatus.org/research/pol icy-briefs/regulatory-accumulation-and-its-costs-0.

Mills M. P. (2019), *The "new energy economy": An exercise in magical thinking*, Manhattan Institute, https://manhattan.institute/article/the-new-energy-economy-an-exercise-in-magical-thinking

Mills M. P. (2022), *The "energy transition" delusion: A reality reset*, Manhattan Institute, 1, https://media4. manhattan-institute.org/sites/default/files/the-energy-transition-delusion_a-reality-reset.pdf

Morrison et al. (2022), pp. 19–23, https://cei.org/wp-content/uploads/2022/06/CEI-Morrison-comment-on-SEC-climate-disclosure-rule-RIN-3235-AM87-final-final-1.pdf

Morrison R. (2021), *Environmental, social, and governance theory: Defusing a major threat to shareholder rights* (Competitive Enterprise Institute), 60–72, https://cei.org/wp-content/uploads/2021/05/Richard-Morrison-ESG-Theory.pdf

Morrison R. (2022, May 3), *SEC's Gensler wants to regulate green funds, but definitions are elusive*, Real Clear Policy, https://www.realclearpolicy.com/articles/2022/05/03/secs_gensler_wants_to_regulate_green_funds_but_definitions_are_elusive_830237.html

Morrison R. et al. (2022, June 17), *Comments of the Competitive Enterprise Institute in the matter of the proposed rule "The Enhancement and Standardization of Climate-Related Disclosures for Investors" before the Securities and Exchange Commission, 87 FR 29059; RIN 3235-AM87*, 6, https://cei.org/wp-content/uploads/2022/06/CEI-Morrison-comment-on-SEC-climate-disclosure-rule-RIN-3235-AM87-final-final-1.pdf

Pears P., Baines T., and Williams O. (2023, July 24), *Greenwashing: Navigating the risk*, Harvard Law School Forum on Corporate Governance, https://corpgov.law.harvard.edu/2023/07/24/greenwashing-navigating-the-risk/

Potter B., Datta A., & Stapp A. (2022, September 13), How to stop environmental review from harming the environment, Institute for Progress, https://ifp.org/environmental-review

Principles for Responsible Investment (n.d.), *What is the Inevitable Policy Response?*, unpri.org, https://www.unpri.org/inevitable-policy-response/what-is-the-inevitable-policy-response/4787.article

Rives K. (2023, July 19), *GOP 'ESG month' yields tense hearings with regulators, questions over campaign*, S&P Market Global Intelligence, https://www.spglobal.com/marketintelligence/en/news-insights/latest-news-headlines/gop-esg-month-yields-tense-hearings-with-regulators-questions-over-campaign-76591291

Sadasivam N. (2022, December 9), *Wall Street's biggest names are backing off their climate commitments*, Grist, https://grist.org/economics/vanguard-asset-managers-net-zero-esg/

Schröder Bosch J. (2023), A roadmap towards greening the European Central Bank, Heinrich-Böll-Stiftung European Union, 16–18, https://eu.boell.org/sites/default/files/2024-01/greening_ecb_web.pdf

Schwartzkopff F. (2024, January 25), US investor exodus deals historic blow to global ESG fund market, *Bloomberg*, https://www.bloomberg.com/news/articles/2024-01-25/sustainable-funds-see-first-ever-global-quarterly-net-outflows?sref=xIpK9uDK

Scott J. C. (1998), *Seeing like a state: How certain schemes to improve the human condition have failed* (Yale University Press).

Securities and Exchange Commission (2001), Investment company names, *Federal Register*, 66(22), 8509–8519, https://www.sec.gov/rules/2001/01/investment-company-names

Securities and Exchange Commission (2002), The enhancement and standardization of climate-related disclosures for investors, notice of proposed rulemaking, *Federal Register, 87*(69), 21334–21473, https://www.govinfo.gov/content/pkg/FR-2022-04-11/pdf/2022-06342.pdf

Securities and Exchange Commission (2002), The enhancement and standardization of climate-related disclosures for investors, *Federal Register, 87*(69), 11, n. 12, https://www.federalregister.gov/docu ments/2022/04/11/2022-06342/the-enhancement-and-standardization-of-climate-related-disclosures-for-investors

Securities and Exchange Commission (2004, March 28), *The enhancement and standardization of climate-related disclosures for investors, Federal Register,* 89(61), 21668–21921, https://www.govinfo.gov/con tent/pkg/FR-2024-03-28/pdf/2024-05137.pdf

Securities and Exchange Commission (2013), Investment company names, *Federal Register, 88*(195), 13, https://www.federalregister.gov/documents/2023/10/11/2023-20793/investment-company-names

Securities and Exchange Commission (2023, September 20), *SEC adopts rule enhancements to prevent misleading or deceptive investment fund names* [press release], https://www.sec.gov/news/press-release/2023-188

Sen. E. J. Markey & Rep. A. Pressley (2023, September 18), *Letter to the honorable Jerome Powell,* congress. gov., https://www.markey.senate.gov/imo/media/doc/letter_to_chair_powell_to_address_climate-related_financial_risks_-_20230918pdf.pdf

Sen. S. M. Capito (2022, May 9), Biden rollback of permitting reform is making his own energy goals impossible, *Washington Examiner,* https://www.washingtonexaminer.com/opinion/2599255/biden-rollback-of-permitting-reform-is-making-his-own-energy-goals-impossible/

Shaw J. (n.d.), *Public choice theory,* Library of Economics and Liberty, https://www.econlib.org/library/Enc1/PublicChoiceTheory.html

Silva Laughlin Lauren (2019, June 20), On ethanol, big corn beats big oil, *The Wall Street Journal,* https://www.wsj.com/articles/on-ethanol-big-corn-beats-big-oil-11561040187

Sindreu J. (2024, March 24), Why ESG investing might never recover, *The Wall Street Journal,* https://www.wsj.com/finance/investing/why-esg-investing-might-never-recover-7aa9e7c9

Skinner (2021), 1305–6.

Skinner C. (2021), Central banks and climate change, *Vanderbilt Law Review, 74*(5), 1301, https://scholarship.law.vanderbilt.edu/vlr/vol74/iss5/4/

Soukup S. (2021), *The dictatorship of woke capital: How political correctness captured big business* (Encounter Books), 55–60.

Spiliakos A., "What does sustainability mean in business," *Business Insights,* October 10, 2018, https://online.hbs.edu/blog/post/what-is-sustainability-in-business

Stigler G. J., The theory of economic regulation, *The Bell Journal of Economics and Management Science,* 2(1), 3–21, https://www.jstor.org/stable/3003160

T. Keith (2014, January 20), *Wielding A pen and a phone, Obama goes it alone,* NPR, https://www.npr.org/2014/01/20/263766043/wielding-a-pen-and-a-phone-obama-goes-it-alone

U.S. Chamber of Commerce (2023, October 24), *The Biden administration's 'whole of government" approach to promoting labor unions,* U.S. Chamber of Commerce, https://www.uschamber.com/employment-law/unions/biden-administrations-whole-of-government-approach-to-promoting-labor-unions-hurts-workers-employers-economy

U.S. Environmental Protection Agency (2018, June 29), *Biofuels and the environment: Second triennial report to Congress,* p. ix, http://epa.gov/epahome/pdf.html

U.S. Environmental Protection Agency (2024, January 23), *Renewable fuel standard program: Overview for renewable fuel standard,* https://www.epa.gov/renewable-fuel-standard-program/program-overview-renewable-fuel-standard-program

United Nations (n.d.), *Renewable energy – powering a safer future,* https://www.un.org/en/climatechange/raising-ambition/renewable-energy

Van Boom D. (2023, April 30), The green revolution is being held back by red tape, *CNET*, https://www.cnet.com/science/the-green-revolution-is-being-held-back-by-red-tape/;

Vollmer A. N. (2022, April 12), *The SEC lacks legal authority to adopt climate-change disclosure rules*, Mercatus Center, https://www.mercatus.org/research/public-interest-comments/sec-lacks-legal-authority-adopt-climate-change-disclosure-rules

West Virginia v. Environmental Protection Agency (2022), https://www.supremecourt.gov/opinions/21pdf/20-1530_n758.pdf

Yandle B. (1983), Baptists and bootleggers: The education of a regulatory economist, *Regulation, AEI Journal on Government and Society, 7*(3), 12–16, https://www.researchgate.net/publication/245588630_Bootleggers_and_Baptists_The_Education_of_a_Regulatory_Economist

Yandle B. (1999), Bootleggers and baptists in retrospect, *Regulation, 22*(3), 5–7, https://www.cato.org/sites/cato.org/files/serials/files/regulation/1999/10/bootleggers.pdf

Yehle E. (2013, August 6), EPA slashes this year's cellulosic targets, *Greenwire*, https://subscriber.politicopro.com/article/eenews/1059985681

About the Editor

John Hill is a consultant, investor, author, and educator who teaches Economics and Finance at the Dolan School of Business, Fairfield University. He earned his degrees from Cornell University and the University of Pennsylvania, where he pursued a PhD in Econometrics under Nobel Laureate Lawrence Klein. John has authored notable books, including *Environmental, Social, and Governance (ESG) Investing* and *Fintech and the Remaking of Financial Institutions*, both published by Academic Press. His career spans senior executive roles at leading financial institutions such as Merrill Lynch, ABN AMRO, the Intercontinental Exchange, and ICAP.

John is deeply committed to charitable causes in education, healthcare, and marine environmental conservation. He serves on the Advisory Council for the Center for Climate, Coastal, and Marine Studies at Fairfield University. In his free time, John enjoys underwater photography and scuba diving, holding certifications as a Dive Master and Assistant Instructor.

https://doi.org/10.1515/9783111178608-015

List of Tables

Table 2.1 Share of institutional investors in equity —— 27
Table 3.1 Types of Corporate ESG Disclosures —— 52
Table 3.2 Examples of Mandatory Corporate ESG Disclosures —— 53
Table 3.3 Common Measurements for Environmental and Social Performance —— 57
Table 3.4 Overview of Methodology in Most Popular ESG Rating Products —— 61
Table 3.5 Limitations of the KLD Ratings Methodology and Suggestions for Improvement —— 66
Table 3.6 Examples of mixed criteria in KLD ratings —— 71
Table 3.7 An illustration of materiality-weighted ESG ratings —— 72
Table 5.1 Frequently Used Terms —— 110
Table 5.2 Stakeholders driving rising expectations for better ESG performance —— 113

https://doi.org/10.1515/9783111178608-016

Index

active ownership 36
Addis, R. 40
Albrecht, D. H. XXI, 47, 49–73
American Clean Energy and Security Act (2009) 159
American Clean Energy Leadership Act (2009) 159
Anantharaman, D. XXI, 47, 49–73
Andrew, J. 73
antimicrobial resistant bacteria (AMR) 14
Asia Investor Group on Climate Change 113
Authority for Consumers and Markets (ACM) XVII
automotive industry 88

Baker, M. 73
Bebchuk, A. L. 127
Benefit Corps 98
Berg, F. 63
Berrone, P. 57
beta activism 14
Bhattacharji, P. XXII, 83, 85–104
Bhutta, U. S. 35
Biden, J. 150, 155
biodiversity loss 31
Blackrock XV, 6
Bloomberg 60
BNP Paribas Group (BNP) 40
Boardroom Access Project (BAP) 17
Boardroom Accountability Project 18
Bolger, B. XXIII, 127, 129–137
Bouten, L. 63, 64
Box, G. E. P. 7
Brockovich, E. 55
Buchanan, J. 146
Burckart, W. 14
Bush, George H. W. 158
Bush, George W. 149
The Business Case for Diversity Backfires (Georgeac and Rattan) 130

California Public Employees' Retirement System (CalPERS) XV, 16, 83, 112
capital markets 3, 10
– institutionalization of 6, 11, 15
– investors' impacts 11–12
Carbon Border Adjustment Mechanism (CBAM) 117
Carbon Disclosure Project (CDP) 55
Carbon Limits and Energy for America's Renewal Act (2009) 159

Carney, M. 157
Carrión-Flores, C. E. 57
Casazza, C. A. XXIII 107, 109–123
Ceres Investor Network 113
Ceres Investor Network Private Equity Working Group 113
Chatterji, A. K. 57, 60, 63
Christensen, H. 54, 73
Clean Energy Standard Act (2012) 159
Clean Power Plan (CPP) 155, 156
Climate Action 100+ 114
climate change 30–31, 39, 156–157
– adaptation 121
– Biden's speech 155
– and biodiversity 159
– CalPERS 16
– risk of 15, 119
Coase, R. 10
Coelho, R. 73
Cohen, M. A. 57
Cohn, J. B. 58
Community Development Financial Institutions (CDFIs) 100
consumer electronics 88
Cooper, M. J. 58
corporate bonds 101
corporate disclosures 51–52
– mandatory 52–54
– types of 52
– voluntary 54, 55
Corporate Sustainability Reporting Directive (CSRD) 117, 129, 133, 136
cradle-to-grave analysis 86–87
– automotive industry 88
– community meetings 90
– consumer electronics 88
– directionality and momentum 89
– distribution and transportation 87
– end-of-life considerations 87
– food industry 88–89
– manufacturing and production 87
– newspapers 90
– nonprofits and watchdogs 90
– peer-relative analysis 89
– product use 87
– raw material extraction 87
– regulatory compliance 88

https://doi.org/10.1515/9783111178608-017

- resource efficiency 87
- sustainability goals 88
- waste reduction 87
- working standards 88
CSRD. *See* Corporate Sustainability Reporting Directive (CSRD)

Darrisaw, E. XXIII, 127, 129–137
Daugaard, D. 23, 25–42
democratic deficit, ESG policymaking
- administrative agencies 155
- Biden's speech, climate change 155
- Clean Power Plan (CPP) 155, 156
- climate legislation 159
- Federal Reserve 156–157
- inevitability 160
- Kyoto Protocol 158
- net-zero policies 159
- Principles for Responsible Investment
    (PRI) 157–158
- regulatory burdens and compliance costs 158
- renewable energy 159
- *West Virginia v. EPA* 156
Deutsche Bank XVIII
Development Financing Authorities (DFAs) 100
diversification 6, 10, 12, 16, 27, 29
diversity, equity, and inclusion (DEI) 48, 99
- stakeholder management 131–132
- value creation process 130–131
divestment strategy XX, XXVI, 94, 127–128
Doyle, T. M. 63, 64
due diligence 119–121
DWS Investment Management Americas, Inc.
    (DIMA) XVIII

economic pillar, sustainability 32, 33
Edmans, A. 5, 58, 131
Energy Independence and Security Act (EISA)
    (2007) 149
Energy Policy Act (2005) 149
engagement ownership 36
environmental, social, and governance (ESG)
    investing
- corporate disclosures 51–55
- definition of 49–50
- diversity, equity, and inclusion (DEI) 130–132
- external information 55–56
- mandatory ESG standards 143–161
- measurements 56–73

- MPT (*see* modern portfolio theory (MPT))
- NAACP Fair Share Model 135
- overlapping principles 135–137
- PE (*see* private equity (PE))
- Rev. Sullivan 133–135
- standardized approach 132–133
- sustainable investing 85–104
- universal ownership 25–42
environmental pillar, sustainability 32, 33
Environmental Protection Agency (EPA) 148–149,
    155, 156
environment-related disclosure 54
ESG Data Convergence Initiative (EDCI) 116
ESG integration 35, 83, 86
- data and metrics 30
- description 9–10
- impact investing 30
ESG investing. *See* environmental, social, and governance (ESG) investing
ESG measurements
- broad *vs.* narrow scope 68
- disclosure *vs.* performance 70
- easy *vs.* difficult targets 68–69
- empirical proxy *vs.* underlying construct 68
- environmental and social performance 56, 57–58
- hard *vs.* soft requirements 69–70
- materiality 70–72
- process-oriented *vs.* result-oriented 69
- research questions 72–73
ESG ratings products 47–48
- disagreement 60, 63–64
- KLD ratings 65–68, 71
- leading 59–62
- obfuscation 64
- oversimplification 64
- rating bias 63–64
European Union (EU) Sustainability Reporting
    Directive XXIV, 130, 134–136
exchange traded funds (ETFs) XIX–XX, 129
exclusionary screening 83, 86

Federal Reserve 156–157
Federal Trade Commission (FTC) XVI–XVII, 154
financialization, economy 3, 5
financial performance
- analyses of XV
- CalPERS 83
- long-term 37, 86
- uncertainty 38

Fink, L. 5
Fiscal Responsibility Act (2023) 150
Flammer, C. 131
food industry 88–89
Freidman, M. 10
Frost, M. 112
fund, definition 110

general obligation bonds 101
General Partners (GPs) XXIII, 107, 112
– acquisitions 120
– cost avoidance 122
– definition 110
– due diligence 119
Gensler, G. 152–153
Georgeac, O. A. M. 130
GHG emissions. *See* greenhouse gas (GHG) emis-
    sions
Gibson, R. 63
Gillian, S. L. 73
Gjølberg, M. 68–70
Global Impact Investing Network (GIIN) 30
Global Reporting Initiative (GRI) Guidelines 55
Global Sullivan Principles 130, 133–134
– community development 136
– corporate responsibility 135
– human rights and social justice 135–136
– stakeholder engagement and voice 136
– sustainability reporting and transparency 136
Glossner, S. 131
Goldin, H. J. 16
Goldman Sachs XVIII–XIX
Gomez-Mejia, L. R. 57
GPs. *See* General Partners (GPs)
Graham, A. 57
green bonds, BNP Paribas 40
greenhouse gas (GHG) emissions 15, 70, 107,
    117–118, 148, 158–159
greenwashing XXI, 47, 54, 145
– deliberate and accidental 91
– examples of XVII
– lack of accountability 38
Grewal, J. 69
Griffin, P. A. 57

Haji, A. A. 54
Harris, J. 11
Hawley, J. P. XX, 3, 5–19
Herman, S. J. XXIII, 107, 109–123

Hertwich, E. G. 57
Hooks, B. L. 135
Housing Finance Authorities (HFAs) 100
human capital-related disclosure 54

impact investment funds, BNP Paribas 40
Inevitable Policy Response (IPR) 157–158
Initiative Climat International (iCI) 115
Innes, R. 57
Interfaith Center on Corporate Responsibility
    (ICCR) 93
International Renewable Energy Agency 150
Investment Company Act (1940) 153
investment decision-making
– long-term value creation 34
– positive impact 34
– regulatory compliance 34
– reputation and stakeholder trust 34
– risk assessment 33–34
– stakeholder expectations 34
The Investor Agenda 114
Investors Group on Climate Change 114

Kahneman, D. 7
Kangogo, M. 23, 25–42
Kappanna, H. 55
KLD ratings 65–68, 71
Konar, S. 57
Kyoto Protocol 158

Lagarde, C. 157
legitimacy 17, 156
Lieberman, J. 158
Lieberman-Warner Climate Security Act (2008) 159
limited market integration 38
Limited Partners (LPs) XXIII, 107, 109, 122
– definition 110
– Europe-based 118
Lubber, M. 9
Lukomnik, J. XX, 3, 5–19
Lydenberg, S. 14

mandatory ESG standards 143–144
– democratic deficit, policymaking 155–160
– examples of 52–54
– investment funds 152–154
– regulatory capture 144–151
– sustainability claims 154–155
Markey, E. 159

Markowitz, H. 6, 11, 15, 19, 26
Marx, K. 10
Matsumura, E. M. 57
McCain, J. 158
microfinance, BNP Paribas 40
Mills, M. P. 149–150
Minow, N. 27
Mission-Related Investments (MRIs) 103
modern portfolio theory (MPT) XX–XXI, 3, 5 See
    also MPT paradox
– economic rationality 7
– efficient market hypothesis 7
– enabling theory 7
– ESG integration 9–10
– relative and absolute returns 8
– security analysis 6
Monks, R. A. G. 27
Morningstar 60, 135
Morrison, R. XXIV–XXV, 128, 129, 141, 143–161
mortgage bonds 101
MPT. See modern portfolio theory (MPT)
MPT paradox
– capital markets, investors' impacts 11–12
– dynamic materiality, arc of 14–15
– legitimacy 17
– politics 15–16
– proxy access 17–18
– systems-level investing 13–14
– universal ownership 12–13
municipal bonds 101

NAACP Fair Share Model 130, 135, 136
National Environmental Policy Act (1969) 150
negative screening 35
Net Zero Asset Managers Initiative 114
Net Zero Asset Owners Alliance (NZAOA) 115
New York University Center for Sustainable
    Business 116
Ni, J. 58
Norwegian Consumer Authority (NCA) XVII

Obama, B. 155
overlapping principles
– community development 136
– corporate responsibility 135
– GDPR privacy laws 137
– human rights and social justice 135–136
– stakeholder engagement and voice 136
– sustainability reporting and transparency 136

Paris Aligned Asset Owners 114
Patamar Capital 41
PE. See private equity (PE)
peer-relative analysis 89
Pitcher, J. XIX, XV
politicization, sustainable investing 91
Portfolio Company, definition 110
portfolio risk 26
positive incentive loans, BNP Paribas 40
positive screening 35
Powell, J. 156
the Practical Energy and Climate Plan 159
Principles for Responsible Investment
    (PRI) 157–158
private debt
– direct 102
– indirect 103
private equity (PE) XXII–XXIII, 107
– acquisitions 120–121
– additionality 97–98
– CalPERS 112
– data sources 97
– definition 111
– description 109–110
– dynamic regulatory and political climate 116–118
– fundraising 119–120
– Initial Public Offering (IPO) 96
– investment approach 118–119
– investment channels 97
– liquidity lock-up 98
– manager, indirect investment 98–99
– navigating exits and impact lockstep 98
– Portfolio Companies 111
– portfolio management 121–123
– stakeholders, rising expectations 112–116
– traditional investing 111–112
– venture capital (VC) 97
Private Equity Climate Risks 115
private equity firm, definition 111
Private Equity Stakeholder Project 115
process-oriented vs. result-oriented measures 69
Program-Related Investments (PRIs) 103
proxy access 17–18
public debt 100
– corporate, mortgage and municipal bonds 101
– corporate engagement 100–101
– managers, indirect investment 102
– revenue and general obligation bonds 101
– types of issuers and authorities 100

public equities 92
– activist takeovers and corporate norms 94
– corporate engagement 92
– divestment 94
– engagement with companies 93
– ESG approach 95
– faith-based investors 93
– interfaith groups 93
– manager, indirect investment 95–96
– shareholder ballots 93
– shareholder voting 92–93
– values-based approach 95

Quigley, E. 13, 27

racial equity audits 132
Ramkumar, A. XIX, XV
Rattan, A. 130
RavenPack 56
Refinitiv 64, 65
regulatory capture
– battery storage 149–151
– biofuel policies 147–148
– cellulosic ethanol 149
– compliance burdens 145
– economic regulation 145, 151
– ethanol program 148–149
– green software movement 144
– greenwashing 145
– market processes 151
– political economy 146
– price impact 144–145
– public choice 145, 146
– renewable energy infrastructure 150
– self-interest 146
– stakeholderism 147
– win/win concept 146, 151
revenue bonds 101
risk reduction process 26

Schoenmaker, D. 29
Schramade, W. 29
Science Based Targets Initiative (SBTi) 114
Securities and Exchange Commission
    (SEC) XVIII–XIX, 47, 52, 54, 70, 152, 154, 155, 158
Serafeim, G. 69
shareholder voting 92–93
Skancke, M. 12
Skinner, C. 156–157

Smith, A. 10
social-and-governance-related disclosure 54
social impact bonds, BNP Paribas 40
social inequities 31
socially responsible investing (SRI) 50
social pillar, sustainability 32, 33
social responsibility movement XXIV, 128, 129
Spiliakos, A. 153
standardized approach 132–133
Stanford Law School 56
Starks, L. T. 73
State Bond Banks 100
Stigler, G. J. 145
Sullivan, L. XXIV, 128
– EU Sustainability Reporting Directive 134–135
– Global Sullivan Principles 133–134, 136
Sunak, R. 159
sustainability
– biodiversity loss 31
– bonds 35–36
– climate change 30–31
– economic pillar 32, 33
– environmental pillar 32, 33
– global challenges 31
– goals 88
– pollution and waste 31
– reporting and transparency 136
– resource depletion 31
– social inequities 31
– social pillar 32, 33
Sustainability Accounting Standards Board (SASB)
    Standards 55, 70–71
Sustainability Financial Disclosure Regulation
    (SFDR) 117
sustainable finance models
– access to funds 37
– balancing trade-offs 38
– engagement and active ownership 36
– enhanced reputation and stakeholder
    engagement 37
– environmental and social impact 36
– externalities 29–30
– ESG integration 35
– financial performance uncertainty 38
– green and sustainability bonds 35–36
– greenwashing and lack of accountability 38
– impact investing 35
– information and data gaps 37
– limited market integration 38

– long-term financial performance 37
– long-term value creation 36–37
– measurement and standardisation 37
– negative screening/exclusion 35
– positive screening 35
– risk management 36
sustainable investing
– cradle-to-grave analysis 86–90
– defined 85–86
– ESG integration 86
– exclusionary screening 86
– greenwashing 91
– impact investing 86
– MRIs and PRIs 103
– navigating 104
– politicization 91
– popularization 85
– private debt 102–103
– private equity 96–99
– public debt 100–102
– public equities 92–96
– resourcing challenges 91
– thematic investing 86
– volatility and risk 90
systemic market risk 26
systems-level investing XX, 3,13–14

Task Force on Climate-related Financial Disclosures
  (TCFD) 55
thematic investing 86
Tsang, A. 73
Tullock, G. 146
Tversky, A. 7

United Nations Environment Programme Finance
  Initiative (UNEP FI) 115
United Nations Principles for Responsible
  Investment (UNPRI) 115, 119–120

universal ownership XXI
– concept of 23–26
– historical roots of 28
– institutional investors 26–28
– investment decision-making, externalities 33–34
– negative impact 29
– sustainability issues 30–31
– sustainability pillars 32–33
– sustainable finance (see sustainable finance
  models)
– systemic market risk 26
– systems-level investing 12–13
University Pension Plan (UPP) 13, 29
Unsal, O. 58
UN Sustainable Development Goals (SDGs) 33, 40,
  141, 152

The value of diversity, equity, and inclusion (Edmans,
  Flammer and Glossner) 131
values-based approach 95
Van Duuren, E. 30
Vanguard Laundry Services 39–40
Violation Tracker 56
voluntary ESG disclosures 54, 55, 160–161

Wadhwa, S. XVIII
Wardlaw, M. I. 58
Waxman, H. 159
Weismann, M. F. 58
Williamson, O. 10
Wong, P. XXII, 83, 85–104

Yandle, B. 146

Zhao, K. XXI, 47, 49–73
Ziolo, M. 32

www.ingramcontent.com/pod-product-compliance
Lightning Source LLC
Chambersburg PA
CBHW081515190326
41458CB00015B/5379